The Logical Character of Natural Laws

The Logical Character of Natural Laws

An Examination of Kneale's View

By

NANDITA CHAUDHURI

MAHA BODHI BOOK AGENCY
4A, Bankim Chatterjee Street, College Square
Kolkata - 700 073, India

The Logical Character of Natural Laws

An Examination of Kneal's View

by

Nandita Chaudhuri

First Published : 2015

Published by :
D.L.S. Jayawardana
MAHA BODHI BOOK AGENCY
4A, Bankim Chatterjee Street, College Square
Kolkata - 700 073, India
Ph : 9831077368, 9831529452
e-mail: mahabodhibookagency@hotmail.com

Printed by
Sagarika Press
Antony Bagan Lane, Kolkata-9

ISBN : 978-93-80336-92-3

Price : Rs. 900

FOREWORD

Nandita Chaudhuri prepared this work, under my supervision, as her thesis in Philosophy for the degree of Ph.D (Arts) of the University of Calcutta. The thesis was submitted in 2007, and she was admitted to the degree in 2008.

Unfortunately for us, however, Dr Nandita Chaudhuri is no more. She died of pneumonia on August 12, 2013.

As for her work in question, it has been sent to the press by her husband, Mr Ajit Kumar Sinha, who has informed me that the work is now at a much advanced stage of publication. It is now a matter of a few days for Nandita's book to see the light of the day.

I feel honoured to be invited by Mr Sinha to write this Foreword for Nandita's work. The work deals with William Kneale's theory of natural necessity, according to which laws of nature as formulated in science, even though they are established or accepted *a posteriori*, yet "are or may be" necessary. It is admitted by him that we (men) have no theoretical insight into the necessity of natural laws; he maintains nevertheless that there are sufficiently strong philosophical considerations to warrant the assumption that they are principles of necessity. For this theory of opaque natural necessity Kneale draws inspiration from Locke's account of laws in the Essay, and, paradoxically enough, from Kant's theory of natural necessity as expounded in the *Critique of Judgement.*

It need hardly be stated that Nandita's work is an important contribution to the literature on the philosophy of inductive logic. The work is so exceptionally well written that it can be read with pleasure and profit by any student of philosophy.

Date : 17.06.2015

Kumudranjan Goswami MA. Ph.D.
Formerly Acharya B.N.Seal Professor
Department of Philosophy, University of Calcutta

Residence :
Merlin Daffodil
Flat no -IA,
10/7 Jyangra Ghosh Para
Kolkata- 700059

PREFACE

William Kneale's theory of natural necessity is an important contribution to the literature on the nature - that is, as he calls it, the logical character - of natural laws. He is extremely cautious in the statement of his view. He takes the view that laws of nature as formulated in science, although they are established or accepted *a posteriori*, have a logical character such as to warrant the assumption that they 'are or may be principles of necessity'.

The word 'principles' contained in the phrase 'principles of necessity', which is sometimes used by Kneale in the statement of his view, is explained in the Introductory Chapter (in 1.5.1).

Nowadays a theory of natural necessity is sometimes called 'natural necessitarianism'. This phrase is accordingly sometimes used in the present work also.

The main objective of this work is to show that Kneale's theory of natural necessity is fairly intelligible and eminently defensible.

The general line of inquiry followed in this work may be briefly described in the following way.

Chapter One is Introductory. Certain preliminary matters are explained and a brief statement of Kneale's theory of natural necessity is given in this Chapter. Some of the main considerations in favour of this theory are stated here and an attempt is made to show that the notion of *a posteriori* necessity is not absurd.

Kneale's theory of natural necessity is derived substantially from Locke's account of natural laws. Chapter Two is accordingly devoted to an exegetical and critical study of Locke's theory of natural necessity, as Kneale and some other scholars find it in his *Essay*.

The Humean objection to the Lockean theory of natural necessity is analysed into two points, and Kneale's reply to the objection with respect to both the points is explained and examined, in Chapter Three. The conclusions drawn in this Chapter are intended to throw light on what has come to be known as Kneale's theory of natural necessity in usual discussions of the nature of natural laws.

The main alternatives to the theory of natural necessity have been considered seriously by Kneale. In Chapter Four his critique of the Humean Regularity theory of natural laws comes up for discussion. What is known as 'Kneale's criticism' in this connection in the literature on the subject is explained and assessed in detail in this Chapter.

To meet Kneale's criticism some sophisticated versions of the Regularity theory of laws of nature have been formulated by critics of the necessity theory. These are examined in Chapter Five.

In Chapter Six, Whitehead's Restricted Generalization theory of natural laws, which is an important alternative to both the Humean Regularity theory and Kneale's Necessity theory of laws of nature, is taken up for an examination.

The Prescription theory of natural laws is opposed to all other theories of laws of nature, in so far as it maintains that law-sentences do not express propositions which are either true or false, but only certain rules or prescriptions for the guidance of our expectations. Kneale's examination of this theory comes to be studied critically in Chapter Seven.

Chapter Eight contains a discussion of some Instrumentalist theories which are not specifically considered by Kneale in his critique of prescriptionism regarding natural laws.

Certain difficulties in Kneale's theory of natural laws are considered and answered in Chapter Nine. Kant's theory of natural necessity, which is formulated in his third *Critique*, and the influence of which on Kneale is not frequently noted, is an important topic treated in this Chapter, where some other matters also are considered.

A Concluding Note on the whole work is added.

The present work has been prepared under the supervision of Dr Kumudranjan Goswami (now retired) Acharya B. N. Seal Professor of Philosophy, Calcutta University. I wish to thank him for his aid, advice, and criticism.

Thanks are due to Professor Norman Swartz of Simon Fraser University, British Columbia, for his advice on certain points and encouragement.

To my colleagues in the Department of Philosophy, Calcutta University, where I am a part-time teacher, I wish to express my thankfulness for the interest they have shown in my work.

I am grateful to the administrative authorities of Shri Shikshayatan College, Kolkata, for kindly granting me study leave for preparation of this work. To the Librarian of this College I remain thankful for allowing me to keep beside me some important books as long as I needed them for use in this work.

I am again indebted to the Librarian, Darsan Bhavan, Visva-Bharati for making easily available to me certain important books and journals which have been utilized in this work.

My thanks are due also to Jessica Thein Tin and Manas Raha for much help in other ways during preparation of this work.

My obligations to previous authors have all been acknowledged in the proper places. If I have dared to criticize some of my superiors in this work, it is because I believe that criticism is another way of paying homage.

Kolkata
July 2007

Nandita Chaudhuri

CONTENTS

CHAPTER ONE

INTRODUCTORY

CHAPTER TWO

ON LOCKE'S THEORY OF NATURAL NECESSITY

CHAPTER THREE

KNEALE'S REPLY TO HUME'S OBJECTION TO THE LOCKEAN THEORY OF NATURAL NECESSITY

CHAPTER FOUR

KNEALE'S CRITIQUE OF THE REGULARITY THEORY OF NATURAL LAWS

CHAPTER FIVE

SOME 'SOPHISTICATED' VERSIONS OF THE REGULARITY THEORY CONSIDERED : AN EXCURCUS

CHAPTER SIX

KNEALE'S CRITIQUE OF WHITEHEAD'S REGIONALISM REGARDING NATURAL LAWS

CHAPTER SEVEN

KNEALE'S CRITIQUE OF THE PRESCRIPTION THEORY OF NATURAL LAWS

CHAPTER EIGHT

SOME VERSIONS OF 'INSTRUMENTALISM' EXAMINED (SOME ADDITIONAL DISCUSSION)

CHAPTER NINE

A FINAL ESTIMATE OF KNEALE'S THEORY OF NATURAL NECESSITY

CHAPTER ONE

INTRODUCTORY

1.1 The Meaning of 'Natural Laws' in Kneale, and the Problem of the Importance of Natural Laws

Kneale states what he himself means by 'laws' - that is, natural laws - as follows :

> ... I understand ... by 'laws' any uniformities in nature such as we assume when making inferences to the unobserved, apart from those which can be established by summative induction. In the usage of the scientists the term is sometimes reserved for uniformities which are considered especially important because many others can be derived from them, but I am deliberately using the word . . . in a wide sense.[1]

Kneale's meaning is clear enough. For him as for many others, natural scientists are interested in making rational inferences from observed to unobserved matters of fact (since we must guide our behaviour by such inferences), but our inferences to the unobserved cannot be rational without at least tacit reliance on laws.

The importance of laws as general principles is sometimes questioned, however. Thus some philosophers argue that we can make inferences directly from particulars to particulars. For example, J. S. Mill does so in his *System of Logic.* He says that 'we much oftener conclude from particulars to particulars directly, than through the intermediate agency of any general proposition'.[2] Thus, he argues, we constantly reason from ourselves to others, or from one person to another, without troubling 'to erect our observations into general maxims of human or external nature'.[3] For example, a village mother whose Lucy got better after taking a particular medicine suggests to another mother that she had better give her child such-and-such a medicine. Kneale has, as is to be expected, given his own comments on Mill's view.

Kneale contends that if Mill means only that we often take laws for granted without explicitly stating them, Mill's view is correct, though the view is incorrect if it is thought that we can make inferences to the unobserved without at least tacitly relying on laws. Kneale says: 'Even astrologers, crystal-gazers, British Israelites, Buckmanites, and people who claim second sight take laws for granted when they make their predictions.'[4] He admits that if we could directly perceive future events, no law would indeed be required as a premiss, but he points out that this sort of clairvoyance would be a kind of perception or observation, not a method of making inferences beyond observation, and so would not come within the scope of the present discussion.[5]

Attention should perhaps be drawn here to 'one truly eccentric view', which, D. M. Armstrong says, has been pointed out to him by Peter Forrest[6]. On this view, although there are regularities or uniformities in nature, there are no laws. According to this view, although nature is not law-governed, we may still make reliable inferences to the unobserved by luck or for some other reason. This view, obviously, evades the above argument. For the view may be called the 'Disappearance view of law'.[7]

It is not difficult to set aside this view, as Armstrong has pointed out. In the first place, what good reason is there for us to think that the world is regular ? In the second place, there is the problem of Induction, which this view has to face. Kneale would particularly insist on this second argument. He says: 'One of the principal aims of natural scientists when they practise induction is to make possible rational inferences from observed to unobserved matters of fact, and, in particular, prediction, or inference to the future'.[8] The expression 'when they practise induction' is noteworthy. It is clear that Kneale would not be disturbed, as Armstrong is not, by the aforementioned 'eccentric' view.

1.2 Types of Laws of Nature

The present work which is concerned with examining Kneale's view about the logical character of natural laws must take into account, not laws of one type, but laws of different types. Some of the older philosophers assumed that all science must be a search for causal laws. For Kneale, this assumption is 'a mistake'.[9] He has clearly pointed out the limits to the notion of cause in natural science. It is, indeed, true that many formulated laws of nature are causal, but scientists have also formulated many other laws of nature which cannot be considered causal laws in any customary sense.

Kneale says:

> Many laws of nature formulated by scientists are indeed laws of causal connexion ... between types of events, e.g. the generalization that friction causes a rise of temperature ... But ... there are many laws of nature which cannot be expressed as causal connexions, for example, that all mammals are vertebrates, and causal laws appear to be more common in the less-advanced sciences.[10]

Although it has been emphasized that many laws of nature are non-causal in order to indicate that an explanation can be quite satisfactory even if the law cited is not in the usual sense causal, the impression, however, must not be left, on the other hand, that examination of causal laws with regard to their logical status in some cases according to the context can have no general bearing on, or value towards, the logical status of non-causal natural laws.

Now as for non-causal laws, there are again many types which are distinguishable. No claim is, however, made that the classification of non-causal laws of nature is exhaustive, and Kneale says that the so-called different types of non-causal laws 'may not even be mutually exclusive'.[11] The classification suggested by him may nevertheless be of some use as showing, as he says, 'that some of the older logicians have over-simplified their accounts of induction'.[12] Kneale's classification is as follows:

1. There are a good number of natural laws which assert 'the *uniform association of attributes*.' All mammals are vertebrates, common salt is soluble in water : these are examples of laws of this type. Such laws are important in the classification of things into natural kinds.

2. There are again laws which assert '*the uniformity of development* to be expected in certain natural processes.' The law, for example, that there are phases in the development of an embryo is such a law. The second law of thermodynamics to the effect that free transference of heat takes place from a body of higher temperature to another of lower temperature till the temperatures of the bodies in thermal contact become equal is presumably also a law of this type.

Laws of this type which assert that a process of some kind goes through a gradual development till a certain course is completed cannot be regarded as causal laws, because, as Kneale says, 'the word "cause" carries with it still some notion of dramatic intervention, of action of one thing on another, which is lacking in these cases'.[13]

3. A third type of law asserts '*functional relations between measurable quantities*.' The word "function" here is used in the mathematical sense. An example is provided by the Boyle-Charles' law for ideal gases. The following is the gas equation:

For any gas

$$pv = kT,$$

where *p* stands for the pressure of the gas, *v* for its volume, T for absolute temperature, and *k* for a constant dependent on the mass and the nature of the gas. The equation means that the product of the pressure and volume of a fixed mass of gas is directly proportional to its temperature in the absolute scale.

The law cited is not a causal law, since it does not assert that a change in the temperature is followed or preceded by a change in the pressure or volume or in both, but that the former change is concurrent with the latter changes. In Nagel's language, 'the relation stated by the law must be distinguished from the sequential order of the events that may occur when the law is tested or used in for making predictions'.[14] He explains the point as :

> ... For example, in testing the law in a laboratory, one may diminish the volume of an ideal gas in such a way that its temperature remains constant, and then note that its pressure increases. But the law says nothing about the order in which the changes may be varied, nor about the temporal sequence in which the changes may be observed.[15]

4. Laws of a fourth type deal with *'numerical constants'* in nature.

Laws about the melting points of chemical substances are the examples in point, e.g. Aluminium melts at 660.1^0 C. Laws about boiling points also may be cited, e.g. Carbon di-sulphide boils at 46.3^0C.

Some laws dealing with numerical constants may, however, be described as laws of functional relations between measurable quantities, and this is the reason why Kneale has pointed out that the types of laws distinguished here are not mutually exclusive. Thus the speed of light which may be regarded as a numerical constant may also be described in terms of functional relationship between measurable quantities. The speed of light may be described as:

All propagation of light is such that

$$s = 299792\ t,$$

where s stands for the space covered in kilometers, and t for the time taken in seconds.

Besides laws of nature, there are also probability rules, which may be considered by some.

1.3 The Formula or Formulae to be used in talking of Laws in Philosophical Discussion

The various types of natural laws have peculiarities which cannot be expressed by making use of any general formula for referring to them. Yet much will be gained if a general formula can be used in talking of laws in the discussion as to the logical character of natural laws.

Kneale in his *Probability and Induction* makes use of the formula 'All α things are β' for purposes of exposition.[16] At times[17] he enunciates a natural law, or what is supposed to be such[18], in the form 'Every F thing is G'. Other writers make use of some formula or other of their own choice. Popper uses the form 'All A's are B's',[19] and Armstrong suggests the form 'Fs are Gs'.[20] All these, however, virtually amount to the same formula. They differ only in the choice of letters or plural signs, but such differences do not matter much. Anyone of these formulae, or, something very much like these, may be used according to the context for expository purposes in the present work.

It might be argued that a formula like 'All α things are β' or 'Every F thing is G', although it suits a law like 'All mammals are vertebrates', cannot cover quantitative laws, such as laws of functional relationship between variable magnitudes (e.g. the gas law): for the latter, something like the form 'the quantities P and Q co-vary in such a way that Q is a certain function of P (Q = f(P))' seems to be more suitable. Kneale, however, would not be perturbed by such an argument. According to him, even functional laws of the type in question are–

> ...universal in two respects, first, as dealing with all specimens of some kind and secondly, as dealing with all the values of some variable magnitudes (or at least all the values within some prescribed range of variation).[21]

For Kneale, it would be wrong to regard functional relations between variable magnitudes as themselves laws, since this would be to miss the fact that such laws are always about some special kinds of things or processes having the variable magnitudes[22]. The formula 'All α things are β' does, indeed, serve to indicate that 'even in quantitative laws there is a reference to all instances of a certain kind, e.g. all specimens of gas, all pieces of copper, all propagations of sounds.'[23] Kneale says that if one decides to use the formula 'All α things are β' (or, if one prefers, 'Every α thing is β'), one may say that

> ...the functional expression used in the statement of a quantitative law is to be thought as part of the expression to be inserted for 'β'. Thus the gas law ... taken ... can be written in the form: 'Every specimen of gas behaves in such a way that its pressure, volume, and temperature are in the relation $pv = k\mathrm{T}$.' [24]

[If one considers probability rules, it will be well to point out that even such rules are *general in form*. Kneale uses the word '"rule" here to suggest an analogy with laws'[25]. He states his view quite clearly:

> ...Very many of our most useful probability statements are themselves established by inductive arguments. When, for example, I say that it is very improbable that Jones will fall into dishonesty since he has a record of twenty years' faithful service, I use a rule to the effect that it is very

> improbable any man with such a record will fall into dishonesty. This rule, which is general in form, has been derived by induction from my own experience and what others have told me. A few men with such records have in the past fallen into dishonesty, but they form a very small proportion of all the cases observed. The probability rule which I bring forward as the justification for my judgement about a particular man bears the same relation to the facts of experience as a law of universal connexion would to an unobserved uniformity.[26]]

It should be clear from the foregoing considerations that a general formula like any of those mentioned before will be useful in talking of laws, for purposes of exposition, in the philosophical discussion about natural laws. It must be pointed out over again that such a formula cannot exhibit the *peculiarities* of the different types of laws (or rules); but 'the peculiar simplicity' of such a formula 'makes it', as Armstrong puts it 'extremely useful for discussing a number of difficult philosophical issues concerning laws'.[27]

1.4 A Few Words on the Major Theories about the Logical Character of Natural Laws Selected for Consideration in This Work

About the logical character of natural laws, many theories have been propounded. Not all of them can be discussed within the prescribed limits of space available to this work. Only the major theories selected by Kneale come within its scope, though the logic of discussion may at times lead to consideration of some related theories. The theories selected for discussion by Kneale are these:

1. ***The Theory of Natural Necessity*:** According to it, laws of nature are, or rather, may be, necessary. Kneale claims to have found this theory in an inchoate form in Locke's *Essay*[28]. He

comes to accept it in its essentials, seeking to defend it against objections. The theory is supported by a number of considerations. In this way what is known as Kneale's theory of natural necessity emerges.

2. ***The Regularity Theory of Natural Laws*** **:** This theory is one of the major alternatives to the necessity theory of laws. In its naïve form the theory is formulated by Hume. It identifies the *unrestricted* uniformities in nature with the laws of nature. Subsequently many refinements upon the Humean regularity theory have been effected. These are certainly deserving of serious consideration in any critical estimate of Kneale's criticism of the regularity theory of laws.

3. ***The Restricted Generalization Theory of (i.e. Regionalism Regarding) Natural Laws*** **:** According to it, natural laws are not unrestricted, but restricted, in scope. The substance of this theory may be given in Kneale's words as: 'laws of nature are, so to say, local and temporary customs established among some constituents of the universe during a "cosmic epoch" '.[29] The theory is held by Whitehead, and is a major alternative as much to the regularity theory as to the necessity theory of laws. The theory along with Kneale's critique of it calls for discussion in the present work.

4. ***The Prescription Theory of Natural Laws*** **:** Some philosophers, on finding difficulties in the above-mentioned theories, have come to hold that the sentences in which laws of nature are formulated express, not any genuine propositions at all, but only rules or prescriptions for our guidance in predicting or anticipating certain events. This theory, as Kneale points out[30], is originally suggested by Ramsey and adopted by some positivists, e.g. Schlick. Kneale criticizes the theory accordingly. Both the theory and Kneale's criticism of it have a title to consideration in this work.

Some writers group Schlick's theory with those of some others and deal with them in a general way under the heading of

'Instrumentalism'[31]. So some principal versions of instrumentalism, not specifically considered by Kneale, have a claim to attention in this work: an attempt needs to be made to see how far Kneale's criticism of prescriptionism can be extended to them.

To prevent confusion that may occur later, it is perhaps necessary to note right here the fact that some philosophers mentioned by Kneale as being advocates of one of these theories are by others mentioned, however, as being advocates of a different theory. Thus, for example, Ramsey whom Kneale regards as the philosopher suggesting the prescription theory of laws is sometimes reckoned among the supporters of the regularity theory[32]. Comment on this apparent anomaly is this: there is in Ramsey's theory an aspect which shows him to be a regularist, and there is an aspect which shows him to be a prescriptionist. He is both this and that according as this aspect and that come to be emphasized.

1.4.1 On the order of exposition followed by Kneale in his treatment of alternatives to the theory of natural necessity, and some justification for a slight departure from that order in this work

In his treatment of alternatives to the theory of natural necessity Kneale no doubt mentions first of all the Humean regularity theory (which he prefers to call the constancy theory) of laws, but in fact discusses Whitehead's theory prior to discussing the Humean theory. His reason for doing so is this: if the theory of natural necessity be rejected, the next consideration is whether statements of laws of nature are only truths of facts. But if they are truths of facts, they are either restricted or unrestricted truths of facts. Now the view that they are restricted truths of facts is adopted by Whitehead, and the view that they are unrestricted truths of facts is the view of Hume and his followers[33]. This is the logic behind Kneale's decision to give a treatment of Whitehead's theory prior to his treatment of the Humean theory.

In the present work, however, a slight departure from the order of treatment followed by Kneale is made, in so far as the Humean regularity theory of laws is discussed here before Whitehead's theory. This is done, first, in order to keep as close as possible to the historical order, and secondly, because it is believed that a better appreciation of Whitehead's philosophy in relevant matters is possible only if a prior account of the Humean theory is already given than otherwise.[34]

In making this departure from the order of treatment followed by Kneale, the logic behind that order is not violated, however. For the alternative he has set down for consideration that statements of laws are either restricted or unrestricted truths of facts might have been also expressed as the alternative that such statements are either unrestricted or restricted truths of facts.

As Kneale himself admits, it 'has commonly been assumed that natural laws are propositions of unrestricted universality...'.[35] This being so, the alternative that such laws, if taken as truths of facts, are unrestricted truths of facts has a certain priority of claim to attention.

1.5 Kneale's Theory of Natural Necessity: A Preliminary Account

An introductory account of Kneale's theory of natural necessity with which, particularly, the present work is concerned may be of some use.

The theory is, as already pointed out in the Preface, based on his view that laws of nature, even though they are – formulated and accepted – *a posteriori*, 'are or may be'[36] yet 'principles of necessity'. Kneale finds no good reason for denying that such laws carry with them a character of necessity. He says at one place that, since this is the only view of such laws which is for him at all plausible, he is led on 'to assume that, if there are any laws of nature such as we try to formulate in natural science, they are principles of necessitation.'[37]

The word 'principles' sometimes used by him in the statement of his view, as in the above passage, needs some explanation.

1.5.1 Kneale's word 'principles' explained

Kneale thinks that the customary distinction between contingent truths and necessary truths is not precise enough, considering the fact that philosophers of the opposed schools have raised many difficulties concerning the notions of contingency and necessity. He comes to suggest accordingly another distinction in place of it[38].

The distinction he recommends in his *Probability and Induction* is a distinction between truths of two different orders. These are truths about *matters of fact* and truths about *principles of modality*. He calls them, for short, *facts* and *principles*. He thinks that the sense of the distinction will be clear from examples. Thus it is a fact that my pen is green, but it is a principle that nothing which is red can be also green all over at the same time. Facts, in this usage, are no doubt identical with contingent truths commonly so called, but principles cannot be simply identified with necessary truths as they are commonly called. For, although all principles are necessary truths, not all necessary truths are principles: some necessary truths are only consequences of principles. Thus the truth that nothing which is red *is* also green all over at the same time–mark the word 'is' used here instead of 'can' is commonly regarded as a necessary truth, but it is not itself a principle of modality, although it is a consequence of a principle, namely, of the principle mentioned above.[39]

Principles, in this usage, are, then, truths about the possibility or impossibility of their being facts of a certain kind. As thus determining what facts there can be or cannot be, principles are, in this respect, more fundamental than facts. Thus the principle mentioned before serves to indicate that there cannot be such a fact as that something which is red is also green all over at the same time. The principle in this way amounts to the principle: 'It is impossible for anything to be both red and green all over'.

John Passmore, in his exposition of Kneale's view, has done well to make one point clear: he makes clear how the character of laws of nature is to be expressed upon Kneale's theory of natural laws. He says:

> ...Some principles – for example, the principle that nothing can be red and green all over at the same time – are, Kneale says, apprehended directly by 'intuitive induction'. Other principles, including laws of nature, cannot be so apprehended. Yet they are clearly principles; for such a law of nature as '*P* is *Q*' does not assert, simply, that 'every *P* is *Q*' but much more - that nothing can be *P* without being *Q*. The 'inductive problem', for Kneale, is to explain why it is rational to believe such non-intuitive principles as laws of nature.[40]

It must be pointed out that Kneale's recommendation of a new terminology in his book under reference need not be taken as a 'decree' that anybody wishing to discuss the subject of the logical nature of natural laws should adopt this new terminology. For him, it is just a recommendation, not a decree.

A brief note now on the way in which Kneale has presented his theory of natural necessity in his *Probability and Induction* may not be inappropriate.

1.5.2 Laws and Law-statements (An incidental note on their distinction and connection)

In his treatment of the necessitation theory of natural laws[41] Kneale sometimes refers to natural laws, and sometimes to propositions or statements about such laws, that is, to law-propositions or law-statements. The impression is sometimes conveyed that, for him, natural laws are necessary, and sometimes that law-propositions or law-statements are necessary. [Some evidence for this is perhaps required. (i) Clear evidence showing that, for him, laws of nature are necessary (not merely principles, which, being *truths* of a certain kind, concern, in the present context, rather statements of natural laws than natural laws themselves) is provided by his expression 'natural necessity' occurring in his phrase 'theory of natural necessity'[42]. 'Natural necessity' means the *necessity of natural laws*[43], and this indicates that natural laws are for him necessary. (ii) As for propositions or statements about natural laws, he says, on a particular occasion, that they are concerned with connections which 'are not evidently necessary'[44]. Mark that he is here saying, not that, evidently, they are not necessary, but that they are not evidently necessary. He is not denying that they are necessary, but only saying that their necessity is not evident (i.e. transparent) to us (men). He says: 'It is true that we often call them laws of necessary connexion, but we cannot in any such case see the necessity of the connexion asserted'[45]. The reason for this opacity of necessary connections in nature will become clear later on at different stages. It is essential to keep it in mind that Kneale's is a theory of opaque necessity. Having furnished evidence in this way for what has been said, it will be easier now to come straight to the point, which is as follows.] Clearly, there is a distinction to be made between laws and statements of laws. Statements of laws are not themselves laws; they are only *about* laws. Now, Kneale need not deny that there is a distinction to be made between them. One need not therefore assume for a moment that there is on Kneale's part, when he is presenting his theory of natural necessity, any confusion between laws and law-statements. His actual position is that, if statements of laws are necessary, this necessity serves to reflect at the same time the necessity of laws, since they are about laws. W. Kneale and Martha Kneale write :

> ...For a correct account of science it is essential to admit that, in a division between the world and those features of language which are man-made, *necessary connexions belong to the world* no less than contingent facts. Unfortunately the influence of the conventionalist theory of necessity which has been derived from Wittgenstein's work is [very] strong ...[46] [Italics not in the text.]

Kneale, as an advocate of a theory of objective necessity holding in nature, has nothing to do with the conventionalist theory of necessity, according to which all necessity is linguistic. His critique of conventionalism will come up for consideration later on (in 9.2).

The important question now is: What are the principal considerations in favour of Kneale's theory of natural necessity ?

1.5.3 Some considerations in favour of Kneale's theory

The following are some of the considerations in favour of Kneale's theory under reference :

First, the theory of natural necessity involves the doctrine of necessary truths which are not known *a priori*, and this doctrine, Kneale says, 'is presupposed by the activity of natural scientists.'[47] Natural scientists speak of laws of nature formulated by them in such a way as to suggest that it would be wrong to analyse their conjectures of laws according to Hume's regularity theory; and, as regards their conjectures of probability in matters of chance also, there is the suggestion that it would be wrong to explain these according to the frequency theory[48], which has, Kneale points out, an 'obvious resemblance'[49] to the regularity theory of natural laws.

Kneale admits that 'some physicists have argued that the quantum theory enables, or even requires, them to dispense with the notion of natural necessity or impossibility', but hastens to point out that 'it is not universally accepted by those most competent to discuss the scientific developments on which it is supposed to the based'.[50] Kneale is aware that some of the laws claimed to have been established are replaceable in physical theory by 'probability rules involving probabilities very near to 1'[51]. He observes, however, on the strength of certain considerations:

> ... So long as we believe that there are or may be principles of necessity or impossibility, we have good reason for conjecturing probability rules, whereas without that belief we should have no reason.[52]

These are matters which are too technical to be discussed in a work with a limited assignment, such as this work. The point is mentioned here to indicate one kind of suggestion on which Kneale's theory of natural necessity is grounded and one line of argument along which he seeks to ward off attack on it.

The primary objective of the present work is to place Kneale's theory under reference within the framework of *philosophical* discussion only and attempt in this way to ascertain, as has been pointed out in the Preface, whether the theory is intelligible and how far it is defensible.

It remains – to resume the thread of discussion – to draw attention to some other considerations that lie at the back of Kneale's theory in question.

Secondly, one of Kneale's principal arguments in favour of his theory is that it is the least unsatisfactory among the theories considered by him about the logical character of natural laws.[53] In this way his argument turns out to be a kind of argument by elimination of alternatives. He concludes that natural laws are or may be necessary, in so far as he is persuaded that they are not as regularists, or regionalists, or prescriptionists (or instrumentalists) construe them to be. It would be too harsh to say that his argument is then at the mercy of the overlooked alternative, because he has also some extra considerations to rely upon to support his theory, for example, his analysis[54] of the peculiar nature of perceptual objects, which (objects) laws of nature are about, besides his interpretation and analysis of the activity of natural scientists.

(It should be clear, by the by, why most of the present work should be devoted to considering the different available main alternatives to the theory of natural necessity and Kneale's criticisms of them.)

Thirdly, it is also pertinent to point out that the theory of natural necessity which Kneale seeks to defend so extensively against his critics cannot be regarded as unintelligible. Karl Popper in one context says, 'I have found Kneale's criticism difficult to understand'.[55] In the same context, however, he acknowledges that Kneale's criticism is a 'most penetrating criticism', saying over again: '... his criticism seems to me most valuable'.[56] These are, however, matters which concern debates (to be left more properly for subsequent consideration) between Kneale and his critics, and do not here appear to be much significant for the question whether or not Kneale's theory is unintelligible in the ordinary sense of being not comprehensible.

Kneale's theory, in so far as it is a theory of *a posteriori* necessity, may be supposed by some to be unintelligible, in the ordinary sense of being not comprehensible, alleging the ground that the notion of *a posteriori* necessity is absurd. Some examination of this notion is therefore required here.

1.5.3.1 On the notion of the necessary *a posteriori*: Kneale and Kripke

Some contemporary philosophers treat the terms 'analytic', '*a priori*' and 'necessary' as coextensive, and some even go to the length of assuming the three terms, as W. Kneale and Martha Kneale put it, 'to be not only coextensive but also synonymous'[57].

These philosophers accordingly tend to regard the notion of *a posteriori* necessity as unintelligible in the sense of being absurd. W. & M. Kneale have of course duly criticized their view. The criticism will be considered in detail later on (in Chapter 9). It will suffice to mention only one point here. It is this: the term *a priori* is taken from theory of knowledge, and the term 'necessity' from metaphysics.[58] So from the fact that something is not known *a priori*, it does not automatically follow that it cannot in its nature be necessary.

The significance of this point cannot be missed. If a truth is necessary, it is so in its own nature, and not in virtue of anybody's knowledge of it. If it is known, and known *a priori*, it not only in fact is necessary, but also comes to be known *as* necessary. Suppose now that it is not known *a priori*, but is simply accepted *a posteriori*. It is then still necessary, which in fact it is in virtue of its own nature; only it is then not known *as* necessary. This is a case for admission of the necessary *a posteriori*.

This general argument can now be applied to the case of laws of nature. Natural laws are not known *a priori*: they are accepted *a posteriori*. It does not follow from this that they cannot in their nature be necessary (supposing that there are reasons, as Kneale believes there are, for assuming that they are necessary). There is, then, nothing unintelligible in the ordinary sense of this word about Kneale's theory of natural necessity.[59]

So far as the *general* question of intelligibility of the notion of necessary *a posteriori* truths is concerned, Saul. A. Kripke has presented an argument which happens to be similar to W. & M. Kneale's argument mentioned above.

Kripke says that 'the notion of *a priority* is a concept of epistemology'.[60] As for the term 'necessary', he first of all points out one sense of it in which it is sometimes used, and then proceeds to indicate the sense with which he himself is concerned here. He says: 'Sometimes this is used in an epistemological way and might then just mean *a priori*'.[61] He is here referring to the view of those philosophers who use 'necessary' interchangeably with the epistemological term '*a priori*'. He then proceeds to say as regards the notion of necessity: 'But what I am concerned with here is a notion which is not a notion of epistemology but of metaphysics, in some (I hope) nonpejorative sense.'[62] The notion of necessity he has in mind is metaphysical, in some nonpejorative sense, in so far as whether or not something is necessary is an issue which is different from the issue whether anyone knows it, and knows it *a priori*. Thus he writes :

> ...We ask whether something might have been true, or might have been false. Well, if something is false, it's obviously not necessarily true. If it is true, might it have been otherwise? Is it possible that, in this respect, the world should have been different from the way it is? If the answer is 'no', then this fact about the world is a necessary one. If the answer is 'yes', then this fact about the world is a contingent one. This in and of itself has nothing to do with anyone's knowledge of anything. It's certainly a philosophical thesis, and not a matter of obvious definitional equivalence, either that everything *a priori* is necessary or that everything necessary is *a priori*. Both concepts may be vague. That may be another problem. But at any rate they are dealing with two different domains, two different areas, the epistemological and the metaphysical.

The import of Kripke's argument is sufficiently clear. If something is necessary, it is so in the metaphysical sense (the term 'metaphysical' being used here in the nonpejorative sense) - that is, in virtue of its own nature. What this is in its own nature is a metaphysical matter which is independent of the epistemological question of whether, or how, it is known. All this is reminiscent of what has been said before in the context of W. & M. Kneale's argument. So nothing further need be added here in this matter.

Kripke says, again, that the philosophers who regard the terms 'necessary' and '*a priori*' as synonymous have virtually identified them without argument, although an argument was required. He says that these two terms 'are *not* obvious synonyms'[63]. He proceeds: 'There may be a philosophical argument connecting them, perhaps even identifying them; but an argument is required, not simply the observation that the two terms are clearly interchangeable.'

One of the reasons for thinking that the terms 'necessary' and '*a priori*' 'must mean the same' may be this, as it is supposed by Kripke, who, however, has not forgotten to add his own comment:

> ... if something not only happens to be true in the actual world but is also true in all possible worlds, then, of course, just by running through all the possible worlds in our heads, we ought to be able with enough effort to see, if a statement is necessary, that it is necessary, and thus know it *a priori.* But really this is not so obviously feasible at all.[64]

Concerning the notion of the necessary *a posteriori*, what has been said above may be expected to indicate that the notion is not unintelligible in the sense of being incomprehensible or absurd. Even then some further discussion on it may be useful. It will be made later on (in 9.3).

As concerns Kneale's theory of natural necessity, some of the main considerations in favour of it have been pointed out. There remains the elaborate work of considering Kneale's criticisms of alternative theories and his replies to objections, and of judging whether other objections are answerable on behalf of him, by organizing the entire discussion within the framework of an ordered exposition.

As has already been pointed out before, Kneale has derived much inspiration for his theory from Locke's account of natural laws. It is therefore advisable to come to Locke's account without any further delay.

Notes

1 W. Kneale, *Probability and Induction*, Oxford, 1949, reprinted 1966, p. 65.

2 J. S. Mill, *A System of Logic*, Longman, London, 1970, Book II, Chapter III, Sec. 3, p. 123.

3 *Ibidem.*

4 Kneale, *op. cit.*, p. 45.

5 *Ibidem.*

6 D. M. Armstrong, *What is a Law of Nature?* Cambridge University Press, 1983, p. 5.

7 *Ibidem.*

8 Kneale, *op. cit.*, p. 45.

9 *Ibid.,* p. 65.

10 *Ibid.*, p. 62; see also Earnest Nagel, *The Structure of Science*, Indian edition, Macmillan India Limited, New Delhi, 1984, pp. 73-78.

11 Kneale, *op. cit.* p. 66.

12 *Ibidem.*

13 *Ibid.,* p. 68.

14 Nagel, *op. cit.*, p. 77.

15 *Ibidem.*

16 Kneale, *op. cit.*, p. 69.

17 See Kneale's article 'Universality and Necessity', *The British Journal for the Philosophy of Science*, 12, August 1961, No. 46, p. 97.

18 The expression 'what is supposed to be such' is used because of the possibility of doubt, which always remains, whether any supposed law of nature is a genuine law. One might say: 'There are no secure paradigms of laws of nature'. Even then it might be said: 'though we can point to no secure paradigms of laws, the scientific theories which we now work with are obviously a reasonable approximation to at least some of the real laws of nature. For if our theories did not nearly grasp the truth at many points, it would be inexplicable that they should permit so much successful prediction.' See Armstrong, op. cit., p. 6. Armstrong says: 'Actually, it seems that even the rough-and-ready generalizations of pre-scientific practical

wisdom represent a reasonable degree of approximation to genuine laws.' *Ibidem.*

19 K. R. Popper, 'A Note on Natural Laws and so-called "Contrary-to-Fact Conditionals" ', *Mind,* 58, N. S. 1949, p. 63.

20 Armstrong, *loc. cit.*

21 Kneale, *Probability and Induction*, pp. 68 f.

22 *Ibid.*, p. 69.

23 *Ibidem.*

24 *Ibidem.* For laws concerned with numerical constants in nature (such as those about melting points of chemical substances), see G. H. von Wright, *The Logical Problem of Induction* (2nd revised edition), Basil Blackwell, Oxford, 1957, p. 40 (last para.).

25 *Ibid.,* p. 118.

26 *Ibid.,* pp 21 f.

27 Armstrong , *op. cit.,* p. 7.

28 Relevant passages from Locke's *Essay Concerning Human Understanding* will be quoted later on.

29 Kneale, *op. cit.,* p. 72.

30 *Ibid.,* p. 76.

31 See, for example, Nagel, *op. cit.,* p. 129n; and, for discussion, pp. 129ff. Nagel is no doubt concerned with theories rather than with laws, but Dewey and Ryle and even Schlick referred to by him use the word 'laws'. See below, Chap 8.

32 See below 5.5 and 7.2.1.

33 Cf. Kneale, *op. cit.,* pp. 71ff. esp. p. 73 (last para., and its continuation on p. 74).

34 Tom L. Beauchamp says: 'Whitehead's account raises afresh, somewhat surprisingly for those who regard him as Hume's opposite on induction, some of the latter's doubts concerning the justifiability of sweeping conclusions reached through scientific inference'. See his paper entitled 'Cosmic Epochs and the Scope of Scientific Laws', in *Process Studies*, vol. 2, 1972, p. 296. Whether, and how far, Beauchamp's interpretation of Whitehead's theory is acceptable will be seen later on; but it makes at least one point clear, namely, that a prior account of the Humean theory would be useful.

35 Kneale, *op. cit.*, p. 72.

36 The whole expression 'are or may be principles of necessity' is borrowed from Kneale; vide *ibid.*, p. 256.

The import of Kneale's words 'are or may be' will become clear as we proceed. It may be helpful, however, to give here a brief indication of his reason for cautiousness:

He admits that we, men, have no *a priori* knowledge of- no direct insight into - the necessity of laws of nature, which are accepted *a posteriori.* He believes nevertheless - on the strength of certain philosophical considerations - that their logical character is such as to suggest the conclusion that they are necessary. In view of the peculiarity of this situation, he chooses to say that they 'are or may be' necessary.

37 *Ibid.*, p. 89.

38 *Vide ibid.*, p. 32.

39 *Ibid.*, pp. 32 -33.

40 John Passmore, *A Hundred Years of Philosophy*, Penguin Books Ltd., England, 1980, p. 421.

41 The expression 'the necessitation theory of natural laws' is taken from Kneale, *op. cit.*, p. 80.

42 For the expression 'theory of natural necessity' *vide ibid.*, p.v.

43 The expression 'the necessity of natural laws' occurs on p. 71 of Kneale's book under reference. *Vide ibid.*, p. 80, for the expression 'the necessity of a natural law'.

44 *Ibid.*, p. 44.

45 *Ibidem.*

46 (William) Kneale and Martha Kneale, *The Development of Logic*, Clarendon Press, Oxford, (1962, reprinted in) 1964, x. 5, 'Necessity and Language', p. 650.

47 Kneale, *Probability and Induction*, p. 254.

48 *Vide ibidem.* For Kneale's criticism of the frequency theory see the same work, § 32 and *passim.*

49 *Ibid.*, p. 151.

50 *Ibid.*, p. 254.

51 *Ibid.*, p. 255.

52 *Ibid.*, p. 256.

53 *Ibid.*, p. 77. (It is on his remarks in the last paragraph of the page just referred to here that the point being developed in the text is based.)

54 On this analysis see below, 3.3. On the importance of understanding 'the peculiarity' of perceptual object terminology for the problem in hand see Kneale's remarks on p. 258 (second para.) of his *Probability and Induction.*

55 Karl Popper, *The Logic of Scientific Discovery*, Hutchinson and Co. Ltd., London, 1959, New Appendices, p. 426.

56 *Ibid.*, p. 427.

57 Kneale and Kneale, *op. cit.*, p. 637 (second para.).

58 *Ibidem* (First para.).

59 Cf. Kneale and Kneale's remark in the first paragraph mentioned in note 58 above.

60 Saul. A. Kripke, *Naming and Necessity*, Basil Blackwell, Oxford, 1980, p. 34.

61 *Ibid.*, p. 35.

62 *Ibid.*, pp. 35f. The next passage cited occurs in the same para. as is being referred to here.

63 *Ibid.*, p. 38.

64 *Ibidem.*

CHAPTER TWO

ON LOCKE'S THEORY OF NATURAL NECESSITY

2.1 Foreword

Kneale finds in Locke's *Essay Concerning Human Understanding* the suggestion of a theory of natural necessity. According to this theory, natural laws may be necessary (as expressing necessary connections), although their necessity remains opaque to us owing to our incurable ignorance of the real essences of substances and of their operations upon one another. This theory is complicated, and cannot be explained all at once. It can be explained only progressively through consideration of a number of related issues. The present Chapter is intended to provide such an explanation. A brief critical appraisal of Locke's theory will also be attempted.

The first thing that needs to be considered is whether Kneale's ascription of a theory of natural necessity to Locke is justified. It is a common practice to regard Locke as an empiricist. So, it seems, a theory of natural or objective necessity is hardly consistent with his basic position. In view of this suspicion, Kneale's interpretation of Locke's theory calls for an examination at the very outset. If it is found that Kneale's interpretation is supported by passages cited from Locke's *Essay*, then of course the suspicion just mentioned can be allayed by holding that the suggestion of natural necessitarianism constitutes after all an aspect of what might be called Locke's *rationalism*[1].

2.2 Is the Ascription of a Theory of Natural Necessity to Locke Justified?

Kneale states what may be called Locke's theory of natural necessity as follows :

> Natural laws are often said to be concerned with necessary connexions, and it is therefore a plausible suggestion that they may be principles of necessitation which for some special reason we cannot hope to establish by intuitive induction. This was apparently Locke's view. In the fourth book of his *Essay on the*[2] *Human Understanding* he says several times that we cannot have insight into the connexions which we assert in natural science; but he holds nevertheless that they may be necessary in the same sense as connexions which we are able to comprehend, and he implies that a sufficiently powerful mind which was furnished with the appropriate ideas of what he calls the real internal essences of things might see the necessity of natural laws.[3]

One can see from the above exposition that, for Kneale, Locke's theory as to natural laws consists, in the main, of two points :

(i) We (men) cannot *comprehend* the connections as asserted in sentences purporting to express natural laws - that is, we cannot *see* or discover the necessity of natural laws - owing to our ignorance of the real internal essences of physical things (substances).

(ii) Nevertheless, natural laws *may be* necessary, and necessary in the same sense in which transparently necessary propositions (say, mathematical propositions) are necessary.

The question is whether these two views are actually Locke's. To settle this question, certain passages need to be cited from Locke's *Essay*.

Locke says:

> ... let our complex *idea* of any species of substances be what it will, we can hardly, from the simple *ideas* contained in it,

> certainly determine the *necessary co-existence* of any other quality whatsoever. Our knowledge in all these inquiries reaches very little further than our experience.[4]

Locke is suggesting here that we cannot discover any *necessary connection* between, e.g. being gold and being malleable (to take this example given by Locke himself a little later on in the same paragraph as that from which the above passage is quoted). This means that, for him, we cannot see the necessity of natural laws, such as 'Gold is malleable'.

To quote another passage:

> ...the simple ideas whereof our complex *ideas* of substances are made up are, for the most part, such as carry with them, no visible necessary connexion or inconsistency with any other simple *ideas*, whose *co-existence* with them we would inform ourselves about.[5]

It is noteworthy that Locke does not say that there is no necessary connection in the case in question: he says only that there is no *visible* necessary connection, or, as he elsewhere says, 'no discoverable connexion'[6]. It is, then, confirmed that, according to him, we do not and cannot *see* the necessity of natural laws.

The reason why Locke says that we cannot see the necessity of natural laws is stated by him in the following passage (to quote only one such passage):

> The complex *ideas* that our names of the species of substances properly stand for are collections of such qualities as have been observed to co-exist in an unknown s*ubstratum,* which we call s*ubstance*; but what other qualities necessarily co-exist with such combinations we cannot certainly know, unless we can discover their natural dependence: which, in their primary qualities, we can go but a very little way in; and in all their secondary qualities, we

> can discover no connexion at all, for the reasons mentioned, *chap iii* viz. (1) Because we know not the real constitutions of substances on which each *secondary quality* particularly depends. (2) Did we know that, it would serve us only for experimental (not universal) knowledge, and reach with certainty no further than that bare instance.[7]

It will have been clear by now that Kneale's ascription to Locke of the first of the two views distinguished above - namely, that we cannot see the necessity of natural laws - is not without textual warrant.

To come now to the second view, namely, that, for Locke, natural laws, though not seen to be necessary, may nevertheless be necessary, and necessary in the same sense as mathematical propositions.

Locke observes:

> I doubt not but, if we could discover the figure, size, texture, and motion of the minute constituent parts of any two bodies, we should know without trial several of their operations one upon another, as we do now the properties of a square or a triangle.[8]

We hasten to point out that in this passage Locke does not aver that natural laws may be necessary; but it is still important as indicating that, for him, if natural laws could be known to be (and so if they were) necessary, they would be necessary in the same sense in which mathematical propositions are. *In bk. iv, ch. vi, sec. 10*, Locke more clearly points this out by comparing the natural law 'all gold is malleable' with the geometrical proposition 'the three angles of all right-lined triangles are equal to two right ones'.

But the crucial question is: Has Locke observed anywhere that natural laws may be necessary? A brief discussion is required in order to answer this question.

Locke observes: 'The ignorance and darkness that is in us no more hinders nor confines the knowledge that is in others, than the blindness of a mole is an argument against the quick-sightedness of an eagle'.[9] So he considers it 'reasonable to think [that] other beings, perfecter than we, have'[10] perhaps the *ideas* which we lack. He suggests that such 'perfecter' beings might see the necessity of natural laws. He thus writes: 'though yet it be not to be doubted that spirits of a higher rank than those immersed in flesh may have as clear *ideas* of the radical constitution of substances as we have of a triangle, and so perceive how all their properties and operations flow from thence: but the manner how they come by that knowledge exceeds our conceptions.'[11] No doubt Locke also adds: 'What faculties . . . other species of creatures have to penetrate into the nature and inmost constitutions of things, what *ideas* they may receive of them, far different from ours, we know not'.[12] The implications of these observations are clear: From the fact that we cannot see the necessity of natural laws, it does not follow that they are contingent. The possibility of their being necessary remains open. 'We cannot see the necessity of natural laws' is quite compatible indeed with 'they may nevertheless be necessary'. Locke seems not only to recognize this possibility, but even to permit it by his talk of perfecter beings.

Moreover, in some passages Locke clearly admits a few necessary instructive propositions about substances such as 'receiving or communicating motion by impulse supposes solidity'[13], 'each particular extension, figure, number of parts, motion, excludes all other of each kind'[14], etc. Woolhouse's remark here is worth considering that when Locke gives these examples, 'he implies, one feels, "these are the necessary connexions that we can discover" rather than "these are the ones that there are" '.[15]

So there are in the *Essay* indications of Locke's inclining towards the view that natural laws may be necessary.

There are some expositors of Locke, however, who maintain that natural laws, for him, are contingent. Thus Gilbert Ryle writes: '... it is not merely that we do not yet see how to demonstrate by rigorous deduction that whatever has the other properties of gold must be soluble in *aqua regia*, but we can already see that there is no such logical implication'.[16] He quotes a passage from Locke [which is shortened here]:

> Thus though we see the yellow colour, and upon trial find the weight, malleableness, fusibility and fixedness that are united in a piece of gold: yet, because no one of these *ideas* has any evident *dependence* or necessary connexion with the other, we cannot certainly know that where any four of these are, the fifth will be there also, how highly probable soever it may be: because the highest probability amounts not to certainty, without which there can be no true knowledge.[17]

Ryle concludes by saying: 'The general propositions of the physical and other inductive sciences rest on the evidence of regularly observed concomitances of properties; and these concomitances are not self-evident or necessary...'[18]

Ryle thinks that, for Locke, there is no necessary connection between, for example, being gold and being soluble in *aqua regia*, and seeks to endorse this interpretation by reference to the above-cited passage from the *Essay*. No doubt in that passage there is the clause 'no one of these ideas has any evident dependence or necessary connexion with the other', but this clause does not mean, as Ryle seems to take it to mean, that no one of the ideas has *any* evident dependence or *any* necessary connection with the other; it rather means that no one of the ideas has any *evident* dependence or any *evident* necessary connection with the other. That is to say, the adjective 'evident' that qualifies 'dependence' also qualifies 'necessary connection'. For, in the immediately preceding sentence that occurs in the paragraph from which Ryle has cited the passage under consideration, Locke has qualified the word 'connexion' with the adjective 'evident'; thus he says: 'For of all the qualities that are co-existent in any subject, without this dependence and evident connexion of their ideas one with another ...' . In the second place, Locke has elsewhere in a passage (already quoted before) clearly said in a similar context that there is 'no visible necessary connexion'. The adjective 'visible' may be noted. Locke's actual position, then, is not, as Ryle maintains, that there is no necessary connection between, e.g. being gold and being soluble in *aqua regia*, but, as has been previously shown, that we do not *see* any necessary connection, although there may be such connections.

It must be pointed out that what has been said above relates only to the final version of Locke's *Essay* (1690), and not to the early drafts (Draft A and Draft B) of this work (1671). Locke says more than once in Draft A of the *Essay*:

> Thus all universal propositions are either certain and then they are only verbal but are not instructive. Or else are instructive and then are not certain.[19]

Passages such as this lend countenance to von Leyden's remark : 'Locke explained that, if universal propositions are to be ... necessary, they cannot be informative'.[20] It appears from von Leyden's interpretation of Locke that natural laws are not, for Locke, necessary. It is argued by von Leyden that, on Locke's view, the fact 'that certain qualities rather than others are normally found together... is a purely contingent fact', and is 'far from being self-evident or necessary'[21]. What von Leyden says is, as has been correctly pointed out by Woolhouse[22], germane indeed to the early drafts of Locke's *Essay*, but not to the *Essay* itself. In the *Essay* Locke does not argue at all that natural laws are *self-evidently* necessary; his view is rather that they may be necessary, even although their necessity is opaque to us.

Kneale's ascription of a theory of natural necessity to Locke is not, then, as far as the *Essay* is concerned, exegetically wrong.

2.3 Locke's Theory of Knowledge

For a detailed explication of Locke's *opaque* necessitarianism regarding natural laws, it may be of use to begin by considering his theory of knowledge. Locke takes knowledge as 'the perception of agreement or disagreement of two ideas'.[23] The clarity of knowledge depends not on the clarity of ideas involved, but on the clarity with which the relation between the ideas is perceived. Locke remarks:

> ...a man that has as clear ideas of the angles of a triangle, and of equality to two right ones, as any mathematician in the world, may have but a very obscure perception of their agreement, and so have but a very obscure knowledge of it.[24]

The concept of idea is one of the more pervasive concepts in the *Essay*[25]. Locke uses the word 'idea' to denote physical as well as mental objects. Ryle has discussed at length the main senses in which Locke opens this 'Pandora's box of a word'.[26] The word 'idea' means feelings or sensations when Locke refers to ideas of sensible qualities, such as hardness, coldness, etc. The word also denotes mental images involved in the process of thinking. At times again, the word means the very act of thinking about something. This sense, Ryle thinks, is very close to the ordinary linguistic usage. When someone says, 'the idea of so-and-so has just occurred to me',[27] this is the sense in which the word is used. Locke uses the word sometimes again in the technical sense of a term, notion or concept. A concept, for Ryle, may be an attribute, quality or character, and conception 'is the apprehension of an attribute, property, quality or character'.[28] Locke also uses 'idea' to mean the mental act of 'considering something to possess certain character'.[29] However, while carrying out his analyses of space, number, substance, power, etc., Locke uses the word to indicate the character itself. It may appear that these variegated different senses in which Locke uses the word 'idea' make his philosophy 'ruinously ambiguous'.[30] Nevertheless, Locke's usage may not be totally unwarranted if one takes into consideration his own definition of idea. He defines an idea as

> Whatsoever is the object of the understanding when a man thinks.[31]
>
> or, later as
>
> Whatsoever the mind perceives in itself, or is the immediate object of perception, thought, or understanding.[32]

For Locke, then, an idea is something that exists or occurs in the mind. Whenever we think, we think in terms of ideas or the mind-dependent entities. Sense-data, images, apprehension of a character, or the characters themselves are all 'species of "ideas" in the sense of being mind-dependent objects'.[33] One be directly aware of the ideas alone, and the natural objects that stand apart from their ideas cannot be known directly. This doctrine of Representationalism has many difficulties. But Ryle thinks that it gives Locke at least one *positive* advantage. If the main purpose of Locke's *Essay* is to 'expose the nerves of the differences between pure mathematical sciences, the natural or experimental sciences, moral and political philosophy and theology', then the purpose is achieved by Locke with his theory of idea. The theory enables him to account for the crucial difference between 'certain generically different types of propositions'.[34] Because of the nature of the involved ideas, the propositions of arithmetic and geometry or moral philosophy are certain and known to be so. The situation is quite different in the case of a natural science where one cannot expect to know the necessity of the propositions, because the ideas are of an entirely different nature. But before this point may be considered, we need to take into account some other facets of Locke's theory of knowledge.

If knowledge is the perception of agreement or disagreement between ideas, then knowledge takes the form of a proposition in which a predicate is either affirmed or denied of the subject. Even though the theory of proposition was not fully developed at the time of Locke, it appears that he has a fourfold classification of propositions in mind. Besides, a proposition is not the only form of expression of agreement between ideas. Aaron points out that to perceive an agreement may mean two things, viz. (i) perceiving an agreement within a proposition, and (ii) perceiving a relation between propositions. As Aaron puts it:

> ...the vague term *agreement* (in Locke's definition of knowledge) covers the relation perceived between the terms of a proposition and also the implication apprehended in inference.[35]

According to the standard meaning of proposition, Locke divides propositions in two groups. A proposition is true but trivial, when the predicate is an idea identical wholly or partly with the idea of the subject. For example, the propositions 'White is white' and 'A triangle is a space bounded by three straight lines' are both trifling. A proposition, again, may be true when its predicate conveys something more than the idea of the subject, e.g. 'All triangles have an angle : sum of two right angles' or 'Gold is soluble in *aqua regia*'. Locke calls such propositions instructive. The necessity of a law of nature, e.g. 'Gold is soluble in *aqua regia*' cannot be known by a mere examination of the terms of the proposition. It is an instructive proposition. This may be viewed as an anticipation of the Kantian distinction between analytic and synthetic propositions.[36] Further, Locke believes that propositions may be certain (necessarily true) or probable. All trifling propositions are certain. But there are indications in his *Essay* that he does not disallow the possibility of instructive certainty. Thus, for him, a law of nature may be instructive and certain at the same time. Locke's stand here, according to Woolhouse, is: There might be such propositions about substances of which we do not have *a priori* knowledge'[37].

Locke admits four possible ways of agreement or disagreement between ideas. They are: (i) identity and diversity, (ii) relation, (iii) co-existence, and (iv) real existence. When Locke speaks of 'relation', it is a form of special relation of agreement. It will be seen later that not all our knowledge is of the same standard. Certainty of the highest degree is possible in the case of knowledge of the first kind. As for relation, we have demonstrative knowledge where the mind apprehends the agreement or disagreement of ideas by intervention of other ideas. But often we may fail to perceive the agreement or disagreement of ideas even if such a relation between the ideas involved may be there. Locke points out clearly:

> Though wherever the mind perceives the agreement or disagreement of any of its ideas, there is certain knowledge; yet it does not always happen that the mind sees that agreement or disagreement which there is between them, even where it is discoverable;...[38]

Locke hereby leaves a scope for further development in mathematical studies.

In cases of co-existence and real existence, however, human knowledge is extremely limited, according to Locke. He observes:

> But whilst we are destitute of senses acute enough to discover the minute particles of bodies and to give us *ideas* of their mechanical affections, we must be content to be ignorant of their properties and ways of operation; nor can we be assured about them any further than some few trials we make are able to reach. But whether they will succeed

> again another time, we cannot be certain. This hinders our certain knowledge of universal truths concerning natural bodies, and our reason carries us herein very little beyond particular matter of fact.[39]

2.4 The Three Pillars of Locke's Theory of Natural Laws

Locke's theory of natural laws rests on three pillars: (i) his theory of substance, (ii) his distinction between primary and secondary qualities, and (iii) his distinction between real and nominal essence. These need to be considered briefly in succession before proceeding to Locke's theory of natural laws.

2.4.1 Locke's theory of substance and mode

Locke distinguishes between substances and modes. By modes, he means such complex ideas as do not contain in them the supposition of subsisting by themselves; but are 'considered as dependences on, or affections of, substances'.[40] His examples of such ideas are 'triangle', 'gratitude', and 'murder', etc. The ideas of substances, on the other hand, are, to put it in Locke's own words:

> ... nothing but several combinations of simple *ideas* co-existing in such, though unknown, cause of their union, as makes the whole subsist of itself. It is by such combinations of simple *ideas* and nothing else, that we represent particular sorts of substances to ourselves; ...[41]

Locke's theory of substance is a peculiar one. According to his epistemology, every idea has to be imported by either sensation or reflection. He concedes that we do not have the idea of substance either by sensation or reflection. Perhaps his rationalistic background compels him to accept the ontological existence of substances even if the idea of substance is not given in sense-experience. In our experience, certain qualities are uniformly found to co-exist. This is inexplicable unless it is presumed that they all belong to one and same thing in which they subsist. In other words, one has to presume that the qualities have a common substratum to which they belong as attributes. The idea of substance is thus obtained as the *explanans* of what is observed in our experience. The idea of a particular substance, e.g. gold, is formed upon observation of certain qualities, like heaviness of a certain degree, yellow colour, malleableness, and fusibility, together. Accordingly, a single name is attached to each such bundle of ideas. The idea of substance in general is obtained by an abstraction of the common elements from the ideas of particular substances, ignoring their special spatio-temporal characteristics and positions. But Locke mentions over and over again that the substratum itself remains unknown. To quote Locke :

> ... if anyone will examine himself concerning his *notion of pure substance in general*, he will find he has no other *idea* of it all, but only a supposition of he knows not what support of such qualities which are capable of producing simple ideas in us; which qualities are commonly called accidents ... . The *idea*, then, we have, to which we give the general name substance, being nothing but the supposed, but unknown, support of these qualities we find existing, which we imagine cannot subsist *sine re substante*, without something to support them, we call that support *substantia*; which, according to the true import of the word, is, in plain *English*, *standing under* or *upholding*. [42]

2.4.2 The distinction between primary and secondary qualities

Locke points out that that there are three types of ideas to constitute our complex idea of a corporeal substance: (1) the ideas of primary qualities, such as bulk, figure, shape, size, etc.; (2) those of the secondary qualities, e.g. colour etc.; and (3) active or passive powers (later referred to as 'powers'), i.e. the dispositional properties inherent in a substance. The primary qualities are really in the objects irrespective of our perception. They are inseparable from the substance, and exist in the substance in spite of all the changes that the substance may undergo. Locke takes these primary qualities as '*real qualities*' in the sense that 'their patterns do really exist in the bodies themselves'.[43] The secondary qualities, on other hand, are '*such qualities*', which in truth is nothing in the objects themselves, but powers to produce various sensations in us by their *primary qualities*, i.e. by the bulk, figure, texture, and motion of their insensible parts, as colours, sounds, tastes, etc.'[44]. An example which Locke furnishes in order to explicate his distinction between primary and secondary qualities is:

> ...a violet, by the impulse of such insensible particles of matter, of peculiar figures and bulks, and in different degrees and modifications of their motions, causes the ideas of blue colour and sweet scent of that flower to be produced in our minds... [45]

In connection with Locke's distinction between primary and secondary qualities, R. Jackson observes:

> ...by primary qualities Locke means not a kind of qualities, but all qualities, and he calls them primary to distinguish them, not from other qualities, but from powers, which are in his view not qualities at all but only wrongly supposed to be qualities. 'Primary' is thus equivalent to 'in the strict sense'.[46]

Jonathan Bennett observes that when Locke says that the secondary qualities of things are not 'of' or 'in' them, he means that they do not belong to a thing 'in the full-blooded sense as their primary qualities', for 'to say of something that it "is purple" is to employ a natural and permissible *facon de parler*, while to say of something that it "is spherical" may be to state a plain fact in a way which requires neither gloss nor apology'.[47]

The secondary qualities are derivative. Buchdahl observes that this derivativeness explains to an extent 'Locke's curious assertion that there is a resemblance between our ideas of primary qualities and the qualities themselves which does not exist in case of secondary qualities'.[48] The secondary qualities depend on the primary qualities, and our ideas of secondary qualities are causally produced by primary qualities. Thus, for Locke, 'what is sweet, blue, or warm in *idea* is but the certain bulk, figure, and motion of the insensible parts in the bodies themselves, which we call so'.[49] Fire, for example, produces the idea of warmth and the sensation of pain. But while the former really is in fire, the feeling of pain is not in it.

Besides the primary and secondary qualities, there is a third element involved in our idea of substance. Every substance possesses certain qualities which can bring about a change in other bodies. For example, fire has heat, which is nothing but the power in fire to produce certain changes in other bodies, namely, the power to melt metal or change the colour and texture of wood, etc. This power is looked upon as a 'part of the qualities of fire' and so made 'a part of the complex *idea* of it'.[50] Later on, power is defined by Locke as

> ... the aptness we consider in any substance to give or receive such alterations of primary qualities, as that the substance so altered should produce in us different *ideas* from what it did before: these are called active and passive powers; ...[51]

Locke admits that bodies around us have powers to produce many changes. However, those changes may remain unnoticed by us, 'because they never appear in sensible effects'.[52] By means of our sense-organs, we can know only the secondary qualities like colour, taste, etc. The connection between the primary qualities of material bodies and the ideas of secondary qualities, that is, the causal mechanism by which the primary qualities produce the secondary qualities, remains unknown to us.

2.4.3 The distinction between real and nominal essence

Locke maintains that our ideas of substances may be of two types: particular and general. Everything that exists in nature is a particular. The idea of the general and universal is obtained by abstraction. Locke embraces Conceptualism at this point. For him, the general words stand for 'a sort of things, and each of them does that by being a sign of an abstract *idea* in the mind; to which *idea*, as things existing are found to agree, so they come to be ranked under that name or, which is all one, be of that sort'.[53] Thus to speak of 'man' or 'horse' is to refer to a single class. A class consists of a group of things sharing a name that represents a universal or class-essence. Sorting of things is important in natural sciences, and that is done because a group of sensible qualities is observed to be shared equally by all members of the sort. Locke calls this group of qualities the nominal essence. And 'the essences of the sorts of things and, consequently, the sorting of things is the workmanship of the understanding that abstracts and makes those general *ideas*'.[54]

Locke makes a distinction between real and nominal essences. The real essence of a thing is its unknown constitution upon which depend all its sensible qualities and their uniform co-existence. We classify things under a general class name because they are observed to possess a common group of observable qualities. This common group of sensible qualities because of which we annex a common name to several things is, as pointed out, the nominal essence. The essence of each genus or sort, then, is only an abstract idea which the general name stands for. For example, the nominal essence of gold is the abstract idea of the observable properties common to all things designated as 'gold'. The real essence, on the other hand, is the insensible constitution of gold owing to which we may have the ideas of some properties of gold like its colour, weight, fixedness, etc. As Woolhouse puts the point:

> It appears then that in those passages where real essences are talked of, substance-ideas are such that to their nominal essences there corresponds a real essence or internal corpuscular constitution. This is a configuration of insensible particles which explains and accounts for the co-instantiation in many particulars of the properties taken account of in the nominal essence–and, of course, for the instantiation of these with all the other properties which just as easily could have been taken account of in the nominal essence.[55]

Locke adds that the nominal essence of substance is **not** made by the mind in an arbitrary manner; it refers to a pattern or unison in nature. The 'mind, in making the complex *ideas* of substances, only follows nature; and puts none together which are not supposed to have an union in nature'.[56] Thus, though the nominal essence of a thing differs from its real essence, the nominal essence conforms to the 'union in nature' that exists objectively. Men in making complex ideas of substances are guided by the conjunction of properties or attributes observed constantly in nature. The ideas of substances have their archetypes in nature. Further, if the real essence of a thing is the primary qualities of its insensible parts, while the nominal essence is a group of observable or secondary qualities of the thing, then, if the secondary qualities of an object are produced by the primary qualities of its insensible parts, this nominal essence is not framed by the mind arbitrarily. One may only observe that set of qualities which the primary qualities of the particular substance are able to produce, and accordingly what can be the nominal essence of a particular kind of substance is only a definite group of qualities, and not any group as we are pleased to make. Though the nominal essence of a substance is an abstract idea formed by the mind, it has an objective reference; it is grounded on the objective qualities of the substance.

There is, however, no distinction between the real and the nominal essence in cases of modes. The modes are, for Locke, their own archetypes, and there is nothing corresponding to the mode-idea in nature. The idea of a mode may be formed by the mind without really coming across any instance of it in experience. And in forming an idea of a mode, the mind is not restricted by the consideration of any regular conjunction or co-existence of properties. The ideas are formed 'without patterns, or reference to any real existence', that is, without examining 'whether they exist so in nature'.[57] The essences of modes are framed arbitrarily by the mind, for 'it is the mind, that combines several scattered independent *ideas* into one complex one and, by the common name it gives them, makes them the essence of certain species, without regulating itself by any connexion they have in nature'.[58]

2.5 Locke's Theory of Natural Laws

In the light of the above discussion of the basic tenets of Locke's philosophy, his view that we cannot know necessary connections in nature seems plausible. He makes a distinction between mathematical knowledge, on the one hand, and our knowledge about natural objects, on the other. One has 'certain', truth in mathematics; for the ideas involved there are mixed modes which are their own archetypes. Pure mathematics is a formal discourse concerning relations between ideas, and there is no need of any reference to the real world. If there is any statement about a circle or a triangle, its truth is independent of the existence of anything corresponding to the idea of a circle or that of a triangle in the world. On the other side, human knowledge concerning things of the objective world always falls short of 'certainty', and however much it can advance, it can never reach the standard of 'certainty' of mathematics. The nature of our ideas in natural science and the powers of human faculties afford only twilight[59]. Natural sciences are concerned with ideas of substances, and very few truths may be known here and most of the so-called knowledge concerning natural objects are only beliefs[60] in the strict sense of the term. In cases of beliefs one is unable to perceive any necessary connections one may only presume[61] them. But, as Woolhouse aptly points out:

> ... what stands in its way is not an ontological difficulty stemming from some feature of its subject matter but rather an epistemological difficulty stemming from 'the weakness of our faculties in this state of mediocrity in which we are in this world'.[62]

All inquiries in natural science culminate in discovering some natural laws, such as 'Gold is soluble in *aqua regia*'. The law, in the example, is a universal proposition having a general term as its subject. It states the co-existence of two properties, that is, the connection between being gold and the quality of solubility in *aqua regia* at all places and times: at all places and times, because it is a universal proposition. It purports to express an objective connection. It is, moreover, an instructive proposition, since our idea of gold does not involve the idea of solubility in *aqua regia.* The important point now is that this proposition is not merely instructive, but presumably is instructively *certain*, where 'certainty' means certainty of truth, not certainty of knowledge. Locke says:

> ...it is fit to observe that certainty is twofold: *certainty of truth* and *certainty of knowledge. Certainty of truth* is when words are so put together in propositions as exactly to express the agreement or disagreement of the *ideas* they stand for as really it is. *Certainty of knowledge* is to perceive the agreement or disagreement of *ideas* as expressed in any proposition. This we usually call knowing, or being certain of the truth of any proposition.[63]

Locke's distinction between certainty of truth and certainty of knowledge, as Pap[64] explains it, amounts to the distinction (to put it in modern terminology) between the necessity of a true proposition and knowing this proposition with certainty. In other words, it is a distinction between 'p is a necessary truth' and 'it is known with certainty that p'. Pap illustrates this distinction, for the sake of clarity, by taking Fermat's famous undecided mathematical theorem, which, if it is true, is a necessary truth, but which mathematicians, who only conjecture it to be true, do not know for certain. 'Being known with certainty' is a time-dependent predicate, in the sense that one can intelligibly say that a proposition is not known with certainty at one time but known with certainty at another time, while it does not make sense to ask *at what time* the proposition is a necessary truth... As for natural laws, then, Locke's view boils down to this, that law-propositions, being about substances, are not known with certainty, that is, not known in the strict sense, even although such propositions may have certainty of truth, that is, may be necessary.

The reason why natural laws cannot be known with certainty is, according to Locke, that, in order to know a universal proposition for certain, the essence of each species mentioned in it must be known. The essence of a species is what constitutes and bounds it. Locke argues:

> This, in all simple *ideas* and modes, is not hard to do. For in these, the real and nominal essence being the same,... the abstract *idea* which the general term stands for being the sole essence and boundary that is or can be supposed of the *species*, there can be no doubt how far the *species* extends, or what things are comprehended under each term;... . But in substances wherein a real essence, distinct from the nominal, is supposed to constitute, determine, and bound the species, the extent of the general word is very uncertain; because, not knowing this real essence, we cannot know what is or what is not of that *species*; and, consequently, what may or may not with certainty be affirmed of it. And

> thus, speaking of a *man* or *gold* or any other *species* of natural substances, as supposed constituted by a precise and real essence which nature regularly imparts to every individual of that kind whereby it is made to be of that *species*, we cannot be certain of the truth of any affirmation or negation made of it. For *man* or *gold*, taken in this sense and used for *species* of things constituted by real essences, different from the complex *idea* in the mind of the speaker, stand for we know not what; and the extent of these *species* with such boundaries are so unknown and undetermined, that it is impossible with any certainty to affirm that all men are rational, or that all gold is yellow.[65]

Locke adds:

> *The names of substances*, then, *whenever made to stand for species which are supposed to be constituted by real essences* which we know not, are not capable to convey certainty to the understanding: of the truth of general propositions made of such terms we cannot be sure.[66]

To be exegetically accurate, there are two principal reasons behind Locke's view that the laws express unknown connections in nature. First, the laws are about substances. But our idea of a substance is an idea of *something* we know not what; and the primary qualities of the minute insensible parts of the substance upon which the secondary qualities depend remain unknown to us. And for this reason 'it is impossible we should know which have a necessary union or inconsistency one with another'. For example, not knowing the size, figure, and texture of parts on which the secondary qualities depend and from which result those qualities which make our complex idea of gold, it is not possible for us to know 'what other qualities result from or are incompatible with the same constitution of the insensible parts of *gold*; and so consequently must always *co-exist* with that complex *idea* we have of it, or else are *inconsistent* with it'.[67] Secondly, we cannot discover any connection between the primary and secondary qualities of a substance. As Locke observes:

> ...there is yet another and more incurable part of ignorance, which sets us more remote from a certain knowledge of the *co-existence* or *in-co-existence* (if I may so say) of different *ideas* in the same subject; and that is that there is no discoverable connexion between any secondary quality and those primary qualities that it depends on.[68]

But it must be emphasized over again that connections may be necessary even if we do not know them. The fact that the human intellect cannot perceive the necessity of laws of nature is no proof that the laws are contingent[69]. Locke laments the limitation of our faculties, but at the same time points out, as has been noted earlier, that had there existed a being more powerful than we are, then it would have been possible for him to possess the perfect idea of a substance; he would also have intuitive knowledge about the real essence of a substance, and about the connection between its primary and secondary qualities. He would thus be able to *see* the necessary connections existing in nature.

2.6 The Merits of the Theory of Natural Necessity

An important question is: what are the merits of the theory of natural necessity? We have regular experiences of groups of sensible qualities, but in the absence of knowledge of the real essence of substances, we do not *see* the reason of this togetherness of the qualities. For example, a certain yellow colour, weight, fusibility, and certain dispositional properties like solubility in *aqua regia* are found together in our experience; and we are led to posit a substance like 'gold' to explain the co-existence of these qualities -a substratum which holds all the qualities together. Even though all we experience in 'gold' is a group of sensible qualities, yet the uniformity of experience cannot be fortuitous. If there be objective necessities in nature, opaque as they may be, that would be a good explanation of the uniformity of our experience. Certain qualities come together in nature because they are then bound by a natural law, i.e. bound by a necessity. The necessity of this connection is objective, and not imposed upon the natural objects by any external force. The necessary connection is natural in the sense that it is consequent upon the real essence or internal constitution of things.

Thinkers like Lewis Carroll believe that the concept of nomic necessity is central to our ordinary discourse. The ordinary concepts of perception, persistence, causation, substance like table, etc., are not nomic concepts, though they have nomic commitments. That natural laws exist is, for Carroll, an essential doctrine. He remarks

> ... if there were no laws of nature, then there would be very little else. If there were no laws, then there would be no causation, there would be no disposition, there would be no true (non-trivial) counterfactual conditionals. By the same token, if there were no laws of nature, there would be no perception, no action, no persistence. There wouldn't be any tables, no red things, no things of value, not even any physical objects.[70]

This needs explaining: Carroll believes that the word 'table' stands for nothing but the dispositional property of 'ability of support' (one may conceive of a table, destroyed immediately after it is made, and hence it never in actuality supports anything). Since no dispositional properties are exemplified unless there is at least one law of nature (for example, wherever there is a thing of a particular variety, 'p', it necessarily possesses a dispositional property, 'q'), we are forced to accept that there is at least one law of nature. Without the presupposition of natural laws, day-to-day functions of life as well as scientific practices become impossible.

Locke's theory of unknown necessity serves to impart rationality to our inductive practices. The uniform co-existence of a number of qualities in the observed instances is the ground for our prediction in the future cases. For example, on perceiving a certain yellow colour, fusibility, weight, and the dispositional property, namely, solubility in *aqua regia*, in some particulars designated by the name 'gold', we infer that all unobserved specimens of gold also have this dispositional property. The process by which we form the opinion is the process of induction, which allows us to pass from knowledge of some cases to knowledge concerning all particular instances of that kind. The process of inference that takes place may be put in the following form:

Instance 1 of a natural kind 'N' has φ and Ψ.

Instance 2 of a natural kind 'N' has φ and Ψ.

Instance 3 of a natural kind 'N' has φ and Ψ.

$\therefore$ All instances of a natural kind 'N' have φ and Ψ.

Obviously this inference does not possess mathematical or deductive certainty. Nevertheless, such inferences are important, as our practical life and scientific procedures are based on them. Any further observation of an instance of the natural kind 'N' having φ and Ψ may be taken as supportive evidence for the conclusion mentioned above. For example, we feel justified in taking a particular (which may be given the number 55) of a natural kind 'N' having φ and Ψ as supportive evidence for the conclusion, 'All instances of a natural kind 'N' have φ and Ψ'. But why is the particular, numbered 55, regarded as evidence for the conclusion ?

Milton Fisk has very interesting reasons to offer. According to him, some data may be taken as evidence in support of a generalization, provided it 'stands a chance of being representative of the way something is', and no data can stand a chance of being representative of the way something is unless there are 'some stable patterns of behaviour'. Thus, some data may be taken to support a generalization only if they are representatives of a uniform pattern in nature. The stable pattern, required in this connection, is not a mere regularity. Fisk argues:

> ... mere regularities are inferior to necessary connections in doing the job that must be done for data to serve as inductive support. The problem is not that data fail to have a chance of being representative of the way things are if there are only regularities in nature, and no necessary connections. It is rather that without any necessary connections, things could happen in so many ways that it would be unreasonable to suppose they happen in one of the relatively few ways in which regularities are preserved. A denial of necessity makes unreasonable an assumption of regularities.
>
> ... only if there are a certain number of unspecified necessary connections believed to hold in nature it is consistent to hold that given data support a given hypothesis.[71]

He adds a little later:

> .... If there were no physical necessities, everything that is logically possible would be possible. Thus the possible worlds are all those compatible with logic. The assumption of regularities in the actual world becomes an extremely strong assumption. ... it is so strong as to be unwarranted. For, even if ... the actual world has shown a high degree of regularity in the past there will be, with logic as the only restriction, an enormous number of possible futures and the proportion of those futures which continue the regularity of the past, or develop new regularities, to those which destroy all semblance of regularity will be exceedingly small indeed.[72]

Further, there is no regress involved if induction is supposed to give us knowledge of natural kinds. Induction gives us knowledge of natural laws stating necessary relations between objects or their properties, and the supposition of necessity rationally justifies our inductive procedures. Fisk explains that 'it is one thing' to adopt an inductive procedure to know *particular* necessary connections and natural kinds, and 'quite another' to suppose *the general fact* that there are necessary connections and natural kinds for adopting an inductive procedure. He says: 'Only if induction relied on an inductive warrant for particular natural kinds and necessities there would be a regress'. Further, if the objection on the score of an infinite regress were valid, then, Fisk observes, that can be also levelled against the weaker supposition of 'mere regularities as a basis of induction'[73].

Fisk raises a question. If we have to accept that there are objective necessities in nature in order to make our inductive practice rational, then how many necessities are exactly required to justify our inductive method? Even those who accept that there are necessary connections in nature would not be able to give any definite answer to this question. Locke is justified in assuming an unspecified number of necessary connections holding in nature. For him, the question about the number of necessary connections in nature is not a legitimate question. This is another merit of Locke's theory. If the number of necessities in nature cannot be determined even for the sake of logical economy, it is cogent to suppose innumerable necessities existing in nature.

Notes

1 R. S. Woolhouse, *Locke's Philosophy of Science and Knowledge*, Basil Blackwell, Oxford, 1970, pp. 25f.

2 *sic*

3 W. C. Kneale, *Probability and Induction*, Clarendon Press, Oxford,

1949, reprinted from corrected sheets of the first edition, 1963, 1966, p. 71.

4 John Locke, *An Essay Concerning Human Understanding,* 4. 3. 14 Yolton, p. 284, [Nidditch, p. 546].

In the above reference '4. 3. 14' after the *Essay* means bk. 4, ch. 3, sec 14 of the *Essay*; 'Yolton, p. 284' means p. 284 in J. W. Yolton's edition of the *Essay* (Everyman's Library, London, 1992), and 'Nidditch p. 546' means p. 546 in P. H. Nidditch's unabridged edition (Clarendon Press, Oxford, 1975) of this work.

All citations from the *Essay* in the present work are from Yolton's edition. The text used in Yolton's edition is that of the fifth edition, 1706, of Locke's *Essay*. The fifth edition of the *Essay* was the last one corrected by Locke in his lifetime. In Yolton's edition *spelling and punctuation have been modernized.*

5 *Ibid.*, 4. 3.10, Yolton, p. 283 [Nidditch, p. 544].

6 *Ibid.*, 4. 3. 22, see also sec. 28.

7 *Ibid.*, 4. 6. 7, Yolton, p. 310 [Nidditch, p. 582].

8 *Ibid.*, 4. 3. 25, Yolton, p. 292 [Nidditch, p. 556].

9 *Ibid.*, 4. 3. 23, Yolton, p. 291[Nidditch, p. 554].

10 *Ibid.*, 4. 3. 24, Yolton, p. 291[Nidditch, p. 555].

11 *Ibid.*, 3. 11. 23, Yolton, pp. 263-264 [Nidditch, p. 520].

12 *Ibid.*, 4. 3. 23, Yolton, p. 291[Nidditch, p. 554].

13 *Ibid.*, 4. 3. 14, Yolton, p. 284 [Nidditch, p. 546].

14 *Ibid.*, 4. 3. 15, Yolton, p. 285 [Nidditch, p. 546].

15 Woolhouse, *op. cit.*, p. 24.

16 G. Ryle, 'John Locke on the Human Understanding', in J. L. Stocks, ed., *Tercentenary Addresses on John Locke*, Oxford University Press, Oxford, 1933, reprinted in C. B. Martin and D. M. Armstrong, eds., *Locke and Berkeley, A Collection of Critical Essays*, Modern Studies in Philosophy, Macmillan, London, p. 36.

17 Cited from Locke's *Essay*, 4. 3. 14, by Ryle, v*ide ibidem.*

18 *Ibid.*, pp. 36-37.

19 John Locke, Draft A of the *Essay,* in R. I. Aaron and J. Gibbs, eds., *An Early Draft of Locke's Essay*, Oxford University Press, Oxford,

1936, p. 50. See also pp. 46-47 and p. 52. Cited by Woolhouse, *op. cit.*, p. 16.

20 Cited from von Leyden, *Seventeenth Century Metaphysics*, London, 1968, pp.160-161 in Woolhouse, *op. cit.*, p.16.

21 *Ibidem.*

22 *Ibid.*, p. 16, also p. 23.

23 Locke, *op. cit.*, 4. 1. 2, Yolton, p. 267 [Nidditch, p. 525].

24 *Ibid.*, 4. 3. 15, Yolton, p. 278 [Nidditch, p. 538].

25 See Yolton, *op. cit.*, p. xx.

26 Ryle, *op. cit.*, p. 17.

27 *Ibid.*, p. 18.

28 *Ibidem.*

29 *Ibid.*, p. 19.

30 *Ibidem.*

31 Lockes '*Essay*' in E. A. Burtt, ed., *The English Philosophers, From Bacon to Mill,* Modern Library, New York, 1939, Introduction, sec. 8, p. 247.

32 Locke, *op. cit.*, 2. 8. 8, Yolton, pp. 57-58 [Nidditch, p.134].

33 Ryle, *op. cit.*, p. 22.

34 *Ibid.*, p. 23.

35 R. I. Aaron, *John Locke,* Clarendon Press, Oxford, 2nd ed., 1955, p. 225.

36 Woolhouse, *op. cit.*, p. 11; also W. Kneale and Martha Kneale, *The Development of Logic*, Oxford, 1962, p. 357, and also A. Pap, *Semantics and Necessary Truth*, Yale University Press, New Haven, 1958, p. 59.

37 Woolhouse, *op. cit.*, p. 21.

38 Locke, *op. cit.*, 4. 2. 2, Yolton, p. 272 [Nidditch, p. 531].

39 *Ibid.*, 4. 3. 25, Yolton, p. 293 [Nidditch, p. 556].

40 *Ibid.*, 2. 12. 4, Yolton, p. 78 [Nidditch, p. 165].

41 *Ibid.*, 2. 23. 6, Yolton, p. 134 [Nidditch, p. 525].

42 *Ibid.*, 2. 23. 2, Yolton, p. 132 [Nidditch, p. 525].

43 *Ibid.*, 2. 8. 15, Yolton, p. 60 [Nidditch, p. 137].

44 *Ibid.*, 2. 8. 10, Yolton, p. 58 [Nidditch, p. 135].

45 *Ibid.*, 2. 8. 13, Yolton, p. 59 [Nidditch, p. 136].

46 R. Jackson, 'Locke's Distinction between Primary and Secondary Qualities', *Mind*, vol. 38, 1929, reprinted in C. B. Martin, and D. M. Armstrong, eds., *Locke and Berkeley, A Collection of Critical Essays*, Modern Studies in Philosophy, Macmillan, London, [year not mentioned], p. 60.

47 J. Bennett, 'Substance, Reality, and Primary Qualities', *American Philosophical Quarterly*, vol.2, 1965, reprinted in Martin and Armstrong, eds., *op. cit.*, p.104.

48 G. Buchdahl, *Metaphysics and Philosophy of Science*, Basil Blackwell, Oxford, 1969, p. 233.

49 Locke, *op. cit.*, 2. 8. 15, Yolton, p. 60 [Nidditch, p. 137].

50 *Ibid.*, 2. 23. 7, Yolton, p. 135 [Nidditch, p. 299].

51 *Ibid.*, 2. 23. 9, Yolton, p. 136 [Nidditch, p. 300].

52 *Ibidem*, [Nidditch, p. 301].

53 *Ibid.*, 3. 3. 12, Yolton, p. 215 [Nidditch, p. 414].

54 *Ibid.*, 3. 3. 12, Yolton, p. 216 [Nidditch, p. 415].

55 Woolhouse, *op. cit.*, pp. 118-119.

56 Locke, *op.cit.*, 3. 6. 28, Yolton, p. 240 [Nidditch, p. 445].

57 *Ibid.*, 2. 22. 2, Yolton, p. 126 [Nidditch, p. 288].

58 *Ibid.*, 3. 5. 6, Yolton, p. 224 [Nidditch, p. 430].

59 *Ibid.*, 4. 14. 2.

60 *Ibid.*, 4. 12. 9-10 [cited by Woolhouse, *op. cit.*, p. 23].

61 *Essay*, 4. 14. 4.

62 Woolhouse, *op. cit.*, p. 23.

63 Locke, *op. cit.*, 4.6.3, Yolton, p. 308 [Nidditch, pp. 579-580].

64 A. Pap, *Semantics and Necessary Truth*, Yale University Press, London, 1969, p. 49.

65 *Ibid.*, 4. 6. 4, Yolton, pp. 308-309 [Nidditch, p. 580].

66 *Ibid.*, 4. 6. 5., Yolton, p. 309 [Nidditch, p. 580].

67 *Ibid.*, 4. 3. 11, Yolton, p. 283 [Nidditch, p. 544].

68 *Ibid.*, 4. 3. 12, Yolton, p. 283 [Nidditch, p. 545].

69 John Biglow, Brian Ellis, and Caroline Lierse have constructed a new model of natural necessity. They write: 'laws of nature must be supposed to exist, and to hold *necessarily*, whether or not anybody knows that they exist, or has any idea of what they are.' [See Biglow, Ellis, and Caroline, 'The World as One of a Kind: Natural Necessity and Laws of Nature', *The British Journal of Philosophy*, vol. 43, 1992, p. 375].

70 J. W. Carroll, *Laws of Nature*, Cambridge University Press, Cambridge, 1994, p. 10.

71 M. Fisk, 'Are There Necessary Connections in Nature?' *Philosophy of Science*, vol. 37, 1970, p. 385.

72 *Ibid.*, p. 392.

73 *Ibid.*, p. 388.

CHAPTER THREE

KNEALE'S REPLY TO HUME'S OBJECTION TO THE LOCKEAN THEORY OF NATURAL NECESSITY

3.1 Foreword

The standard objection to the view that natural laws are necessary is that we can always conceive the contradictory of a supposed law of nature and that therefore such a law cannot be necessary. Kneale observes that this objection 'was formulated by Hume' and 'is an extremely formidable objection', and that 'it is not surprising that many modern philosophers have taken it to be a conclusive refutation of the suggestion that natural laws are principles of necessitation'.[1] As Kneale considers this objection to be primarily Hume's objection, it is understandable why he seeks to reply to it with reference to Hume's philosophy. Hume's objection and Kneale's reply to it are considered in this Chapter.

3.2 Hume's Objection to the Theory of Natural Necessity

Hume's famous objection to the supposed necessity of causal connection may be extended with equal efficacy to natural necessity in general. According to him, to think of something is to have an image of it, and when we have an image of something, we are engaged in the thought of it. Now, certainly it is possible to imagine the opposite of a law. It may be a law, for example, that salt dissolves in water[2]. But there is nothing, so far as we know, in the nature of salt to necessitate its dissolving in water; we can always think of or imagine some salt that does not dissolve in water. Likewise, we may conceive the contradictory of any scientific law.

The objection to natural necessity is that there would be no contradiction in maintaining that the regular connection between two things or events, experienced so far, may cease to hold. A law, stating a causal connection, or, for that matter, any law proclaiming a connection between two relata, is not indicative of any necessity, because it is possible to imagine the contradictory of the law. If the contradiction of a law is conceivable, then the contradiction is a possibility and accordingly the law is contingent[3].

What does Hume mean by 'contradictory'? Contradiction involves two objects or states of affairs such that by logic the presence of the one excludes the possibility of the other. In other words, a self-contradictory statement involves words denoting incompatible states of affairs, that is, states of affairs which cannot both be true at the same time. This nature of contradiction foils our attempts to comprehend its meaning and, as has been stated earlier, our understanding involves ideas, and to have ideas, for Hume, is to have mental images. Understandably, nobody succeeds in thinking of a contradiction because it is impossible to have simultaneous images of two things when they cancel each other. If one tries to conceive the impossible, one 'would not succeed in conceiving anything'.[4] Therefore, if the contradiction of a law is conceivable, then the contradiction is a possibility and accordingly the law is not to be viewed as necessary.

Hume has great faith in the dictum that 'it is impossible for us to *think* of anything, which we have not antecedently felt...'. In his *Enquiry* he says:

> ...When we entertain, therefore, any suspicion that a philosophical term is employed without any meaning or idea (as is but too frequent), we need but enquire, *from what impression is that supposed idea derived*? And if it be impossible to assign any, this will serve to confirm our suspicion.[5]

The proper application of this dictum, Hume hopes, would enable us to achieve clarity and precision in cases of philosophical reasoning. If there be any obscurity or ambiguity in any complex idea, then we have to define, that is, enumerate, the simple ideas that compose the idea.[6] But, even after the definition is 'pushed up' to the simplest ideas, if some confusion or vagueness still remains, then Hume's suggestion is to produce the impression or the original sensation of which the idea is a copy. With this principle in mind, Hume goes about searching for the impression of necessary connection, but all he can find in experience is an *exceptionless* regularity of a relation. The unfruitful search leads him to conclude that the ideas of cause and effect (and similarly all the ideas involved in our thought about necessary connection) are separable in the sense that the idea of the one does not include that of the other. Thus, Hume says in his *Treatise*:

> ... as all distinct ideas are separable from each other, and as the ideas of cause and effect are evidently distinct, 'twill be easy for us to conceive any object to be non-existent this moment, and existent the next, without conjoining to it the distinct idea of a cause or productive principle. The separation, therefore, of the idea of a cause from that of a beginning of existence is plainly possible for the imagination; and consequently the actual separation of these objects is so far possible that it implies no contradiction nor absurdity; and is therefore incapable of being refuted by any reasoning from mere ideas, without which 'tis impossible to demonstrate the necessity of a cause.[7]

When Hume denies the necessary connection between cause and effect, or between any two features connected by a law of nature, he has obviously logical necessity as his model of necessity. Had there been a necessary connection, it would have been known *a priori*. But can we know the necessity of causal connection by conceptual analysis, that is, by the mere examination of the idea of cause? Certainly not. In perception of the cause for the first time, we do not see its necessary connection with the effect. Even if the cause and the effect are both present before the senses for the first time, that is, even if we are witnessing their conjunction for the first time, we do not know any necessary connection holding between them at that moment. Hume says:

> ... The mind can never possibly find the effect in the supposed cause, by the most accurate scrutiny and examination. For the effect is totally different from the cause, and consequently can never be discovered in it. Motion in the second billiard-ball is a quite distinct event from motion in the first: nor is there anything in the one to suggest the smallest hint of the other.[8]

What, then, is the source of this idea of necessity? There is no impression of necessary connection in the perception of the objective world. Because of the regular co-presence of the two relata in our experience and no experience of any exception to the regularity, the mind is 'determined by custom' to consider its usual attendant whenever any one is experienced, and it is this determination which enables us to talk of necessity. Hume's reason for denial of necessary connections in nature may be analyzed into two points. These are:

1. The things or states of affairs involved in the so-called necessary relation are separate. For the connection is not seen as a necessary one when the connection is perceived for the first time. Upon experiencing any one of the kind for the first time, it is not possible to infer or predict the other. This *impossibility of prediction* of one from the other suffices to prove that they are separate, and if they are separate then there is no necessary connection between them.

2. It is possible to imagine the things bound by a law of nature as separate. That is, it is always possible to conceive one in separation from the other. This means that a change in the course of nature described by a law is conceivable. Though bread, for

example, has always nourished in the past, we may very well think of a piece of bread which does not possess this property. *Conceivability of the opposite* suffices to prove the absence of necessity of natural laws.

Incidentally, it may be mentioned that Kneale, in his exposition of Hume's view, does not distinguish the two points stated above, though some present day thinkers, like Evan Fales, contend that actually Hume 'provides two distinct criteria for assaying the existence of necessities in nature'[9]. Taking logical necessity as the paradigm of necessity, a statement may be taken to convey a necessary connection, for Hume, if (i) its opposite is inconceivable, and (ii) it states a connection between two things or states of affairs such that it is possible to infer each of the connected ones from the experience of the other. The failure of natural law to comply with these two conditions, namely, the 'inconceivability of the opposite' and the 'possibility of prediction' leads Hume to conclude that laws are not expressive of necessary connections existing in nature. Fales, however, remarks that in Hume's argument the two criteria are deemed as 'interchangeable'[10] and that Hume himself has been found to conflate the two. So Kneale's exposition does not after all dilute the essence of Hume's argument.

3.3 Kneale's Reply to Hume's Objection

In Kneale's reply to Hume's objection two points may be distinguished. We proceed to consider these points one after another.

3.3.1 The first point in Kneale's reply

The first point in Kneale's reply to Hume is this. When Hume maintains that we can *conceive* the contradictory of a supposed law of nature, what he can be taken to mean is that we can *imagine* its contradictory. To conceive or think of a *matter of fact* is, for him, to imagine it. An idea, he says, is an image. An image is a copy of an impression. An impression in Hume's terminology is what is called in modern terminology a sensum. It follows that, according to him, we can imagine (that is, have an image of) a sensum or sensa only. When we imagine, e.g. lightning, we really imagine a bright visual impression which is a sensum. When we imagine thunder, we really imagine a loud auditory impression which again is a sensum. When, therefore, we imagine the contradictory of the law, for example, that lightning causes thunder, we really imagine that a bright visual sensum is not sometimes[11] followed by a loud auditory sensum. But the difficulty is that a natural law is not a statement about sensa. It is a statement about perceptual objects. Indeed, when we speak of lightning, we are speaking about a public event which can be perceived by other people or photographed. When we speak of thunder, we are indeed speaking about a public event which again can be perceived by other people or recorded in a machine. A natural law being in this way a statement, not about sensa, but about perceptual objects, Hume's objection ultimately proves to be irrelevant.

This point is stated succinctly by Kneale in the following words:

> ... we should not allow ourselves to be impressed by the argument that, since we can always imagine a perceptual object behaving in a manner contrary to supposed laws of nature, these latter can never be principles of necessitation. For to imagine a perceptual object is only to imagine the sensa which one would expect to sense in perceiving the object, and natural laws are not concerned with sensa but with perceptual objects....[12]

Certain questions arise at once, namely, what is meant by 'perceptual object', what is the distinction between sensum terminology and perceptual object terminology, and most importantly, whether statements about perceptual objects are not reducible to statements about sensa. If, indeed, statements about perceptual objects are found to be reducible to statements about sensa, Hume's objection cannot be brushed aside as above on the ground that natural laws are statements not about sensa, but about perceptual objects.

Kneale has duly considered these questions, and sought to highlight the *peculiarity* of the perceptual object terminology. The peculiarity of perceptual object terminology consists, according to him, in its irreducibility. He has tried to show, by way of a critique of phenomenalism, that statements about perceptual objects are *not* reducible to statements about sensa. Kneale's critique of phenomenalism and the related questions will come up for consideration in the sequel. Meantime, we proceed to take notice of the second point in Kneale's reply to Hume's objection.

3.3.2 The second point in Kneale's reply

The second point in Kneale's reply is stated by him in the following words (the passage is often cited in philosophical writings):

> In any sense of the word 'conceive' which is relevant to the argument, an ability to conceive the contradictory of a supposed law of nature does not disprove the suggestion that the supposed law is a principle of necessitation. This can be seen from consideration of a mathematical analogy. In 1742 Goldbach, an otherwise unknown correspondent of the Swiss mathematician Euler, suggested that every even number greater than two is the sum of two primes. This conjecture has been confirmed for all the even numbers for which it has been tested, but during the past two centuries no one has succeeded in demonstrating its truth. The attitude of the mathematicians towards it can, therefore, be expressed by the statement 'Goldbach's conjecture looks like a theorem, but it may conceivably be false'.[13]

Kneale admits that there is an important distinction between Goldbach's conjecture and the case of natural laws; for, unlike a mathematical proposition, a natural law is not ever in principle demonstrable. He points out that this difference only strengthens his argument. 'If the conceivability of the contradictory is not to be taken as a disproof of necessity in mathematics, where proof is attainable by *a priori* reasoning, why should it be supposed to furnish such a disproof in natural science'?[14]

Kneale's argument has been explained not exactly in the same manner by different writers. Goldbach's conjecture, falling short of demonstrative proof, is not known to be true or false. But if subsequent demonstration proves Goldbach's conjecture to be necessarily true, what then? If it is necessarily true, then its contradictory is necessarily false, and therefore surely *inconceivable* according to Hume's principles. For Hume, in the case of a mathematical proposition, its negation is inconceivable in the sense of involving a contradiction. But if it is inconceivable, how can it still be *conceivable* (as it is required to be, if Kneale is to be right)? Here one may utilize a point made by Karl Popper in the course of his criticism of Kneale's argument. One may say that the contradictory of Goldbach's conjecture, if the conjecture is necessarily true, can still be *conceived* in the sense in which we, in an indirect proof, start by *conceiving* a proposition to be true and end by concluding that this proposition is nevertheless inconceivable. Popper says: 'Indeed, an indirect proof may well be put thus: "*Conceive* that *a* is true. Then we should have to admit that *b* is true. But we know that *b* is absurd. Thus it is *inconceivable* that *a* is true." '[15]

Here when it is said to be *inconceivable* that *a* is true, 'inconceivable' means the same as 'leading to a contradiction'. When, however, the indirect proof starts by *conceiving* that *a* is true, *conceive* does not mean what does not lead to a contradiction. The word is used in a different sense. This sense is, as Popper points out, 'a little vague and ambiguous'. But it would be misleading to say that it is *not conceivable* that *a* is true, 'considering that we did start by conceiving, precisely, the truth of a'.[16] It will have been clear by now that the contradictory of Goldbach's conjecture, supposing that it is proved to be necessarily true, is after all *conceivable* (in some sense), even though, it is inconceivable in the sense of leading to a contradiction.

But if one utilizes Popper's point in the above way, Kneale's argument cannot be expected to give general satisfaction. This is indeed the view of Popper, who says:

> ... Thus 'inconceivable' in logic and mathematics is simply another word for 'leading to an obvious contradiction'. *Logically* possible or 'conceivable' is everything that does not lead to an obvious contradiction, and logically impossible or 'inconceivable' is everything that does. When Kneale says that the contradictory of a theorem may be 'conceivable', he uses the word in another sense... .[17]

The implication of Popper's observation is that Kneale's argument 'operates with a sense of "conceivable" different from the one intended'[18] and is not therefore satisfactory.

Ayer, who is also critical of Kneale's argument, does not, however, contend that Kneale, in saying that we can conceive the contradictory of Goldbach's conjecture, operates with a sense of 'conceivable' which is different from the intended sense. Ayer argues that in so far as Goldbach's conjecture has not been *demonstrated* as either true or false, both the conjecture and its contradictory are conceivable. As he puts it:

> ... It may happen, in doing logic or pure mathematics, that one formulates a statement which one is unable to prove or disprove. Surely in that case both the alternatives of its truth and falsehood are conceivable.[19]

Accordingly Ayer concludes that 'Kneale makes his case'[20]. But Ayer hastens to point out that Kneale's argument has no force against Hume's primary doctrine. Ayer emphasizes that a proper interpretation of any philosopher must refer to the total system that he constructs and that each individual statement made by him ought to be understood with reference to its context. He points out:

> ... Hume is not primarily concerned with showing that a given set of propositions, which have been taken as necessary, are not so really. This is only a possible consequence of his fundamental point that 'there is no object which implies the existence of any other if we consider these objects in themselves, and never look beyond the idea which we form of them'[21], in short, that to say that events are distinct is incompatible with saying that they are logically related.[22]

With regard to this last contention of Ayer's, it may be observed that Kneale's present concern is to make the point that in mathematics there may be necessary truths which are not yet discovered as necessary and that in such cases their opposites or contradictories are equally conceivable. Since Ayer has, as seen, already granted this point, that should suffice for the present. Whether Kneale's argument touches some other part of Hume's theory (considered by Ayer to be of primary importance) that natural necessity is not logical necessity is beside the point. Kneale in his reply to Hume under consideration is not concerned with that.

Michael Hooker in his assessment of Kneale's argument observes, however, that 'Kneale does not make his case strong enough' although 'it can be so made'.[23] Kneale thinks that the contradictory of Goldbach's conjecture is conceivable since the conjecture has not been *proved* false. But simply because a proposition has not been *proved* false, it cannot be held that it or its contradictory is conceivable. There are indeed 'some constraints on the conceivability of a proposition beyond not knowing it to have been shown false'.[24] As for Goldbach's conjecture, at least some acquaintance with its contents is required in order that it or its contradictory may be allowed to be conceivable. Hooker points out that a sufficiently informed person *is* in a position to conceive the truth or falsity of the conjecture. Thus he can 'conceive or imagine'[25] that the conjecture is false. For example, we can imagine that a computer comes to discover a counter-example to the conjecture, that much discussion follows, that philosophical examples come to be revised subsequently, and so on. In this way a sufficiently informed person may be able to conceive the contradictory of Goldbach's conjecture.

It is time to return to the first point in Kneale's reply to Hume's objection. This point raises a number of issues, as noted before. Kneale's treatment of those issues is now up for consideration.

3.3.3 Kneale's treatment of the issues raised by the first point of his reply to Hume's objection considered

According to Hume, we can always imagine the contradictory or contrary of a supposed law of nature, which therefore cannot be necessary. Kneale has argued that what we can imagine, on Hume's theory, are only sensa, and that natural laws are not about sensa, but about perceptual objects. The question arises, what does Kneale mean by 'perceptual objects'? Kneale says: ' ... the phrase "perceptual object" has a wider range than "material object" '[26]. He explains this observation first.

3.3.3.1 The meaning of 'perceptual objects'

In ordinary language, such verbs as 'see', 'feel', 'hear', and 'taste' are often used with such nouns as 'stick', 'stone', 'explosion', and 'sugar' for their objects. For convenience' sake, Kneale proposes to use the word 'perception' as an umbrella term to cover seeing, feeling, hearing, and tasting, in this sense, and also proposes to introduce the phrase 'perceptual objects' to denote objects which we perceive, or may perceive, in the indicated sense of 'perceive'. Perceptual objects, in this sense, are publicly observable phenomena, that is, such items as are accessible to other people too. Obviously, the class of perceptual objects is wider than that of material objects. Sticks and stones, which are perceptual objects, are also material objects; but lightning flashes which also we claim to perceive are not material objects like stones and sticks, even although they are perceptual objects. Even noises and smells are sometimes mentioned by plain men in ordinary speech as publicly observable items. Thus, for example, a plain man sometimes asks his friends to listen to a funny noise coming from a machine.

3.3.3.2 Perceptual object terminology and sensum terminology

There are circumstances in which the common way of speaking gives rise to difficulties. In order to avoid such difficulties, philosophers have thought fit to introduce a new terminology, which may be called sensum terminology, and to recommend a 'new and more fundamental sense' for the use of such words as 'see', 'feel', 'hear', etc.

Thus, a plain man sometimes reports to his doctor that he hears a noise in his head. Surely, this noise is not a constituent of the public world. The doctor cannot hear it with his stethoscope. This is no doubt an abnormal case, but there are also normal circumstances in which the use of such a word as (for example) 'see' does not seem to fit into the ordinary way of talking about what we see. Thus, a straight stick half immersed in water looks bent. The bent appearance of the stick is *public*, and yet there is the need here to distinguish between what we see and what is assumed to exist independently of perception. In the usual perceptual sense of the word, 'see', to say that we see a stick or stone is to imply that it is over there as it is seen; but when a stick, which is half in water and half out of it, looks bent, to say that we can see a bent stick is not to imply that a bent stick is over there.

To get out of the difficulties of the above sort, philosophers think it necessary to distinguish between perceptual objects and sensa or sense data. They maintain that when (e.g.) a man reports that he hears a noise in his head, what he hears is a sensum, and that when we see a stick half immersed in water to be bent, what we see is, not a perceptual object, but a sensum. Hearing and seeing in this special use mean sensing, and not perceiving.

Kneale admits that the suggested distinction between sensation and perception, or, for that matter, between sensum terminology and perceptual object terminology, is valuable, as suggesting a way out of the difficulties into which our ordinary mode of speech leads us. But he points out that 'it has unfortunately given rise to some new misunderstandings'[27]. Philosophers in their over-enthusiasm for their new usage for such a word as 'see', have gone the length of saying that sticks and stones are things which we do not *really see*. Kneale concedes that we do not see sticks and stones in the same sense in which we see sensa such as after-images, but he contends that 'it is surely a gratuitous creation of paradoxes to maintain that our ordinary usage of the word "see" is mistaken'. He argues:

> ...We learnt to speak of seeing sticks and stones long before we thought of using the word to stand for a mode of pure sensation, and we cannot help continuing to speak in this way, however hard we may try.[28]

Kneale does recognize the need for distinguishing between the two different terminologies, stressing at the same time that it is an important and by no means easy philosophical problem to explain the relations between them. He has accordingly subjected to criticisms certain views regarding the relations between the two terminologies. His criticism of the phenomenalistic doctrine, which seeks to replace perceptual object terminology entirely by sensum terminology, is particularly important, as having a direct bearing upon what has been called before the first point in his reply to Hume. It is also important in a general way as having a bearing upon his assessment of the theory of natural necessity. To this, therefore, we may turn next.

3.3.3.3 Critique of phenomenalism

According to phenomenalism, a perceptual object is a logical construction from sensa. It is not suggested that perceptual objects are composed of sensa as a house, for example, is composed of bricks. What the view in question means, on the usual interpretation, is that sentences or statements about perceptual objects are in principle reducible to sentences or statements about sensa. This in its turn means that sentences which mention perceptual objects can always in principle be replaced by, or translated into, different but equivalent sentences which do not mention perceptual objects but mention only sensa. To bring the matter into clearer focus, Kneale gives an example:

> ... Thus the statement that there is a penny on the table is to be taken as equivalent to a complex statement to the effect that if anyone sensed sensa of certain kinds, e.g. kinesthetic sensa such as he would have in approaching the table and putting out his hand, he would also sense sensa of certain other kinds, e.g. factual sensa such as he would have in handling the penny.[29]

Kneale refers to Mill, who has defined matter 'as a permanent possibility of sensations'. It becomes clear that if the phenomenalist programme of reduction is to be carried out, *possible* sensa have to be taken into account. Accordingly, Kneale contends that if a perceptual object statement is to be reduced to a series of sense data statements, the series must be an infinite one 'to allow for all the infinite variety of possible sensa which are relevant'.[30] There may be innumerable possible situations involving a particular perceptual object and, so innumerable possible sensa in connection with it. For example, a penny on the table may be viewed differently from different positions or in different illuminations. But an infinite sequence, Kneale points out, cannot be specified except by providing a rule for its construction, and the only rule that can be given in this context is the rule stating that the required set of hypothetical statements about sensa are those which would be true if there were a perceptual object of a certain kind at a certain place. Thus the phenomenalist would fail to eliminate perceptual object statements altogether in the manner required by his programme.

The phenomenalist programme of reduction, then, fails. Kneale says that the phenomenalist might now abandon the programme of reduction and content himself with saying that a perceptual object statement *entails* some sense data statements. Kneale admits that plain men no doubt regard perceptual object statements as indications of the course of sense experience which may be expected[31], but he contends that even this 'reformed version of phenomenalism'[32] makes difficulties. For to say, with regard to the penny on the table (in the example given before), that if I had had certain experiences involved in putting out my hand, I should have had certain other experiences of the sort involved in handling the penny, is to mean apparently that

> ... there were certain facts, not further specified, which in conjunction with an experience of the first kind would have necessitated an experience of the second kind. This is something for which the phenomenalist can find no place in his scheme.[33]

This part of Kneale's criticism is not, however, clear. Particularly, the phrase 'certain facts, not further specified' is left unexplained. The question whether a perceptual object statement *entails* a sense-datum statement or statements needs a clear-cut answer.

Chisholm, in the course of his criticism of C. I. Lewis's phenomenalist thesis, clearly points out that the entailment does not hold. He says: 'Professor Lewis believes that "This thing is red" entails as analytic consequences an unlimited number of statements referring solely to what might appear'.[34] Chisholm argues to show that this belief is mistaken. He asks us to consider the following perceptual object statement which he calls the thing statement[35]—

This is red (P)

and the following sense-datum statement

Redness will appear (R)

The question is whether P entails R. Obviously, there is no contradiction in affirming P and denying R. However, P does entail R if P is taken in conjunction with some other thing statement which refers to observation-conditions. This other thing statement might be[36]

> This is observed under normal conditions; and if this is red and is observed under normal conditions, redness will appear. (Q)

But Chisholm adds, P entails not-R if P is taken in conjunction, not with the above-mentioned thing statement Q, but with still *another* thing statement S which also refers to observation-conditions. This other thing statement S might be[37]

> This is observed under conditions which are normal except for the presence of blue lights; and if this is red and is observed under conditions which are normal except for the presence of blue lights, redness will not appear. (S)

Obviously, the thing statement S is logically consistent with P. Since P and S are logically consistent, the conjunction P and S entails whatever P entails and cannot entail anything which is logically inconsistent with what P entails. So Chisholm concludes: 'If P and S entail not-R, it is impossible that P entail R. Hence "This is red" (P) does not entail "Redness will appear" (R).'[38]

Lewis does not maintain, however, that a thing-statement such as 'This is red' entails a *categorical* sense-datum statement, such as 'Redness will appear'. What is entailed, in his view, is a complicated conditional sense-datum statement. So Chisholm has thought fit to consider one of Lewis's own examples. In discussing Lewis's view, Chisholm utilizes again the letters P, R, S. Now, the following is Lewis's own example of a thing statement:

There really is a doorknob in front of me and to the left. (P)

For Lewis, the following conditional sense-datum statement might be an analytic consequence of the above thing statement:

> If I should seem to see such a doorknob and if I should seem to myself to be initiating a certain grasping motion, then in all probability the feeling of contacting a doorknob would follow (R)

Chisholm here contends that if R is an analytic consequence of P– that is, if P entails R-, it is logically impossible that there be any statement S such that S is consistent with P and such that P and S entail not-R. But clearly there are many such statements S. Thus S might be the following statement:

> I am unable to move my limbs and my hands but am subject to delusions such that I think I'm moving them; I often seem to myself to be initiating a certain grasping motion, but, when I do, I never have the feeling of contacting anything (S).

Chisholm points out that it does not matter whether the statement S is *true*; for Lewis's theory is concerned, not with the truth, but with the *meaning*, of thing statements. Now, S and P are logically consistent. But the conjunction of P and S entails not-R. Hence, in accordance with the argument previously stated, it is impossible that P entails R.

The view that a thing statement, or, as Kneale calls it, a

perceptual object statement, *entails* some sense-datum statements cannot, then, be accepted.

It has been seen that the phenomenalist programme of reduction cannot possibly be carried out and that even the reformed version of phenomenalism is not tenable.

3.4 Conclusions from the Above Considerations

(1) The Humean objection that we can always imagine the contradictory of a supposed law of nature is irrelevant, because, on Hume's principles, to imagine a perceptual object is only to imagine certain sensa, whereas a natural law-statement is a statement, not about sensa, but about a perceptual object or objects. Nor can any statement about a perceptual object be reduced to statements about sensa. Accordingly Kneale observes:

> ... I conclude, therefore, that there is no good reason for denying that laws of nature are principles of necessitation.[39]

(2) The critique of phenomenalism has shown that the nature of a perceptual object 'is not, and cannot, be manifested in any single perception nor yet in any sequence of perceptions, however long'.[40] Hence, if we, defying the long philosophical tradition, think fit to say that we *know* the existence of some perceptual objects, we may still admit that such knowledge of the existence of a perceptual object is 'quite compatible with a great deal of ignorance about it even in respect of matters which could be determined by perception, e.g. its internal constitution'.[41] Accordingly, there is no good reason for denying that there can be such truths about perceptual objects as remain opaque to us. In this way the Lockean theory of *opaque* natural necessity comes to be intelligible to us.

What is known as Kneale's theory of natural necessity is a theory of opaque necessity for which he has derived inspiration from Locke and, as will be seen in 9.4, also from Kant.

NOTES

1 Kneale, *Probability and Induction*, pp. 71f.

2 *Ibid.*

3 A contingent proposition has been defined as 'any proposition which not only is true in some possible worlds, but also is false in some possible worlds' in N. Swartz and R.Bradley, *Possible Worlds: An Introduction to Logic and Its Philosophy*,
Indianapolis, Hackett, 1979, p. 14.

4 Kneale, *op. cit.*, p. 72.

5 David Hume, *Enquiries Concerning Human Understanding and the Principles of Morals*, ed. P. H. Nidditch, 3rd ed., Clarendon Press, London, 1975, Sec. II, p. 22.

6 *Ibid.*, p. 62.

7 David Hume, *Treatise of Human Nature*, ed. L. A. Selby-Bigge Oxford, 1888, p.80.

8 *Enquiries*, p. 29.

9 E. Fales, *Causation and Universals*, Routledge, London, 1990, p. 22.

10 *Ibidem.*

11 The expression 'not sometimes' is used here, because the proposition involved is an 'O' proposition which is logically the contradictory of an 'A' proposition. The words 'some not' of an 'O' proposition may be treated as 'not sometimes' , just as the word 'all' in the corresponding 'A' proposition may be treated as 'always'. 'Not always' logically amounts to 'not sometimes'.

This note would not have been inserted at all unless an important scholar of the USA, who had kindly agreed to read the first draft of this chapter, had objected to the use of the expression 'not sometimes' here and suggested that the better expression should be 'not always'.

12 *Ibid.*, pp. 89.

13 *Ibid.*, pp. 79-80.

14 *Ibid.*, pp. 80.

15 K. R Popper, *The Logic of Scientific Discovery*, Hutchinson, London, 1959, p. 429.

16 *Ibidem.*

17 *Ibidem.*

18 *Ibidem.*

19 A. J. Ayer, 'What is a Law of Nature?' in *Revue Internationale de Philosophie*, no. 36, 1956, reprinted in Ayer, *The Concept of a Person*, Macmillan, London,1964; here taken from B. A. Brody, ed. *Readings in Philosophical Analysis*, Prentice Hall, New Jersey, 1970, p. 42.

20 *Ibidem.*

21 Cited from Hume's 'Treatise', I, iii, vi, *vide ibidem.*

22 *Ibidem.*

23 M. Hooker, 'Descartes's Denial of Mind-Body Identity', in M. Hooker, ed. *Descartes: Critical and Interpretative Essays*, The John Hopkins University Press, Baltimore, 1978, p. 177.

24 *Ibidem.*

25 *Ibidem.*

26 Kneale, *op. cit.*, p. 81.

27 *Ibid.*, p. 82.

28 *Ibidem.*

29 *Ibid.*, p. 85.

30 *Ibid.*, p. 86.

31 *Ibidem.*

32 *Ibidem.*

33 *Ibid.*, p. 88.

34 R. Chisholm, 'The Problem of Empiricism', *Journal of Philosophy*, vol. 45, 1948, p. 513.

35 *Ibidem.*

36 *Ibidem.*

37 *Ibidem.*

38 *Ibid.*, p. 514.

39 Kneale, *op. cit.*, p.89.

40 *Ibid.*, p. 257.

41 *Ibid.*, pp 89.

42 *A detailed discussion of Hume's critique of causal necessity by the author may be found under Appendix-I of this book (287-326).*

CHAPTER FOUR

KNEALE'S CRITIQUE OF THE REGULARITY THEORY OF NATURAL LAWS

4.1 Foreword

The strongest and most impressive opposition to the theory of natural necessity comes in the form of the regularity theory, or, as Kneale prefers to call it, the *constancy* theory, of natural laws. Kneale takes Hume as the chief proponent of this theory, though it is a matter of controversy for recent scholarship[1] whether Hume really had advocated the regularity theory of natural laws. This point, however, is beyond the purview of the present discussion. We, here, after Kneale, take Hume to be the chief opponent of the necessity theory[2], and examine whether the regularity theory can sustain Kneale's objection to it.

The point at issue between the necessity theorist and the regularist is the strength with which the predicate is ascribed to the subject in a law statement. For the regularist, laws are *merely* truths of facts of unrestricted generality, whereas for the necessity theorist, laws are *stronger* than mere general statements of facts; over and above being universal truths, laws contain an element of *necessity*. A brief statement of the regularity theory follows.

4.2 The Regularity Theory of Natural Laws Briefly Stated

Both the regularist and the necessity theorist admit that natural laws are not discoverable *a priori*. For Hume and his followers, however, such laws are mere contingent truths. As for Hume, he considers causal laws particularly, but, according to his followers, his view can in principle be extended to other natural laws. On the Humean interpretation, statements of such laws are statements about matters of fact, and as such do not enjoy demonstrative certainty like mathematical propositions. At the time of experiencing an A and a B for the first time, we do not apprehend the regular relation that may hold between them. Only after finding their 'constant conjunction' in our experience, the mind is psychologically determined to consider their relation to be a regular one and pass in thought from one of them to the other. The lawlike relation holding between A and B is asserted owing to the constancy of experience and the resultant mental disposition formed as a 'custom' or 'habit'. On the Humean view, as Kneale expresses it: 'To assert a law of nature is, then, only to assert a constant conjunction without restriction to the field of our experience'.[3] Hume's theory, considered in its generality, allows of being summarized as: Statements of natural laws are contingent statements about matters of fact and are statements of unrestricted generality.

A modern version of the Humean regularity theory is as follows: *s* is a statement of natural law if and only if:

1. *s* is universally quantified,
2. *s* is omnitemporally and omnispatially unrestricted in scope,
3. *s* is omnitemporally and omnispatially true, and
4. *s* is contingent.[4]

4.3 Kneale on the Regularity Theory

Kneale has rejected the Humean or naive regularity theory by means of an argument which has come to be known as Kneale's argument[5] against this theory. Before turning to this argument, however, it may be of some use to consider his defence of the regularity theory with respect to the point that natural laws - that is, the statements expressing such laws - are *unrestricted* in scope. This may serve as an indirect confirmation of his rejection (to be considered later) of Whitehead's theory which holds that such laws are *restricted* in scope.

Kneale says:

> It is often objected against this theory [i.e. the Regularity or Constancy theory] that there cannot be facts of unrestricted universality or, to put the matter in another way, that sentences which purport to state such facts are meaningless.[6]

Evidently, Kneale here has in mind the early logical positivist view that a sentence is factually significant - that is, empirically meaningful - if and only if it expresses a statement which is (non-analytic and)[7] completely verifiable by experience. It follows from this view that a natural law-statement is not expressed by any factually significant sentence, for such a statement is of *unrestricted* universality and no unrestricted universal statement is completely verifiable by experience. Clearly, on this view, the regularity theory of laws stands refuted. But the point with respect to which the regularity theory stands refuted by this view is a point on which Kneale is, as already mentioned before, in full agreement with the regularists - namely, the point that natural law-statements are of unrestricted universality. So Kneale proceeds to reject the view. He says: 'I do not find this argument convincing. It depends on the use of a criterion of significance which I see no reason to accept, ... '[8]. He grants that there may be some argument against the possibility of empirical statements of unrestricted universality; he hastens to point out, however, '[But] I have seen none.'[9]

It is high time that we turned to Kneale's argument *against* the regularity theory. This argument may well be characterized as the argument from the counterfactual import of statements of laws.

The main problem is to distinguish a natural law from an accidental generalization. Unlike an accidental generalization, a law-statement, for Kneale, has a counterfactual import. The point is illustrated by Kneale by the dodo example in his *Probability and Induction.*[10] Let it be understood that dodos lived on the earth during a certain period till the end of the eighteenth century. Let it be supposed, for argument's sake, that an organized group of bird-watchers kept records of all the dodos from the origin to the extinction of the species. It may be supposed once again that the records say that every dodo had a white feather in its tail. On this supposition, this universal statement has been established by summative induction by complete enumeration. The question is whether this universal statement 'All dodos have a white feather in their tails' is to be regarded as a law of nature. Or is it only an accidental generalization? If the Humean regularity analysis of laws is correct, the universal statement of facts 'All dodos have a white feather in their tails' is to be regarded as a law. But Kneale argues that if it is to be a law that all dodos have a white feather in their tails, then if there had been any dodos other than those mentioned in the records, they also would have had a white feather in their tails. 'But', Kneale contends, 'an unfulfilled hypothetical proposition of this kind cannot be derived from a proposition which is concerned only with the actual.'[11] He observes:

> ... A contingent universal proposition can always be expressed in the form 'there are in fact no α things which are not β', and from such a proposition it is impossible to deduce that if something which was not in fact α had been α it would also have been β.[12]

That is, the universal statement of matters of fact [on the above-mentioned supposition] that all dodos have a white feather in their tails is expressible as 'There are in fact no dodos which are not white-feathered in their tails', and from this it cannot be deduced that if something which was not in fact a dodo had been a dodo it would also have been white-feathered in its tail. The point of this argument is that no mere statement of fact, even if it is universal, can be a statement of law: a law is concerned not only with actual instances of a certain description, but with anything which *might have* satisfied the description.[13]

4.4 The Kneale–Popper Controversy on the Logical Nature of Natural Laws

4.4.1 Popper's observations in 1949 on Kneale's argument

In an article[14] contributed to *Mind*, Popper seeks to refute certain arguments such as Kneale's, concerning natural laws and their logical import, by pressing a demand for a non-modal extensional language to express the force of laws. Apparently, a law enjoys a logical force not found in an accidental generalization. From a mere general statement 'All A's are B's' follows an indicative conditional stating 'If x were *identical with* one of the A's, then x would be *one of* the B's'. But from this general statement, one is not entitled to deduce: 'If x were *added* to the A's then it would be one of the B's'. Popper explains his point with an example of an accidental generalization, namely, 'All my friends speak French'. This statement does not warrant the inference that if Confucius were a friend of mine, that is, if the name of Confucius were *added* to the list of my friends, then Confucius would have spoken French. From the accidental generalization we are only allowed to deduce a statement to the effect that 'if Confucius had been *identical* with one of x's friends, then... '.

However, this difference, Popper thinks, is not due to any difference in the logical form or import of a law-statement. The difference is rather due to the difference in the nature of the terms involved in lawlike and in other generalizations. The terms involved in a law 'are not defined by enumeration of the elements belonging to them, this is what makes the law "strictly universal" '.[15] On the other hand, the subject-term of an accidental generalization is either defined or definable by enumeration of its elements. Popper calls a statement of this sort 'numerically universal'. The modern riddle centering the logical import of a law and the difference of a law from a mere universal statement may be explained, Popper thinks, by reference to the extensionality and intentionality of terms and a fallacy described by Aristotle. The terms of a law are 'strictly universal or qualitative or ... intentional terms', and those of numerically universal statements are 'numerically universal (or enumerative or individual or singular or particular or ... extensional) terms.' 'The ambiguity in question arises from using the same expression as a name for terms of both kinds'.[16] Popper says that the phrase 'If x were an A' can be interpreted in one or the other of two ways: If A is a term in a strictly universal law, the phrase is to be interpreted to mean 'If x has the property of A'; but if A is a term in an accidental or numerically universal statement, the phrase is to be interpreted as 'If x is identical with one of the elements of A'. The phrase being interpreted thus, a subjunctive conditional is deducible, according to Popper, from any universal statement whatever, whether it is a universal law or a merely accidental or numerically universal statement. However, Popper warns: if 'we interpret the phrase in the second case qualitatively, as we are permitted to do in the first, then we simply change the extension, and therefore the meaning of the term (committing what classical logic called a fallacy of ambiguity). No wonder that we find that the resulting inference is invalid...'[17]

4.4.2 Kneale's observations in 1950 on Popper's argument

Kneale, while replying to Popper's argument, as presented above, first of all paraphrased Popper's argument in something like the following way[18] : Once the distinction between numerically universal or enumerative or extensional terms and strictly universal or qualitative or intensional terms has been made clear by Popper, there should in Popper's opinion be no serious objection to maintaining that natural law-statements are equivalent to universal material implications, since a universal material implication containing qualitative or intensional terms (that is, unrestricted descriptions) does indeed allow inference to counterfactual (or subjunctive) conditionals.

Kneale in his turn now proceeds to show that 'universal material implications have no relevance to contrary-to-fact conditionals.'[19] For this purpose he presents the formula:

$$(x) \ . \ \text{raven} \ (x) \supset \text{black} \ (x),$$

and says that we are apt to read it as if it were an abbreviation for :

Anything, if it is a raven, is black.

This second expression, he avers, begs the issue by giving the statement the look of a law-statement through the word 'if' and the use of timeless present, which are the usual devices for the statement of laws. This can be avoided, he thinks, by first transforming the original formula into its equivalent formula:

$$\sim (\exists x) \ . \ \text{raven} \ (x) \ . \sim \text{black} \ (x),$$

and then taking it as an abbreviation for:

> There has never been a raven that was not black, and there will never be a raven that is not black.

This is, in Kneale's view, 'an accurate rendering of the original formula into ordinary English'.[20] In this rendering the statement does not look much like a law-statement; for the word 'if' and the use of timeless present are avoided; on the contrary there is here an explicit distinction of times. Still the question needs to be considered whether it allows inference to any contrary-to-fact conditional.

The second part of the statement which refers to the future - 'there will never be a raven that is not black' - is not useful to a man who is interested in a counterfactual situation and considers whether in conditions which did not in fact prevail there would have been non-black ravens. Nor is the first part - 'There has never been a raven that was not black' - of any more use. For even if it is a fact that there had never been a raven that was not black, this is quite well compatible with some ravens' inhabiting very snowy regions and producing descendants that were white although still otherwise raven-like. Hence even if we could know that there had never been a raven that was not black, inference to the contrary-to-fact conditional 'If some inhabitants of snowy regions were ravens, they would be black' would not be allowable.

Kneale finds that philosophers wedded to the thesis that statements of law are universal material implications do not admit any *unrealized* physical or natural possibility. Upon their account of the matter - as Kneale puts it with reference to the present example - 'either (i) it is a law of nature that all ravens are black, or (ii) there has been or will be somewhere at some time a raven that was not or is not black.'[21] The reason why they are committed to this is that (i) is the contradictory of (ii) and that therefore both (i) and (ii) cannot be denied at once without violating the logical law of the excluded middle. Popper in his paper under reference shows himself to be dimly aware of this when he says at the end of that paper:

> ... It may be useful and, for some purposes, necessary to assume a general principle stating that every kind of event that is compatible with the accepted natural laws does in fact occur in some (finite) space-time region.[22]

But Kneale objects that with Popper the general principle cannot be a *mere assumption* that it is useful and necessary to make for some purposes. 'It is', Kneale asserts, 'a direct consequence of his [Popper's] thesis that statements of law are universal material implications; and if it is unplausible, so too is that thesis'.[23] Kneale holds not only that Popper's principle is 'unplausible', but that it 'is inconsistent with our ordinary view of natural law'. He illustrates his point by means of two examples taken from different fields.

The first example is this: we can conceive that there has never been a chain reaction of plutonium in a strong steel shell containing heavy hydrogen, and also that there never will be. But it can hardly be supposed in that case that there is a law of nature precluding such events. Nor can it be supposed, for that matter, that the possibility of such a reaction has been or will be realized at some time. The prevention of such an occurrence in the past and also in the future is very well conceivable and is explicable in terms of human planning and the ordinary belief that the consequences of the occurrence would be disastrous.

As for the second example offered by Kneale, this is it: it may be supposed that a musician is lying on his death bed and composes a complicated tune in his imagination, murmuring to himself before breathing his last in a voice too low to be audible to anybody 'None has ever heard or will ever hear this tune', where 'this tune' is to be understood as an intricate pattern of sounds describable in general terms. Clearly, the statement is not regarded by the musician as a statement of natural law, and it cannot be supposed, in the circumstances described, that the possibility that somebody has heard or will hear the tune is therefore a *realized* possibility.

Kneale concludes by observing:

> ...For my purpose it is sufficient that we can conceive an unrestrictedly universal material implication without regarding it as a statement of law. In short, we do not ordinarily believe that every natural possibility must be realized somewhere at sometime.[24]

4.4.3 Popper's view in 1959 about natural laws

In the New Appendices to *The Logic of Scientific Discovery* of 1959 Popper observes: 'I am prepared to accept Kneale's criticism in so far as I am prepared to accept the view that there exists a category of statements, the laws of nature, which are logically stronger than the corresponding universal statements.'[25] He (Popper) concedes that natural laws possess a natural or physical necessity that distinguishes a statement of law from other universal statements - but, unlike Kneale, he does not take the meaning of necessity to be the same everywhere. For him, natural necessity differs from logical necessity. He considers it 'intuitively acceptable' that the laws as 'principles of necessitation' are *prohibitions* forbidding certain events. Natural laws restrict 'the (logically) possible choice of singular facts. They are thus principles of 'impossibility with respect to these singular facts'.[26] Still a law is contingently necessary; for its necessity hinges on the structural property of the world. Popper compares it to the musical necessity that imposes restrictions on a musician in his composition. The musician is free to choose any rhythmic pattern for his composition, but once the choice is made, he is restricted by the pattern of his own choice. For example, anyone choosing a four-beat pattern of rhythm cannot end his musical score on the third beat. Nevertheless, there is no law prohibiting the musician from composing a musical score ending on the third beat. He could have very well done it, had he chosen some other rhythmic pattern, which in fact he had not. Similarly, natural necessity or impossibility 'imposes *structural* principles upon the world. But it still leaves a great deal of freedom to the more contingent singular facts - the initial conditions'.[27]

The important question now is: How does Popper define natural necessity? Popper offers the following definition of it:

> *A statement may be said to be naturally or physically necessary, if, and only if, it is deducible from a statement function which is satisfied in all worlds that differ from our world, if at all, only with respect to initial conditions.*[28]

The significant thing about this definition is that it is, in intention, - that is, so far as its wording is concerned - a definition of natural necessity in terms of *universality*, the suggestion being that no modal notion is invoked. It is this suggestion that serves to distinguish Popper's notion of natural necessity, as expressed so far, from Kneale's notion of it.

As far as Popper is concerned, he is of the opinion that, from the point of view of his methodology - that is, his theory of falsification - it matters little whether natural laws are treated as just 'strictly universal statements' or as 'necessary'; for 'in both cases', he says, 'we can only test our conjecture by attempted refutations'.[29] He argues that we can never know for certain whether a conjectured law of nature is really a law or only one that looks like a law while depending in fact on some special initial conditions obtaining in our actual world. His definition of natural necessity allows, he thinks, of being applied *negatively* by finding initial conditions under which a conjectured law turns out to be invalid; for if it turns out to be invalid, it can then be said that the conjectured law is not necessary and not a genuine law of nature. In this way, he says, his definition fits in with his methodology very well.[30]

It is time to turn next to Kneale's estimate of Popper's position in *The Logic of Scientific Discovery* stated above.

4.4.4 Kneale's assessment of Popper's view of 1959 as to natural laws

Kneale agrees with Popper that we can never know for certain whether a supposed law of nature is a genuine law; for 'to say this is only to admit that we cannot establish a law of nature *a priori*'.[31] Kneale's view is that the laws of nature, although they are - or rather, may be - necessary, are established or accepted *a posteriori*. In other words, his is a doctrine of *opaque* natural necessity. Anyway, the present problem is to determine whether Popper's overall position in *The Logic of Scientific Discovery* is tenable. According to Kneale, as it will be clear by and by, it is not.

Kneale calls attention to a passage in *The Logic of Scientific Discovery*, which occurs just before Popper's definition of natural necessity already quoted before. The passage is:

> As Tarski has shown, it is possible to explain *logical necessity* in terms of universality: a statement may be said to be logically necessary if and only if it is deducible (for example, by particularization) from a '*universally valid*' statement function; that is to say, from a statement function which is *satisfied by every model.* (This means, true in all possible words).
>
> I think that we may explain by the same method what we mean by natural necessity...[32]

After this, Popper goes on to offer his own definition of natural necessity (already quoted in the preceding subsection). In the passage just now quoted (to be referred to in this subsection as the first passage from Popper) he proposes to define natural necessity, as Tarski has defined logical necessity, in terms of *universality*. But what makes difficult is the expression 'This means, true in all possible worlds' added by Popper in brackets to explain the immediately preceding phrase '*satisfied by every model*'. Kneale contends that if Tarski's programme is to explain logical necessity in terms of universality, as Popper says at the outset of the just quoted passage that it is, Tarski can have nothing to do with *possible worlds* at all.[33] If Popper's clarification (as added in brackets) of Tarski's position is correct, Tarski's professed explanation of logical necessity in terms of universality turns out ultimately to be an explanation of it in terms of what is true in all possible worlds. And Popper's professed definition of *natural necessity* along the line of Tarski's explanation of logical necessity likewise turns out ultimately to be a definition of it in terms of truth in all possible worlds. It emerges that Popper in his account has not after all succeeded in dispensing with *modal* notions. Kneale accordingly observes:

> ...I hold therefore that Popper is mistaken if he thinks, as apparently he does, that he has succeeded in improving on the Humean account of natural laws while remaining true

> to the principle that necessity can be explained without remainder in terms of universality. In fact, he has only defined one modal notion [sc. that of necessity] in terms of another [sc. that of possibility]; but he has hidden this from himself for the moment by talking of all worlds, which differ from our world, if at all, only in initial conditions.[34]

This is, for Kneale, one instance of Popper's uncertainty about his own commitments. And there is another. Kneale this time cites the following passage from Popper:

> ...I regard, unlike Kneale, 'necessary' as a mere word - as a label useful for distinguishing *the universality of laws* from 'accidental' universality. Of course, any other label would do just as well, for there is not much connection here with logical necessity. I largely agree with the spirit of Wittgenstein's paraphrase of Hume: 'A necessity for one thing to happen because another has happened does not exist. There is only logical necessity.'[35]

This passage is to be referred to in this subsection as the second passage from Popper. Now, with reference to this passage and the first passage from Popper, Kneale says: 'As they stand, these two passages are inconsistent'.[36] In the first passage Popper recommends an account of natural necessity along the line of Tarski's account of logical necessity, whereas in the second passage Popper says that there is not much connection between natural necessity and logical necessity. Kneale's suggestion is that one can consistently recommend an account of natural necessity along the line of some account of logical necessity if only one commits oneself to the view that there is after all some important connection between natural necessity and logical necessity.

Kneale points out further that in the second passage Popper indicates his acceptance of Wittgenstein's account of logical necessity and shows thereby that he is not aware of the fact that

Tarski himself has rejected the Wittgensteinian account of logical necessity as unsatisfactory.[37] One cannot consistently do two things at once: to indicate one's acceptance of Tarski's account of logical necessity and also to indicate one's acceptance of Wittgenstein's account of it; for it is a fact that Tarski's account emerges from his rejection of the Wittgensteinian account. There is, then, either some confusion or some lack of commitment on the part of Popper.

Kneale in the end points out that the notion of necessitation should be taken as *fundamental*[38], and that any attempt to reduce necessity completely to universality is unjustified. Formal logic gives us the general principles of necessitation. In addition to these formal principles of necessitation, we have the non-formal principles of necessitation pertaining to various subject matters. In natural science the laws are such non-formal principles of necessitation. Popper, Kneale urges, does not understand the exact nature of these non-formal principles. It is his failure to understand these principles which has made Popper unnecessarily worried that the admission of such principles would involve him in a 'terrible evil called essentialism'. To this Kneale's reply is that 'a non-formal principle of necessitation would be exactly what he [Popper] has allowed a law of nature to be, namely, a generalization which holds for all possible worlds of some kind...'.[39]

[Nerlich and Suchting also have criticized Popper's definition of natural necessity. To avoid criticisms, Popper has presented a 'revised' definition of natural necessity, but even this revised definition has been criticized by Suchting. These matters cannot be treated here in detail for fear of being carried far afield. Hence these are touched upon in the Notes for the sake of a fairly complete treatment.] [40]

4.4.5 A note on Popper's difference from Kneale with respect to counterfactual conditionals

So far occasion has not arisen to refer to and comment on Popper's difference from Kneale with respect to counterfactual, or, as he says, subjunctive, conditionals. As is well known, a counterfactual conditional, for Kneale, is a conditional of which the antecedent is false, that is, contrary to facts. Popper, in his *Logic of Scientific Discovery*, points out: 'I do not think that this usage is to be recommended'[41]. In his article in *Mind* 58, N.S., 1949 - an article already referred to in 4.4.1, though the present point was not then noted - Popper has observed that subjunctive conditionals 'do not imply that the antecedent is false, but leave this question open'[42]. It has to be decided whether it is Popper's usage or Kneale's usage, as regards a counterfactual or subjunctive conditional, which is the more acceptable.

In his *Logic of Scientific Discovery* Popper explains that it is upon his own view as to subjunctive conditionals that he has admitted, in his article in *Mind* 58, N.S., 1949, 'that . . . subjunctive conditionals must be deducible from natural laws.'[43] He then refers to Kneale's article in *Analysis* 10, 1950 - an article also referred to before, in 4.4.2, although the point to be mentioned now was not mentioned there - , and says that Kneale there attributes to him the view that a subjunctive, or contrary-to-fact, conditional is of the form '$\sim \phi(a) \,.\, (\phi(a) \supset \Psi(a))$'. Popper remarks that this attribution is 'difficult to understand', seeing that he has already admitted that subjunctive conditionals must be deducible from natural laws. He observes: 'I wonder whether Kneale realized that this expression of his was only a complicated way of saying "$\sim\phi(a)$"; for who would ever think of asserting that "$\sim\phi(a)$" was deducible from the law "$(x)(\phi(x) \supset \Psi(x))$" ?'[44]

To come back now to the question whether Kneale's usage as to subjunctive or counterfactual conditionals is acceptable. It will suffice here to call attention to Mackie's comment on the point. Mackie regards Kneale's usage as after all justified. He refers to two types of subjunctive conditionals: (i) those conditionals the antecedents of which are unfulfilled, and (ii) those the antecedents of which are believed by the speakers as unlikely. The latter are open conditionals, and even an accidentally true universal statement would entail them. Mackie observes: 'It is only the conditionals whose antecedents are unfulfilled that even look like the exclusive property of nomic universals'[45].

Although Mackie's comment has been utilized above in support of Kneale's usage about counterfactual conditionals, his (Mackie's) own treatment of counterfactual conditionals and of natural laws is different, and is both interesting and important, and is worth considering. The reason why his view may be considered in this Chapter is that he has made some observations on Kneale's theory of natural necessity itself. It may be of some use to come to Mackie's view through a brief note on Goodman's truth-functional analysis of counterfactual conditionals.

4.5 Mackie's Treatment of Counterfactual Conditionals and of Natural Laws Considered

As stated just now, it may be useful to come to Mackie's analysis of counterfactual conditionals after some brief consideration of Goodman's analysis of them.

4.5.1 A brief note, in passing, on Goodman's analysis of counterfactuals

In *Fact, Fiction and Forecast* Goodman has searched for a criterion of truth for counterfactual conditionals so that the problem of counterfactual conditionals may be given a proper solution. In the process, he is led to impose one restriction upon another on a set of statements sustaining counterfactuals, and finally he comes to offer no satisfactory solution in this matter. In course of his argument Goodman has laid down the stipulation that a set of statements, S, sustaining a counterfactual must be not only *compatible* but also *coherent* with the antecedent of the counterfactual. Yet his solution is not free from difficulties. Co-tenability itself is a matter depending on causal connection, and hence to explain causality in terms of co-tenability is to get involved in circularity. Mackie thinks that this has led Goodman to a very serious trouble. In order to know whether an antecedent 'A' is co-tenable with the set 'S', we are to determine the truth of another counterfactual. Goodman himself acknowledges that 'to establish any counterfactual...we first have to determine the truth of another'.[46] To concede this is to face an infinite regress. Obviously, the problem of counterfactual remains unresolved in Goodman's hands.

The situation looks grave, and, considering the problems that arise in connection with the logic of counterfactuals, (even if it is not exactly the problem of circularity or infinite regress faced by Goodman). Nicholas Rescher wishes that the *logical* problem of contrary-to-fact conditional 'may be laid to rest' because 'its solution is inevitably an extra-logical matter'.[47] Mackie is of the opinion, however, that there is no reason to be pessimistic on this point. In fact, a solution is available to the problem of interpreting counterfactuals - a solution that will also explain why a law *appears* to sustain a counterfactual, while an accidental generalization does not.

4.5.2 Mackie's approach to counterfactual conditionals

Mackie claims to offer a solution to the problem of the counterfactual significance of laws 'within the framework of a regularity theory'.[48] He observes that Kneale's objection to the regularity theory appears, indeed, to be insurmountable and conclusive, and to project a real problem for the regularists. If laws are 'unrestrictedly general contingent truths' descriptive of the actual world, how can they support counterfactual conditionals 'which look like an extension of the law into merely possible worlds'?[49] If a counterfactual conditional is interpreted to be a journey to the possible world, 'how can it be reasonable to carry with us, in our baggage for this journey, a statement that merely describes the actual world'?[50] Mackie answers by showing that this is only an appearance of the nature and role of a counterfactual conditional. A law-governed counterfactual 'seems to extend the scope of a law beyond the actual facts'.[51] In reality, however, the counterfactuals are not statements about the possible world- '... they only look like this'. Mackie emphasizes that 'we should resist the temptation to take uncritically the suggestion that the counterfactual describes one or more possible worlds'[52].

Instead of offering a truth-functional analysis of counterfactual conditionals, Mackie recommends that a counterfactual conditional may be taken as a 'condensed and incomplete argument' -a 'telescoped' argument[53]. Upon this interpretation, since a counterfactual is not true (or false), Goodman's problem of finding an apposite criterion for the truth of a counterfactual does not arise. It may be observed here that Mackie's solution has already been suggested by Henry Hiz in his paper entitled 'On the Inferential Sense of Contrary-to-Fact Conditional' contributed to *Journal of Philosophy*[54]. Hiz analyses contrary-to-fact conditionals as metalinguistic statements, suggesting to us what may be inferred from a set of premises.

For Mackie, a counterfactual conditional, being neither true nor false, differs from a statement. To take an example of a counterfactual conditional: 'If this piece of paper were gold, it would have been malleable'. Mackie finds that, prima facie, it refers to an imaginary situation pointing out, at the same time, that it is imaginary. Yet

> ... this description is not a purely imaginative exercise... How can we describe non-imaginatively an imaginary situation ? Only by an inference from something else that we know or believe. And yet to state a counterfactual is not to give an inference in full: we do not give all the premises and intermediate steps. A counterfactual, then, is a condensed and incomplete argument.[55]

The assertion of a counterfactual is regarded as advancing or understanding an argument without completing it. If the argument, expressed enthymematically in the form of a counterfactual, be stated fully, one of the premises comes to be the *supposition* of the antecedent of the counterfactual taken along with some other premises that are known or believed. The conclusion is the consequent of the counterfactual. Chisholm points out that the purpose of advancing a counterfactual is to draw our attention to 'one or more of the premises which, taken with the antecedent, logically imply the consequent'[56]. The other premise, or one of the premises, *presupposed* is a law. Thus if somebody believes, as a law, that all gold is malleable, he can advance a counterfactual: 'If this piece of paper were gold, it would have been malleable'. Analogously, Mackie observes: '...the counterfactual conditionals, which emerge from the analysis of causal statements, though not themselves true, are surrogates for clusters of statements which can be true'.[57] In advancing a counterfactual, all the premises of the elliptical argument are not specified. Nevertheless, there is an inference made from the supposition to the conclusion that 'lies within the scope of the supposition'.[58] To advance a counterfactual, for example, 'If this bit of potassium had been exposed to air, it would have burst into flame' is to say: 'Suppose that this bit of potassium has been exposed to air; then (within the scope of the supposition) it has burst into flame'.[59] Thus a counterfactual or a non-material conditional is *sustained*, and not *implied*, 'by the premiss or premisses which, with the antecedent as a further premise, entail the consequent of the conditional'.[60] Mackie adds:

> ...It is true that if certain premisses, together with a supposition P, entail a conclusion Q, then these premisses alone entail the material conditional $P \supset Q$. So wherever true premisses validly sustain a non-material conditional, the corresponding material conditional is true. But the non-material conditional corresponds not to the conclusion $P \supset Q$ but rather to the whole argument within the scope of the supposition, from which we infer $P \supset Q$ by the principle of conditional proof.[61]

What is expected of a general proposition to sustain a counterfactual? A generalization, according to Mackie, sustains a counterfactual if the reason for accepting the generalization is not undermined by adding the supposition. That is why it is reasonable to assert only those counterfactual conditionals which are sustained by the laws of nature, and not others. To explain fully: Mackie compares the example of the counterfactual cited above with another counterfactual 'If this bit of potassium had been exposed to air, it would have turned into gold'. Since it is a law of nature that potassium exposed to oxygen bursts into flame, the law sustains the former in the sense that the law combined with the supposition that this bit of potassium is exposed to air and the fact that air contains oxygen allows us to validly infer the consequent that the potassium bursts into flame. On the other hand, a singular material conditional, '(this bit of potassium is exposed to air) ⊃ (it is turned into gold)', which is only vacuously true, does not sustain the second counterfactual. A material conditional, coupled with the supposition that the antecedent obtains entails, indeed, the consequent. But it is not reasonable to combine the supposition with the conditional which is regarded as true on the sole ground that the supposition is false. This is only to combine a statement and its negation as premises and draw a conclusion from them in a serious argument. In formal logic, a contradiction 'p. ~p' may be taken to lead to any conclusion validly. However, 'no one supposes for a moment that this is a sensible way of *arguing*'.[62]

Without having presupposed an element of necessity in laws, this account of a counterfactual conditional claims to offer a point of distinction between a law and an accidentally true general proposition. Mackie takes the following example of an accidental generalization: 'All coins in my pocket are shiny'. It does not sustain the counterfactual that 'if that other coin had been in my pocket, it would have been shiny', because it is not reasonable to retain, along with the counterfactual supposition that the other coin is in my pocket, a universal proposition that has been established upon an exhaustive check of all the coins in my pocket. It is further possible to show that an accidental generalization, the truth of which is not known by complete enumeration, does not sustain a counterfactual conditional. Mackie gives an example of such a statement: 'No stones in the box are radioactive'. This is a fact because a Geiger counter established nearby shows no indication. This universal statement does not sustain the counterfactual 'if that other stone were in the box, it would not have been radioactive', because some other stone in the box 'undermines the evidence of the Geiger counter as a reason for believing the universal along with the supposition'.[63]

Attempts have been made earlier by some regularists to distinguish a law from a true generalization of facts in terms of the difference 'in the attitude of those who put them forward'.[64] But if the attitude towards a law-statement is a criterion that distinguishes law-statements from other universal statements, this cannot be a purely subjective or an irrational decision. What makes an attitude rational? Mackie seeks to provide the answer. He points out that the inductive evidence supporting, confirming, or corroborating a natural law also justifies our belief that the law holds equally in unobserved cases and that the same also supports a counterfactual conditional. There is 'some formal relation between the body of evidence and the new proposition which it supports',[65] and that also constitutes the justification for advancing a counterfactual conditional. The universal truth 'All coins in X's pocket are made of silver' would not sustain the counterfactual 'If the penny were in X's pocket, it would have been made of silver'. The evidence supporting this general truth is obtained by examination of each of the coins in X's pocket. Since it has been found that none of them are pennies, it is incongruous to suppose that at least one coin in X's pocket is a penny. In the case of a law, on the other hand, all the instances covered by the law are not observed, nor is it required to observe all the cases coming under the class denoted by the subject-term to reach such an inductive conclusion. The evidence supporting the conclusion, e.g. 'Gold is malleable', allows us to presume malleability in every case of gold, observed or unobserved. That evidence also supports the argument we advance in a counterfactual conditional. Accordingly, Mackie remarks :

> ...Formally all that is required to let a law sustain counterfactuals is that there should be the same logical relation (i) between the evidence and the proposed law (covering unobserved instances) as things are, and (ii) between the evidence and the proposed law with things otherwise the same but with additional instances of the law's subject term. And this holds for all ordinary inductive reasoning.[66]

He adds:

> ...Inductive evidence is, by definition, projective; inductive evidence for a law provides a ground for believing that law which is not impaired either (i) by the supposition that there is an instance of the subject term which has not been included in the evidence, or (ii) by the supposition that there are additional (contrary-to-fact) instances of the subject term. The sustaining of counterfactuals by laws or 'nomic universals' is nothing more than the projective force of inductive evidence in a new guise.[67]

If it is a law that potassium, exposed to oxygen, ignites, there must be a sufficient number of positive instances supporting the law. Such a number of instances also support that if an unobserved bit of potassium is exposed to oxygen at any point of time, it ignites. The same evidence also supports that had this potassium, which in fact is not exposed to oxygen, were so exposed, it would have ignited. The evidence bears the same logical relation to the counterfactual case as it bears to the unobserved cases. This makes it reasonable to make a counterfactual supposition.

With this, Mackie comes to think that the problem of analysis of counterfactual conditionals is resolved and that the power of law-statements to sustain counterfactuals is explained in a satisfactory manner.

4.5.3 Mackie's view as to natural laws

For Mackie, the mystery about the special contents of law-statements, over and above the common contents of other universal statements, ceases to bother us any more. There is no difference in the contents of lawful and accidental generalizations. The difference between them lies in how we *use* them. To use a statement as a law is to combine it with suppositions about unobserved cases along with suppositions that change the extension of the subject-term. In this sense, a law warrants counterfactual inferences. The reason for this, as seen above, is the inductive evidence. Thus the problem of sustaining a counterfactual conditional by a law is nothing but the problem of induction. Mackie observes:

> ...'A asserts a nomic universal' will then be shortened for 'A asserts a contingent actual universal statement on (ultimately) inductive evidence and is also ready to assert the counterfactuals which are related to that evidence in the same way as are (actual) instances of the universal statement'. If we could adhere to this understanding of the phrase, it would be harmless. But for that very reason, it would no longer justify Kneale's further claim that laws of nature are principles of necessitation, that in asserting them we are somehow claiming that there is, in what goes on in the world, something like a logical requirement (although we do not know enough to be able to explicitly see it as such...[68]

So far Mackie appears more as a regularist than as a supporter of Kneale. But simply for that can we consider him a regularist? Beauchamp and Rosenberg refer to some passages in Mackie's writings that appear to be Humean in spirit. They remark that though Hume himself has not written them, Hume would 'no doubt have been pleased to have written' them himself. They add that 'it is traditional misunderstanding of Hume's views about induction that might blind one to the similarities between the theory Mackie advances and Hume's own discussion of the role played by evidence and confidence in the distinction between lawlike and accidental generalizations'.[69] If Mackie sounds like Hume, that only shows that it is possible to make a distinction between lawlike and accidental universals within Hume's philosophy without conceding that a law is anything more than a simple universal. For Beauchamp and Rosenberg, Mackie 'attempts to reconstruct Kneale's argument' and 'Mackie's willingness to advance the discussion by putting it on an empirical basis and providing further arguments certainly seems an improvement over the obscure status of natural necessity in Kneale's writings'.[70]

One needs, however, to delve deeper into Mackie's view. Mackie believes that his theory so far has only been able to show why a law sustains a counterfactual conditional without giving up the regularist position. But the question persists: how do we ultimately distinguish a law from an accidental generalization? The regularists might reply that a nomic generalization is 'explainable or derivable' from higher or fundamental laws, while an accidental generalization has no such basis. Mackie finds this solution unacceptable, for this 'explains the lawfulness only of the derived or derivable laws'.[71] If this solution be accepted, we have either to accept an infinite regress in derivation or to maintain that some basic laws, because they are basic, are not derivable from any higher laws and as such really are not laws. Yet they must be laws, since what are derivable from them are laws. The regularists may try to solve the puzzle by turning their theory upside down and maintaining that basic laws are called laws not because they are derivable from other laws, but because other laws are derivable from them. But this hardly provides an adequate criterion for distinguishing between law-statements and statements of accidental generalities. Yet another possible answer is examined by Mackie. He refers to Mill who thinks that laws are unrestricted generalities with a wide range of application. Mill talks of 'laws of working' and 'collocations'. The laws of working are discovered by induction. The collocations, on the other hand, are to be discovered by complete examination. We test whether something is not 'independent of a collocation by changing the collocation and seeing if it still holds'.[72] This shows that a law of working rests on a stronger basis than a collocation. But what makes the basis stronger for a law of working? The answer is suggested to Mackie by Kneale's theory of natural necessity.

As for Kneale, he maintains, as has been seen before, that Hume's objection is based on a wrong theory of perception and that the rejection of phenomenalism is sufficient to diffuse the force of Hume's objection. Mackie finds that Kneale adopts the realist point of view of Locke and suggests that truths concerning perceptual objects are not open to inspection. He (Mackie) holds that this vindication of realism is not so important in present times; nevertheless he admits the truth of this conclusion 'without question'. He comments, however, that even if Kneale's position that truths about perceptual objects remain unknown to us is accepted, this is not to take 'all the force out of Hume's doubt about objective necessities of the kind proposed'.[73]

Mackie thinks that Hume's main objection only proves that there is no logical connection between two events that are causally connected. But Hume's objection, according to him, has bearing only upon 'causation *so far as we know about it in the objects*'. However, it 'leaves room for "several qualities, both in material and immaterial objects, with which we are utterly unacquainted" [*Treatise*, I, iii, 14, Selby-Bigge, p. 168]'[74]. Now coming to induction, why does it support a law? A satisfactory answer may be provided only if we go beyond mere regularity and 'conjecture that there really is some causal mechanism underlying the succession and explaining it'. Mackie asks here:

> ....must this be a matter of conjecture, of *transcendent hypothesis*? Would it not be even better to uncover and observe the mechanism? And yet, if we did so, would not Hume's criticisms again have force ... ?[75]

Mackie agrees with Hume that all we can see in causal mechanism is a succession of events. For Kneale, the cause has a structure which is unobservable. The effect also has an unobservable structure. The necessity of development of one structure into the other would be evident provided we knew the structures. Science can only hypothesize about these structures. These are mere conjectures which get corroborated by 'their success in relating observed regularities to intelligible structure development'.[76] For Mackie, what lies at the bottom of causal mechanism is a kind of *qualitative structural continuity* or *natural persistence*. Two events may appear to be distinct. A match is struck on a matchbox and there is a flame. Apparently the effect has nothing in common with the cause. But Mackie writes:

> ...if we were to replace the macroscopic picture with a detailed description of the molecular and atomic movements with which the perceived processes are identified by an adequate physico-chemical theory, we should find far more continuity and persistence. And this is part of the point of micro-reduction, of the transcendent hypotheses of which Kneale speaks.[77]

If there is a structural continuity or natural persistence between A and B, it will not only be true to say that all unobserved A's are B's. It will also be possible to assert with confidence that had anything been an A, it would have been a B. For Mackie:

> Qualitative or structural continuity of process, then, may

> well be something in the objects, over and above the complex regularity, which provides some backing for the conditional and especially counterfactual statements that emerge in the analysis of our ordinary causal concept.[78]

This theory, Mackie thinks, is 'built upon foundations provided in Kneale's theory'[79]; yet it has 'strayed rather far from the sort of theory Kneale proposes'. Kneale, Mackie says, belongs to the rationalist tradition; 'his transcendent hypotheses reveal only continuities and persistences; these are an empirical counterpart of the rationalists 'necessity'.[80] Mackie, like Kneale, maintains that we can only hypothesize that the actual laws of working reveal structural continuities. Further, since the laws are inductively established the law statements are synthetic objective statements. The natural persistence proves that causal connection is not due to mind, it is *an objective connection existing in the realm of facts.* In order to distinguish between the causal and the non-causal relation we need a theory of natural necessity, as reinterpreted in the indicated way. In a causal sequence there is a qualitative or structural continuity. This can be located 'once we move from the events at the perceptual level to the "transcendent hypothesis" with which those events are, on a scientific realist view, identified, and by which they are explained'.[81]

But Beauchamp and Rosenberg contend that if Mackie talks of natural persistence, the problem of induction remains unresolved; for 'persistences are inferred from experience and in particular from experiences of regularities'.[82] The identification of persistence presupposes a causal determination, and, therefore, persistence cannot distinguish, without circularity, the causal from non-causal sequences. They write:

> ...The persistence involved in or underlying causal sequences is not a matter either of *a priori* expectedness or intelligibility. ...What is it, we may ask, that distinguishes persistences from non-causal sequences? Hume's challenge is still unanswered.[83]

They add a little later:

> ...Is there anything in persistence that constitutes what Mackie describes as 'the long-searched-for link between individual cause and effect which a pure regularity theory fails, or refuses, to find'? If we are correct that persistences are experimentially derived from constant conjunctions, the answer is 'no'. And since Mackie has rightly rejected Kneale's transcendent hypothesizing in favor of empirical laws of working, his interpretation of Kneale provides no transcendent ground for objecting to Hume. Interpreted as a refutation of Hume, Mackie's non-rationalist reconstruction of Kneale's theory is thus rendered implausible by the argument that Mackie himself advances.[84]

What follows from the above is that the attempt made by Mackie to explain the distinction between lawlike statements and accidental generalizations ultimately goes beyond the scope of the regularity theory. If there is only regularity, and no necessity, amongst natural phenomena, what is the justification of the inductive procedure? Beauchamp and Rosenberg accept Mackie's solution to explain the counterfactual import of laws. For them,

> ...if the language of possible cases is exhaustibly analyzable in terms of suppositions and suppressed, non-modal premises, then from the fact that lawlike generalizations sustain counterfactuals, no conclusion whatever follows in support of natural necessity. At most it follows that lawlike generalizations are used to make 'inferences beyond the actual'. These are hypothetical suppositions moving from known data to inductively insufficient conclusion. ...Inductive sufficiency cannot be obtained for such conclusions, for the lawlike generalization is being used to project beyond the actual world into the so-called possible worlds that are counter to fact. These hypotheticals do not

> report what is the case; they are mind-dependent projections. ... lawlikeness and counterfactual support alike can be treated as a function of the degree of confidence generated by and vested in the supporting evidence.[85]

But can we regard what is possible or impossible as solely determined by the mind? For Molnar, these are metaphysical issues and the Humean suggestion seems counter-intuitive. The question still remains how, according to the regularity theory, are laws to be distinguished from mere regularities of a cosmic scale, that is, 'a universally instanced cosmic accident ...that survives all attempts at falsification and all changes in the order of nature'? One may admit, as Beauchamp and Rosenberg did, that 'there is indeed, so far as we know, no difference whatever. An allegedly "accidental" universal that meets the tests of survival... is a universal of law'.[86] But can there be tests of survival carried out in a conclusive manner to prove the law-status of a statement? Kneale, as previously seen, has spoken of certain statements like the one about music composed by a musician on his deathbed, which would pass the test of survival, yet they are not laws. A Humean, at this point, might be tempted to say that, in a deterministic universe, where all events are determined by causal laws, 'any allegedly accidental universal truths like those suggested by Kneale, hold, if they hold at all, in consequence of laws, and should therefore be regarded as laws themselves'.[87] But what justifies the suggestion that the universe as deterministic?

Beauchamp and Rosenberg turning to Kneale accuse him of circularity: they hold that laws are explained by Kneale in terms of counterfactuals, 'which themselves rely on an implicit appeal to laws'. Thus 'the supposed death-knell of the regularity theory ultimately goes unexplained'.[88] This seems to be a misunderstanding of Kneale. Kneale has not explained laws in terms of counterfactuals. He no doubt holds that the laws are necessary and that they possess a counterfactual import. He would be certainly begging the question if he had *explained* the necessity of laws in terms of their counterfactual import. But he has not done that. That laws have a counterfactual import is undeniably true, and even some regularists accept it. Kneale has just referred to this fact while examining the regularity theory of laws. As to the necessity of natural laws, the view that such laws are, or may be, necessary comes to be advocated by him on the basis of a number of considerations. The view is suggested to him, as seen so far, by Locke. And it has been seen that he has sought to defend this view against some serious objections to it. When this study is finished, it will be seen that this view is further strengthened for him through his consideration and rejection of some serious alternatives to it, and it will also be seen that he has not forgotten to refer to Kant from whom a kind of backing is available for a theory of natural necessity and that he has added the final consideration that the theory of natural necessity does indeed serve to make intelligible the belief that (ampliative) induction is after all a *rational* policy. All this goes to show that the charge of circularity leveled by Beauchamp and Rosenberg against Kneale is unjustified.

It has been seen that the regularity theory, as explained so far, does not satisfactorily explain the distinction between a law and an accidental generalization. The next task is to examine some further attempts which have been made to salvage the regularity theory from Kneale's criticism. Armstrong calls them the 'sophisticated versions' of the regularity theory. If it is found that Kneale's objection is not applicable to such sophistications, then, surely, the regularity theory may be reinstated on fresher grounds.

Notes

1 K. P. Winkler in an article entitled 'The New Hume', contributed to *The Philosophical Review*, vol. C, no. 4 (1991), gives an excellent presentation of this neo-Humean interpretation, specially advocated by Galen Strawson in *Secret Connexion: Causation, Realism and David Hume*, Clarendon Press, Oxford, 1989 to show that this new interpretation is not a proper representation of the Humean

position in the light of his entire work. T. L. Beauchamp and A. Rosenberg in *Hume and the Problem of Causation*, Oxford University Press, Oxford, 1981, describe Hume as a revisionary philosopher who gives a new meaning of the phrase 'necessary connection' instead of denying it, in its ordinary sense, as a part of meaning of causal relation.

2 Cf. Kneale, *Probability and Induction*, Oxford, 1966, p. 71.

3 *Ibid.*, p. 74.

4 T. L. Beauchamp, 'Cosmic Epochs and the Scope of Scientific Laws', *Process Studies*, vol. 2, 1972, p. 296, and cf. D. M. Armstrong, *What is a Law of Nature?* Cambridge University Press, Cambridge, 1987, p. 12.

5 See Armstrong, *ibid.*, p. 17.

6 Kneale, *op. cit.*, p. 74.

7 See Carl Hempel, 'Problems and Changes in the Empiricist Criterion of Meaning', R. R. Ammerman, ed. *Classics of Analytic Philosophy*, TMH Edition, Bombay - New Delhi, 1965, p. 217.

8 Kneale, *op. cit.*, p. 74.

9 *Ibidem.*

10 *Ibid.*, p. 75.

11 *Ibidem.*

12 *Ibidem.*

13 Achinstein maintains that if S is taken as the subject of a law-statement, then a law says that anything that is an S satisfies a consequent condition C, if it satisfies an antecedent condition A. But he asks: does the law imply that anything that satisfies the subject-term S is such that if it were to satisfy the antecedent condition A, then it would have satisfied the consequent condition C? Or, can we interpret the law to imply that anything is such that if it were to satisfy the subject-term and the antecedent, then it would also satisfy the consequent? Achinstein argues that a law implies that 'if *i* which is an S were to satisfy A, it would satisfy C *without the need for any further assumptions* (i.e. beyond that *i* is an S which does not satisfy A)' and this type of counterfactual is the 'central' one implied by a law though it may not be the only one implied by a law. Achinstein believes that a law supports the counterfactual by way of semantical entailment. The law 'All S under A satisfies C' *means* 'If an item,

which is an S and does not satisfy A, were to satisfy A, then, it would satisfy C'. Achinstein asserts:

> The present feature of laws, that there is a semantical entailment between a law, a statement about a particular item, and a counterfactual of a certain type, is one in virtue of which laws can be said to express what is necessary. [P. Achinstein, *Law and Explanation*, Clarendon Press, Oxford, 1971, p. 51]

For Kneale, however, a law of nature is not a statement the necessity of which is a matter of semantics. Kneale regards a law as expressing natural necessity which often remains unknown to the intellect.

14 K. R. Popper, 'A Note on Natural Laws and so-called Contrary-to-Fact Conditionals', *Mind*, vol. LVIII, 1949, pp. 64-66.

15 *Ibid.*, p. 64.

16 *Ibid.*, p. 65.

17 *Ibidem.*

18 See Kneale, 'Natural Law and Contrary-to-Fact Conditionals', *Analysis*, 1950, reprinted in Margaret Macdonald, ed. *Philosophy and Analysis*, Basil Blackwell, Oxford, 1954, p. 228, and also his 'Universality and Necessity', in *The British Journal for the Philosophy of Science*, No. 46, 1961, p. 13.

19 'Natural Laws and Contrary-to-Fact Conditionals', *Philosophy and Analysis*, p. 228.

20 *Ibid.*, p. 229.

21 *Ibidem.*

22 Popper, *op. cit.*, p. 66.

23 Kneale, *op. cit.* p. 230.

24 *Ibidem.*

25 K. R. Popper, *The Logic of Scientific Discovery*, Hutchinson of London, 1959, p. 432.

26 *Ibid.*, p. 430.

27 *Ibid.*, p. 428.

Norman Swartz takes Popper's usage of the phrase 'initial conditions' as a deviation from the 'common parlance of scientists and engineers'. Swartz finds Popper interpreting the term in a special or extended sense. By the allowing of diversity of initial conditions is meant that there may be variations from world to world in respect of singular historical facts among the possible worlds that share the same nomologically necessary laws. [N. Swartz, *The Concept of Physical Laws,* Cambridge University Press, Cambridge, 1985, p. 133.]

28 *Ibid.*, p. 433.
29 *Ibid.*, p. 437.
30 *Ibid.*, p. 433.
31 Kneale, 'Universality and Necessity', *The British Journal for the Philosophy of Science,* No. 46, 1961, p. 15.
32 Popper, *The Logic of Scientific Discovery,* p. 432.
33 Kneale, *op.cit.,* p. 17.
34 *Ibid.*, p. 18.
35 Popper, *op. cit.*, p. 438. Quoted by Kneale *also* in W. Kneale and Martha Kneale, *The Development of Logic*, Oxford, p. 650.
36 Kneale, *op.cit.*, p. 16.
37 *Ibidem.*
38 *Ibid.*, p. 18.
39 *Ibid.*, p. 19.
40 Nerlich and Suchting, in a paper commenting on Popper's definition of natural necessity, observe that Popper's definition of natural necessity virtually concedes that a law of nature is something logically stronger than a true unrestricted universal statement and that the latter is neither logically sufficient nor intuitively adequate to describe a law-statement. Further, the definition is viewed as verbally defective. In order to eliminate some universal statements which are true of our world from the purview of natural laws, Popper has used the device of a range of worlds which differ from our world only with respect to initial conditions. However, this is not enough. Nerlich and Suchting show that some accidentally true generalizations, like Popper's moa-example, are not excluded by his definition of physical necessity.

Nerlich and Suchting suggest a re-statement of his definition:

> ...the intent of his definition may be expressed as follows: a statement may be naturally or physically necessary if, and only if, it is deducible from a statement function which

> is satisfied in all worlds which instantiate the properties and relations of our world but which may differ from our world with respect to initial conditions. ['Popper on Law and Natural Necessity', *The British Journal for the Philosophy of Science*, vol. 18, 1967, p. 234]

They have raised another important question: what is the criterion to delimit the possible range of variation of initial conditions? Only two alternatives seem plausible: either (i) there is some logical criterion which imposes a restriction on the initial conditions, or, (ii) it is some physical possibility that sets a limit to the variation of initial conditions. The first alternative is tantamount to reducing natural necessity to logical necessity, and this turns out to be the position from which Popper wants to distance himself. On the other hand, if the second alternative is accepted, that would make the definition circular; 'for it would now read: a statement may be said to be naturally or physically necessary if, and only if, it is deducible from a statement function which is satisfied in all worlds which instantiate the properties and relations of our world but which may differ from our world with respect to physically possible initial conditions, i.e., initial conditions which are not inconsistent with a naturally or physically necessary statement'.[*Ibid.*, p. 235.]

In the face of the above criticism, Popper reiterates that his position differs radically from Kneale's. In response to the objection of circularity, he replies that he is already aware of it. He has talked about this circularity in the very Appendix in which he offers a definition of natural necessity. However, he believes that the circularity is not vicious. At the same time he admits that there is a 'verbal defect' in the definition and offers a revised definition as follows:

> (N) *a* is a naturally or physically necessary fact (or statement, or statement function) of our own world T if and only if *a* is satisfied in every *logically* possible world which satisfies a set M of 'separated' and universal facts, consisting of every fact *b* such that to *b* corresponds an axiom *b'* with the following properties: (1) *b'* belongs to one or another independent set A of 'separated' universal

axioms *which are satisfied in every possible world differing from our world (if at all) only with respect to initial conditions (in the wider sense)*; and (2) *b' is not* satisfied in every possible world *W* in which all the other axioms of *A* are satisfied, even if it is stipulated that *all those initial conditions* hold in *W* which hold *in our own world*. ['A Revised Definition of Natural Necessity', *The British Journal for the Philosophy of Science*, vol. 19, 1968, p. 321]

However, even this revised definition cannot take care of all the problems raised earlier. Suchting says: if the properties are instantiated by individuals and there is a limited number of individuals, then 'there can be no naturally necessary statements on Popper's account'['Popper's Revised Definition of Natural Necessity', *The British Journal for the Philosophy of Science*, v. 20, 1969, p. 352] in a spatio-temporally infinite world or a finite world in which every part is not occupied by an individual.

41 *The Logic of Scientific Discovery*, p. 434.

42 *Mind*, 58, N.S., 1949, p. 62.

43 *The Logic of Scientific Discovery*, p. 434 note.

44 *Ibidem*.

45 J. L. Mackie, 'Counterfactuals and Causal Laws' in R. J, Butler, ed. *Analytic Philosophy*, Series - I, Oxford, 1966, p. 66. Also in *The Cement of the Universe*, Clarendon Press, Oxford, 1974, p. 197 ff.

46 N. Goodman, *Fact, Fiction and Forecast*, Bobbs-Merrill, Indianapolis, New York, 1973, p. 23.

47 N. Rescher, 'Belief-Contravening Suppositions', *Philosophical Review*, v. LXX, 1961, p.196.

48 Mackie, 'Counterfactuals and Causal Laws', p. 67.

49 Mackie, *The Cement of the Universe*, p. 203.

50 *Ibid*., p. 201.

51 Mackie, 'Counterfactuals and Causal Laws', p. 66.

52 Mackie, *The Cement of the Universe*, p. 203.

53 Mackie, 'Counterfactuals and Causal Laws', p. 68.

54 Henry Hiz, 'On the Inferential Sense of Contrary-to-Fact Conditional', *Journal of Philosophy*, vol. 48, 1949, pp. 586-87.

55 Mackie, *op.cit*., pp. 67-68.

56 R. M. Chisholm, 'Law Statements and Counterfactual Inference',

Analysis, 15, 1955, reprinted in E. Sosa, ed. *Causation and Counterfactuals,* Oxford University Press, Oxford, London, 1975, p. 151.

57 Mackie, *The Cement of the Universe*, pp. 229-230.

58 Mackie, 'Counterfactuals and Causal Laws', p. 69.

59 Mackie, *The Cement of the Universe*, p. 201.

60 Mackie, 'Counterfactuals and Causal Laws', p. 69.

61 *Ibidem.*

62 Mackie, *The Cement of the Universe,* p. 200.

63 Mackie, 'Counterfactuals and Causal Laws', p. 72.

64 Ayer, 'What is a Law of Nature?' p. 51.

65 Mackie, *The Cement of the Universe,* p. 202.

66 J. L. Mackie, *Truth, Probability and Paradox,* Clarendon Press, Oxford, 1973, pp. 117-18.

67 *Ibid., p.* 118.

68 Mackie, *The Cement of the Universe*, p. 203.

69 T. L. Beauchamp and A. Rosenberg, *Hume and the Problem of Causation*, Oxford University Press, Oxford, 1981, p. 148.

70 *Ibid.*, p. 126.

71 Mackie, *op. cit.*, p. 206.

72 *Ibid.*, p. 214.

73 *Ibid.,* p. 215.

74 *Ibidem.*

75 *Ibid.*, p. 217.

76 *Ibidem.*

77 *Ibid.*, pp. 221-222.

78 *Ibid.*, p. 224.

79 *Ibid.*, p. 228.

80 *Ibid.*, p. 223.

81 *Ibid.*, p. 228.

82 Beauchamp and Rosenberg, *op.cit.*, p. 129.

83 *Ibid.*, p. 130.

84 *Ibid.*, pp. 130-31.

85 *Ibid.*, p. 151.

86 *Ibid.*, p. 156.

87 Mackie, *The Cement of the Universe*, p. 198.

88 *Ibid.*, p. 157.

CHAPTER FIVE

SOME 'SOPHISTICATED' VERSIONS OF THE REGULARITY THEORY CONSIDERED: AN EXCURCUS

5.1 Foreword

Kneale's criticism of the regularity theory of natural laws has brought to light the problem of explicating the true character of natural laws from the pure regularity point of view. A satisfactory answer to Kneale's objection is not found at least in Hume's own work.

The main point of Kneale's objection is, as has been seen, that a law of nature has a counterfactual import and is on that account logically stronger than an accidental generalization. It is by this counterfactual import that a law of nature can be distinguished from a universal statement of facts.

The regularists also have felt the need to distinguish a law from a non-law, though the naïve version of the regularity theory, as considered before, fails to offer a satisfactory criterion for this purpose. There are also other difficulties for the theory. Armstrong has shown that there are laws which do not satisfy the Humean stipulations. Again, there are many universal statements which the Humeans themselves would refuse to call laws, even though they satisfy all the Humean stipulations for a law. Various attempts have been made, on behalf of the regularists, to bring improvements upon Hume's theory to avoid these difficulties. In this way certain sophisticated versions of the regularity theory have arisen. The present Chapter, as its title indicates, is devoted to a discussion of some such versions.

Before proceeding to consider the sophisticated versions of the regularity theory, a brief look at Molnar's restatement of Kneale's argument against this theory may be of some interest.

5.2 Molnar's Presentation of Kneale's Argument against the Regularity Theory

Molnar begins with the Humean definition of a law of nature:

D_1: p is a statement of a law of nature iff

i) p is universally quantified.

ii) p is true omnitemporally and omnispatially.

iii) p is contingent.

iv) p contains only non-local empirical predicates, apart from logical connectives and quantifiers.

A state of affairs is empirically possible if it does not contradict a law of nature. A state of affairs is an unrealized possibility, if it is possible but does not occur. Thus one comes to another definition.

D_2: If p is a statement asserting the existence of a state of affairs, then what it says is possible, provided p is not inconsistent with any law of nature.

Obviously, p is a statement of possibility iff what p says is possible. Hence one comes to a third definition:

D_3: p states an unrealized possibility (a state of affairs which is conceived as 'neither actual nor impossible') iff

i) p is a statement of possibility, and

ii) p is false.

With these definitions in mind, Molnar restates Kneale's argument in the format of a formal proof. There are ten steps in Molnar's presentation of the argument[1] :

1. 'Something is F' is false. (Assumption)
2. 'Nothing is F'. (1 Equivalence)
3. 'Nothing is F' is a law of nature. (2, D_1)
4. 'Something is F' is inconsistent with 'Nothing is F'. (Tautology)
5. 'Something is F' is inconsistent with a law of nature. (3, 4)
6. 'Something is F' is not a statement of possibility. (5, D_2)
7. If 'Something is F' is false, then 'Something is F' is not a statement of possibility. (1-6 Conditional Proof)
8. It is not the case that both 'Something is F' is false and that 'Something is F' is a statement of possibility. (7 Equivalence)
9. 'Something is F' is not a statement of unrealized possibility. (8, D_3)
10. For any x, if x is an unrestricted empirical existential proposition, then x is not a statement of unrealized possibility. (9, UG)

The conclusion of the above argument, Molnar claims, proves that 'no contingent unrestricted existential proposition containing only empirical predicates' can be both false and 'consistent with every law of nature', and 'Kneale's argument thus pits the Regularity Theory of Laws of Nature and the definition of a statement of unrealized possibility against each other'.[2] However, the conclusion that there can be no unrealized possibility is obviously counterintuitive. Ordinarily, many statements are believed to be false but empirically possible.

The regularists are also faced with difficulties with probabilistic laws, uninstantiated laws, and infinitely qualified laws.[3] In examining the sophisticated versions of the regularity theory, it has to be seen how far free from difficulties they are.

5.3 A Classification of the Sophisticated Versions of the Regularity Theory

The attempts to improve upon the regularity theory have been broadly classified by Armstrong under two heads: (i) those versions which introduce 'an external criterion' to distinguish laws from non-laws, and (ii) the versions which give 'an internal criterion' - a characteristic belonging to the very nature of laws demarcating laws from non-laws. Suchting construes the rationale that might have dwelled in the regularists' minds to have led them to choose any of these two alternative modes of sophistication. He observes that since, for the regularists, a law-statement cannot be anything more than a mere contingent universal statement about matters of facts, the only way in which a law can be distinguished from other universal statements is by an appeal to 'certain specific relations that they bear to other items'.[4] The other item in the relation may be either the persons entertaining the statements as laws, or, some other statements. As the improvement attempted in terms of the former appeals to certain epistemic matters, viz. the attitude towards the uniformities, the nature of evidence supporting the laws, etc., this version of sophistication upon the regularity theory is called by Armstrong the epistemic version. Suchting calls it 'the pragmatic version',[5] because the attitude towards a law is reflected in the special way in which a law-statement is used in guiding human action. This is the kind of explanation offered by Goodman, Ayer, and Strawson, besides Braithwaite and Ramsey. The latter alternative has again taken two forms: (i) the resiliency version offered by Brian Skyrm, and (ii) the systematic version adopted by Ramsey, Lewis, and others. The systematic version seeks to distinguish a law-statement from a universal statement of fact by means of some logical relation which obtains between a law-statement and some other statements. On this interpretation, the laws are, as Suchting puts it, 'objects of certain characteristic human attitudes, expressed ... in the uses made of them and not others, in guiding human action. But these attitudes are taken not to constitute, but rather to be a consequence of, their being law-statements'.[6]

The above classification of the different attempts to improve upon the regularity theory is not intended to suggest that one version is an exclusive alternative to the other. The different versions are often found to go hand in hand. Suchting has mentioned Walters who has combined two versions. Mention may also be made of Braithwaite. In an article published in *Mind* (vol. 36, 1928) he has sought to explain the distinction between a law and a non-law in terms of belief. However, after twenty-four years in his *Scientific Explanations* he has justified people's belief in laws by reference to the relation a law-statement bears to the total system of believed or accepted statements. This explanation, he claims, is far superior in subtlety to his earlier solution, and this combines the epistemic version with the systematic one.

5.4 The Epistemic Version of Sophistication

Beauchamp and Rosenberg maintain that there is a circularity in the sort of objection that Kneale has urged against the regularity theory of natural laws from the point of view of the counterfactual import of laws. Laws, according to Kneale, are distinguished from statements of accidental generalizations in that they support counterfactuals, but the notion of counterfactuals in its turn depends on an implicit understanding of the concept of laws. Hence, they contend, 'the supposed death knell of the regularity theory ultimately goes unexplained by Hume's opponents'. On the other hand, 'the Humean avoids a circular explanation of lawlike generalizations and counterfactuals by analysing *both* in terms of epistemically warranted attitudes'.[7] They further write: 'Lawlikeness and counterfactual support alike can be treated as a function of the degree of confidence generated by and vested in the supporting evidence'.[8]

The origin of this interpretation of law may also be traced in

Hume. Hume regards the notion of a necessary connection as the most important component of our idea of causal connection. He recommends that this idea of necessary connection be understood as being due to habit, that is, a psychological fact 'about human beings and other animals, viz. propensities to associate in a reflex-like manner certain impressions with certain ideas'.[9] It would be more interesting, however, to see how this Humean way of explaining the idea of necessary connection in *psychological* terms has been developed further by Hume's followers in later years.

Thus Braithwaite suggests that the distinction between a law of nature and the other kind of universal statements may be explained on the ground of people's 'rational corpus of knowledge and reasonable belief'.[10] A law of nature, for him, is a subset of true statements. The honorific title of 'law of nature' is reserved only for those true statements which one has some special reason to believe. As he puts it:

> ...This account of natural law makes the application of the notion dependent upon the way in which the hypothesis is regarded by a particular person at a particular time as having been established: 'lawlike' may be thought of as a honorific epithet which is employed as a mark of origin.[11]

He specifies the conditions in which a statement is believed to be a law of nature. A law is accepted or believed on non-demonstrative grounds, that is, on grounds other than the complete enumeration of its instances. A statement is a law if it is supported by direct observation of some of its instances and is also indirectly supported by instances of other hypotheses which are subsumed with the first statement under a higher-level hypothesis. The statement 'All men are mortal' would not be called a law if the only evidence available in its support were the instances of men. There must be other reasons for believing in the law than the evidence of its instances alone. If the above statement is deduced from a higher-level hypothesis, namely, 'All animals are mortal', then the evidence supporting other general propositions, like 'All horses are mortal', 'All cats are mortal', etc., which are placed along with the general statement 'All men are mortal' on the same level and subsumed under the higher-level hypothesis 'All animals are mortal', would constitute its indirect evidence. Thus the statement 'All men are mortal' is accepted as true upon direct observation of the mortality of some of its instances and also on such other pieces of evidence that horses have died, cats have died, etc., and is for this reason regarded as a law of nature.

Braithwaite admits that this explanation has a paradoxical consequence. Upon it, a statement like 'All men are mortal' would be regarded as a natural law because 'it occurs in an established scientific deductive system at a lower level than a hypothesis (e.g. 'All animals are mortal') which has other lower-level hypotheses under it which are directly confirmed by experience...'.[12] Paradoxically, the higher-level hypothesis, 'All animals are mortal', would not be considered a law because the only evidence supporting it is the evidence of its own instances. Braithwaite thinks that the paradox corresponds to the way a law of nature is generally put to use. A law is usually understood to provide an explanation of the instances coming under it. If the sole reason for believing a general statement is the 'direct knowledge of the truth of its instances', it is 'a poor sort of explanation of these instances'. On the other hand, if the general statement, besides its direct evidence, is also supported by indirect evidence, it has a greater explanatory power. The law, in that case, provides the grounds for believing the truth of its instances 'independently of any direct knowledge of such truth'.[13] Thus Braithwaite goes on to define lawhood in the following manner:

> The condition for an established hypothesis *h* being *lawlike* (i.e. being, if true, a natural law) will then be that the hypothesis either occurs in an established scientific deductive system as a higher-level hypothesis containing theoretical

> concepts or that it occurs in an established scientific deductive system as a deduction from higher-level hypotheses which are supported by empirical evidence which is not direct evidence for *h* itself.[14]

The formulation of lawlikeness, in so far as it is a formulation in terms of deducibility from higher-level hypotheses, has two obvious advantages. It provides an account that puts due emphasis upon the explanatory character of a law of nature. Secondly, though a law is distinguished from a non-law by means of the reasonable belief on the part of individual subjects, it does not reduce lawfulness to a purely subjective notion varying from person to person. As the 'rational corpora of many people with the same scientific education and culture agree in the scientific deductive systems at a given time',[15] there would be a general agreement that some statements, if true, are statements of laws of nature and that some others are accidental generalizations, though 'each of the people will mean something different by his statement'.[16]

Braithwaite also includes hypotheses containing theoretical concepts in the class of laws; for these hypotheses, though not deduced from higher-level hypotheses, are not established by the process of induction by complete enumeration. The hypotheses containing theoretical terms are obtainable by the hypothetico-deductive method - the method of formulating the hypothesis and then deducing testable consequences from it.

Both forms of hypothesis mentioned by Braithwaite have an explanatory role - they explain their instances, besides covering them. A true statement, then, is regarded as a statement of law after considering the 'way in which it could enter into an established scientific deductive system'[17].

From Braithwaite who started with an epistemic version and, realizing its difficulties, developed it further into a systematic version, it is time to move on to some other philosophers, like Goodman and Ayer, who have suggested that the distinction between a law and a non-law be interpreted as being due to the circumstance leading to the acceptance of a statement as a law or the attitude towards a law. Goodman thinks it 'unscientific' to distinguish a law from a non-law 'by reference to a causative force'. Again, 'no syntactical criterion can be adequate for even the most special descriptions of particular facts can be cast in a form having any desired degree of syntactical universality'.[18] A law, e.g. 'All butter melts at 150^0 F', is accepted as true when many cases that may come under it still remain undetermined. The description of a contingent fact like 'All coins in my pocket are silver', however, is accepted as true only after determining all the cases coming under it. Goodman points out that by determination of all instances, he means the test of all things satisfying a particular description by direct examination or any other means to find out whether they also possess another feature. This determination, of course, is not the 'final discovery of truth'; it is just 'enough examination to reach a decision as to whether a given statement or its negate (*sic*) is to be admitted as evidence for the hypothesis in question'.[19] Even if all the instances covered by the law are not determined, the laws are used to predict what happens in unexamined cases. A universal proposition describing a truth of fact, on the other hand, is not used to predict the case of any of its instances. Our decision to use certain general statements in a particular way explains the special feature of a law - its counterfactual import. In short, Goodman believes:

> ...the principle we use to decide counterfactual cases is a principle we are willing to commit ourselves to in deciding unrealized cases that are still subject to direct observation.
>
> ...a law is a true sentence used for making predictions. That laws are used predictively is of course a simple truism, and I am not proposing it as a novelty. I want to emphasize the Humean idea that rather than a sentence being used for prediction because it is a law, it is called a law because it is

> used for prediction; and that rather than the law being used for prediction because it describes a causal connection, the meaning of the causal connection is to be interpreted in terms of predictively used laws.[20]

This criterion, Goodman claims, excludes vacuous principles as laws. If the laws possess counterfactual import, then they must be based on supportive evidence. Further, it should not be thought that only statements that have been actually used for prediction are the laws and that a true statement, previously used for prediction, would cease to be a law when it becomes completely tested to leave none of its instances undetermined. He restates the definition of lawlikeness as:

> A general statement is lawlike if and only if it is acceptable prior to the determination of all its instances.[21]

Goodman apprehends a possible objection to the above definition. He considers again the true but unlawlike generalization: 'All coins in my pocket are silver'. It does not support the counterfactual 'If P were in my pocket, then it would have been silver'. But a difficulty still remains. This statement as a non-law has no predictive use. Nevertheless, if the subject of the statement is broadened strategically, then it can be shown to have a counterfactual import. For example, the subject of the general statement, 'All coins in my pocket are silver', may be extended so that the original statement becomes 'All coins that are either in my pocket or are dimes are silver'. Since all dimes are not examined before the assertion of this reformulated statement, it is a predictive statement. In this manner, the subject of any statement may be expanded to make the statement lawlike. Thus a further change in the definition of lawlikeness becomes necessary. Goodman gives the following one as the revised definition of lawlikeness:

> A sentence is lawlike if its acceptance does not depend upon the determination of any given instance.[22]

The definition is refurbished to exclude from the class of laws those statements that are accepted on the determination of any given instance. This criterion excludes the statement 'All coins that are either in my pocket or are dimes are silver' from the class of laws, for the acceptance of the statement demands the examination of all the coins in the pocket.

Goodman's account of lawlikeness uses the notion of acceptability of a statement as dependent on 'some given knowledge'. In his words: 'the acceptance of a given statement depends upon a certain kind and amount of evidence'.[23] In the case of a statement like 'All coins in my pocket are silver', even testing of all but a single instance and getting positive result in each case would not lead us to accept the statement as true and predict that the remaining single instance would be similar to the observed instances. On the other hand, in the case of a statement like 'All butter melts at 150^0 F', the determination of a few instances suffices for accepting the statement as true and making further predictions in accordance with the statement with confidence.

Goodman has noted another factor that distinguishes a law from an accidental generalization. He finds that only laws are capable of being confirmed by its instances. An accidental generalization does not receive confirmation from any instance of it. If a particular piece of copper is found to conduct electricity, this observation is accepted as a confirming instance of the law, 'Copper conducts electricity', and this fact further increases the credibility of the law in predicting the behavior of other pieces of copper. On the other hand, the fact that a particular person present in the room is the third son does not in any manner increase the faith that the other men present in the room are also third sons; neither does it confirm the general statement 'All men in the room are third sons'.

Goodman introduces his famous 'grue problem' here. He points out that observation of all emeralds before a point of time, *t*, is believed to support the general statement 'All emeralds are green'. He then imagines a predicate 'grue' that is applicable to 'all things examined before *t* just in case they are green but to other things just in case they are blue'.[24] At time *t*, then, for each evidence-statement expressing that a given emerald, *a*, is green, 'there is a parallel evidence-statement asserting that the emerald is grue'.[25] Thus all pieces of evidence supporting the hypothesis 'All emeralds are green' would also support the hypothesis 'All emeralds are grue'. Accordingly, the prediction that the next emerald observed is green and the prediction that the next emerald observed is grue are equally confirmed by the evidence-statement describing the same observation. If later on an emerald is found to be grue, it is blue and therefore it cannot be green. Of the two incompatible and contrary predicates, one is surely known to be present in the emerald. However, according to Goodman's present definition, both are confirmed equally. Similarly, we have equal confirmation for any prediction about anything in the world on the basis of the same observation. We are caught in a paradoxical situation here, where 'anything confirms anything'.[26] It has already been explained above that, to Goodman, 'only predictions subsumed under lawlike hypotheses are genuinely confirmed'.[27] He realizes that his definition of lawlikeness includes certain unwanted cases and in effect excludes nothing, and that some further refinement on his definition is still awaited.

Goodman uses the notion of *projectibility* in order to explain the lawlikeness of a hypothesis. The problem of prediction from past to future cases is part of the problem of 'projecting from any set of cases to others'.[28] Any general proposition sets the mind in motion to make future predictions. And Goodman finds that the predictions are made spontaneously in various directions. The mind gradually rectifies later on and learns to distinguish between valid and invalid predictions. But how do we distinguish a valid from an invalid prediction? Goodman explains:

> A valid prediction is, admittedly, one that is in agreement with past regularities in what has been observed; . . . such agreement with regularities in what has been observed is a function of our linguistic practices. Thus the line between valid and invalid predictions (or inductions and projections) is drawn upon the basis of how the world is and has been described and anticipated in words.[29]

It is important to note that lawlikeness is described here as being due to the general agreement of people to use certain general statements. Whether a general statement is a law or not is decided by reference to certain 'background hypotheses' which 'depend for their effectiveness upon projectibility'.[30] Goodman admits that this theory of lawlikeness is far from complete; nevertheless, he claims that it enables the Humean rejection of objective necessary connection in nature to withstand the attacks from its opponents. The notion of necessary connection, Goodman finds, is no longer 'sacrosanct', and he decides to discard it altogether. Before critically examining this version, two other views which seek to demarcate a law from a non-law on epistemic grounds may be considered.

P. F. Strawson begins his exposition of law-statements with the observation that if a statement is a law then it must be true omnispatially and omnitemporally. Any person uttering a law-statement anywhere at any point of time is uttering a true statement. Thus an ideal law-statement contains no such words the reference of which 'depends in any way upon the situation in which they are uttered'.[31]

Strawson distinguishes a law-statement from a mere general statement which is not a law. Contingent general statements, according to him, are of two types: (i) restricted generalizations, that is, generalizations about a closed class, and (ii) unrestricted generalizations, that is, generalizations about an open class. To take, e.g. the statement 'All cats like fish': many of us would be inclined to regard this statement as expressive of unrestricted generality. Strawson, however, points out that the statement is not about an open class. He observes:

> ...But it would be possible to say: 'It *used to be true* that all cats like fish; but now X has bred a new strain of cats which detest fish.' When the pre-X talkers uttered the sentence, they made a true statement; but when the post-X talkers uttered it, they made a false one. So the class referred to was not ideally open.[32]

A law-statement, on the other hand, is a statement about an open class, and is, therefore, 'independent of contextual conditions'.[33]

To regard statements as expressions of laws 'is both to emphasize the unrestrictedness of their application and to say something about the nature of evidence by which they are supported'.[34] The evidence for the truth of a law-statement, or, the evidence for the acceptance of a law, should in no way indicate that the law is about a class of which the members are 'limited in a very definite temporal sense'. The assertion of the law 'All S is P' should not depend on the evidence 'that there will be no more members, and that there never were more than the limited number of which observations have been recorded' of S. Finally, Strawson adds that the 'evidence which is both permissible and adequate to establish a law will ... be adequate to establish also the related unfulfilled conditionals'.[35]

Strawson admits that some contingently true generalizations of the form '(x) (Sx ⊃ Px)' are not laws. But from this it does not follow that no law-statements are contingent, that is, that no law can be of the form '(x)(Sx ⊃ Px)'. Strawson takes up the objection raised by Kneale. Kneale maintains that laws are not mere unrestricted generalizations, but are stronger than these. The counterfactual import of laws remains unexplained in the regularity account. An accidental generalization, 'All S is P', standing on the evidence that (i) there is a limited number of members of S and (ii) that there would not be any more added to this number, will not permit us to say that had there been another S then it would have been P. Thus the evidence that there is no S that is non-P does not suffice to make the statement, 'All S is P' a statement of law. Strawson seeks to explain the counterfactual import of laws within the regularity scheme. He maintains:

> An *essential* part of the evidence for the conclusion that there (omnitemporally) is no *s* which is not *p* in our imagined case consists of evidence that the class of members of the species is limited in a very temporal sense; i.e. evidence that there will be no more members, and there never were more than the limited number of which observations have been recorded. All we need to add to our characterization of natural laws is the requirement that such evidence as this shall not be an essential part of our grounds for accepting them. Evidence which is both permissible and adequate to establish a law will then be adequate to establish also the related unfulfilled conditionals.[36]

To use law-statements, for Strawson, 'is both to emphasize the unrestrictedness of their application and to say something about the nature of evidence by which they are supported'.[37] This is considered to be an epistemic version of the sophisticated regularity theory by Armstrong and Suchting[38].

The exposition of the epistemic version remains incomplete without a brief reference to Ayer. His view has been noted in the previous chapter. He has sought to explain the distinction between a statement of law and a generalization of fact not in terms of the fact that makes the statement true or false, but in terms of the attitude people have in proposing the law. He maintains that the factual content of every form of general proposition is the same. But a law, as distinguished from an accidental generalization, has a counterfactual import. The scope of a law is not restricted to the actual; it extends equally to the possible. Understandably, then, the law is not different from a mere generalization in terms of what actually happens. The difference is only a difference in attitude. Ayer proposes 'to explain the distinction between generalization of law and generalization of fact, and thereby to give some account of what a law of nature is, by the indirect method of analysing the distinction between treating a generalization as a statement of law and treating it as a statement of fact'.[39]

Ayer does not claim to provide a definition of natural law. He is well aware that there cannot be a one-one correspondence between every proposition that expresses a law of nature and a particular attitude that people actually have towards it. There may be natural laws that remain unknown to the human intellect. Such laws then may exist, but the laws being unknown, people do not have any attitude towards them. However, Ayer claims that the notion of unknown laws is not inconsistent with his theory that seeks to explain the distinction between a law and an accidental generalization in terms of people's attitude. Ayer does not explain this point. In the next section, the reason Ayer possibly has in mind will be examined. This exposition of Ayer's view may be concluded by noting what, according to him, are the specialities of the attitude towards a law. He writes:

> ...for someone to treat a statement of the form 'if anything has ϕ it has ψ' as expressing a law of nature, it is sufficient (1) that subject to willingness to explain away exceptions he believes that in a non-trivial sense everything which in fact has ϕ has ψ, (2) that his belief that something which has ϕ has ψ is not liable to be weakened by the discovery that the object in question also has some other property X, provided (a) that X does not logically entail not -ψ, (b) that X is not a manifestation of not-ψ, (3) that the discovery that something had X would not in itself seriously weaken his

belief that it had ϕ, (4) that he does not regard the statement 'if anything has ϕ and not-X it has ψ' as a more exact statement of the generalization that he was intending to express.[40]

5.4.1 Some difficulties of the epistemic version

The prima facie difficulty of the epistemic version is the explanation of unknown laws. Ayer has admitted the possibility of unknown laws, and Suchting believes that other thinkers, as mentioned before, 'implicitly' accept them. The problem is: If the epistemic version does not rule out the possibility of unknown laws, can it explain lawlikeness in terms of people's attitude?

It is generally believed that the laws of nature are independent of human minds. They obtain irrespective of the existence of human beings and their knowledge. It is quite possible that some of the laws remain unknown to human minds. Thus Suchting maintains that 'it is unnecessary for the obtaining of laws that any law-statement ever be known or believed by any human being'.[41] But the recognition that there may be law-statements towards which people have no attitude undermines the very theory of laws that makes an essential reference to people's attitude. In the epistemic version, what would be the status of the unknown law-statements towards which people do not possess the special attitude which they have for other, that is, known, laws? The epistemic version faces this problem here: A statement, S, which was not a law previously when the law was unknown and accordingly there was no attitude towards it, becomes a law when it is known and people develop an attitude towards it. This has led Ayer to make a modest claim that the explanation of the distinction between a law and a mere generalization in terms of people's attitude may at most be taken as an explanation in terms of the sufficient condition and not a necessary condition of lawlikeness. Though Ayer has not spelled out his position about unknown laws within the framework of his epistemic version, Suchting conjures up the possible reason which Ayer could have provided. The reason may be stated in the following words:

> ...to say that there is an unknown law expressible by sentence S is to say that what would normally be asserted by S is true, though nobody in fact asserts S, and that there are certain situations which would be the subject-matter of evidence-statement E relevant to S, such that if someone were to be in possession of E, and also consider S, then that person would have an attitude to S satisfying conditions on laws'.[42]

Thus the only way the epistemic version can tackle the problem of unknown laws is by an introduction of the subjunctive mood as to what people would have believed under unfulfilled conditions. Under the explanation provided by the epistemic version, a law is a statement of uniformity, if either we actually possess a certain attitude, A, towards it, or, if certain other (epistemic) conditions had been fulfilled, we would have the attitude, A, towards it.

Armstrong points out that the introduction of the language of counterfactuals would not really help the epistemic version. The counterfactuals of the epistemic theorists 'apparently demand the existence of certain laws about epistemic attitudes'.[43] Only some laws like 'Whenever there is a law, L, people have an attitude A towards it under circumstance, C' can justify their counterfactuals. But these laws themselves are regularities, and people must have a certain attitude to them. Thus the use of counterfactuals by the epistemic theorists makes their theory open to the charge of circularity.

Armstrong observes that even though it is not clear whether the attempt to sophisticate the regularity theory by the introduction of an epistemic condition can survive the charge of circularity, the following objection can be brought against it in any case:

> ...It is clearly possible that there should be a universe governed by laws, and one in which there were some Humean uniformities which we would not wish to account laws, but in which there were no minds. . . . But in this universe there would be no Humean regularities involving epistemic attitudes, and hence, according to the Epistemic theorist, no laws.[44]

How in the knowerless world do we distinguish between a law and a non-law? One might answer that in a knowerless world the distinction is not of any great significance. Nevertheless, one cannot deny that there is a difference, and if there is a difference at all, then what is the differentiating criterion? In the epistemic version, the concept of unknown laws is explained in terms of subjunctive conditionals about human behaviour, and this in turn is explained in terms of laws about human behaviour. Consequently, in a knowerless world where there is no human being, there cannot be any unknown law. Again, as Suchting points out, in such a world, there would be no known laws either, for there are no human beings to possess any attitude towards them. Therefore, in a knowerless world there would be total lawlessness.

The epistemic theorists may desire to treat the laws of a law-governed knowerless universe as uninstantiated laws. But what is the explanation of uninstantiated laws? The explanation of uninstantiated laws provided by the regularity theory is 'parasitic' upon, or deduced from, instantiated laws. As explained above, the knowerless world is a lawless world. There may be some regularities in the knowerless world from which the hypothetical regularities about human behavior may be deduced, but this would be by sheer chance. Thus, Armstrong observes, 'any attempted escape *via* uninstantiated laws seems blocked'.[45]

Armstrong mentions another problem in the epistemic theory faced by Michael Tooley. The problem is related to the explanation of the distinction between laws and non-laws provided in terms of counterfactuals based upon laws. We may conceive of a natural law that prevents the possibility of any knowing mind - a law that allows only the existence of very simple things. What a law says, according to the epistemic theorist who is a regularity theorist, is a contingent matter. Thus he must allow the possibility of laws 'which make minds nomically impossible. But he can give no account of these in his terms'.[46] There is also the problem - the direct threat of circularity. Any attempt to explain knowledge or rational belief involves an appeal to the notion of law. Thus the concept of law cannot be reduced to the concept of human knowledge or belief.

Besides, it is not clear why certain regularities are objects of the epistemic attitudes appropriate for laws, but not others. If this difference of attitude is not arbitrary, there must be a 'real or supposed difference in the objective nature of the uniformities in question'.[47] But recognition of an objective difference undermines the epistemic version itself. If there are objective differences, they should be enough to differentiate a universal statement of law from a universal statement of fact.

Armstrong writes:

> This last objection shows that an attempt to modify the Epistemic view by talking only about the regularities which it would be *rational* to treat in certain epistemic ways, must appeal to differences in the regularities which make rational the difference in epistemic attitude. The modification therefore passes over into one of the Objectivist or internal solutions although in a concealed manner.[48]

Molnar argues that necessity and possibility are not epistemic concepts: what is necessary or possible does not depend on the knowledge of any one scientist or all the scientists of all times or the manner in which scientific knowledge is acquired or the evidence supporting scientific knowledge. The concepts of 'necessity' and 'possibility' and the distinction between a law and an accidental generalization are metaphysical issues. A law sets a limit to possibility, and the world is restricted by laws irrespective of our knowledge of the laws. How do we distinguish, for example, between the falsity and the impossibility of the statement: 'Nothing is a river of Cocacola'? It has to be determined by reference to metaphysics, and not by epistemology.

We find that the epistemic theory does not succeed in explaining the difference between a law-statement and a statement of fact. Earlier a fusion of the epistemic and the systematic version has been observed in Braithwaite. Ayer's version of the theory has been found to be incomplete. The epistemic version of sophistication on the regularity theory ultimately hinges on some objective factor, an internal characteristic of the law-statement in contradistinction from a mere regularity. The epistemic version thus glides into the resiliency or the systematic version.

Before discussing the resiliency version, attention may be drawn to another difficulty of the epistemic version. If the laws, following the epistemic version, are statements to which we have a special attitude, then, Suchting says 'the members of law-statements depend on *de facto* modes of functioning of human organisms'. Here arises a problem. The behaviour-pattern of people is not logically a fixed phenomenon; it may change owing to many factors. It is also possible to think about a world that has everything identical with our present world except the way people form their beliefs there and use those beliefs in regulating their lives. Again, there may be two different behaviour-patterns in the same world. But the epistemic view seems to disallow this. If the status of a law ultimately depends on people's attitude or the inductive policy people decide to adopt, then Suchting surmises, 'membership of the class of law-statements would be, logically, a matter of convention'.[49] If, instead of maintaining that a statement may be used for predictive purposes because it is a law, it is maintained, as Goodman does, that a statement is a law because of its predictive use, then 'there are as many possible sets of law-statements as there are possible predictive practices'.[50] This is, however, hardly acceptable as a satisfactory account of natural laws.

Another difficulty crops up especially in connection with Goodman's theory, though the difficulty casts its shadow over every form of the epistemic version in some way. Goodman maintains that a statement like 'All coins in my pocket are silver' is a contingent statement. For it is accepted after the determination of all its instances and has for this reason no predictive function. But what happens if the phrase 'coins in my pocket' is used to mean a very large class, e.g. all coins that are ever in my pocket at any point of space and time? It is not evident whether this statement has then any predictive role. That is, when the class of coins is a very large one, it is not clear whether, from an examination of some coins in one's pocket and finding them to be silver, one infers or not that the next coin is silver. If the statement is used for prediction, it fulfils the condition of a law, even though it is not explicable in terms of a wider generalization about people's habit.

Again, Suchting imagines a world where there are only a few pieces of butter all of which are stored in a particular place. What would be status of the statement 'All butter melts at 150°F. in that situation? Suchting maintains that in that case we are changing the number and distribution of instances of the universal in question in imagination. But the number and distribution of instances of a generalization is an accidental matter, and the status of lawhood is not dependent on these factors.

In defence of the epistemic theory, it may be urged that the criticism to the effect that if lawhood is explained in terms of people's attitude then there would be different laws for people with different habits or attitudes is not really damaging. If people's habit changes in the world, then the new world is not identical with the previous world, even though other physical elements remain the same. Likewise two worlds having identical elements except people's behaviour-patterns are not the same. And if the worlds are not the same, the laws in them need not be the same. Suchting replies that this is contrary to the commonly accepted theory of laws. A statement is a law of nature not in any special individual world inhabited by a special group of people. Once a statement is accepted as a law of nature, its status would remain unchanged even after a different set of people with different behavior-patterns enter into the universe. The status of a law is independent of the existence of any individual. And if a theory is found to be inconsistent with the ordinary understanding, the inconsistency may be regarded as an objection to the theory.

It is time to pass on to the second version of sophistication upon the regularity theory.

5.5 The Resiliency Version of Sophistication

Brian Skyrm wishes to replace the modal notion in the expression of natural laws by the concept of resiliency. High resiliency, for Skyrm, 'can be thought of as a statistical notion of necessity'.[51] Let us take the statement 'All Fs are Gs' as expressing a law. There is a certain probability for an F to be a G, and this probability is invariant under varying circumstances. In other words, if Fs are Gs regularly then there is a certain limiting frequency of Gs among Fs, and this limiting frequency is maintained through the variation of circumstances accompanying Fs.

The concept of resiliency, for Skyrm, provides an insight into the nature of universal laws. A universal law may be understood to assert that everything falling within the scope of its quantifier has the '*propensity of one*' not to be a counter-example. For example, if it is a law that 'All ravens are black', it means 'Every raven has a propensity of one to be black'. Negatively speaking, the law has the propensity of one to deny the existence of any counter-example, that is, a non-black raven. Thus the law means that everything has a propensity of one to be either black, or not a raven, or both.

Skyrm urges that a law may be understood to state something irrespective of any objectification process. If the probability-value of a sentence is highly resilient over a set of sentences, the probability-value of that sentence will be approximately the same in all probability distributions which we get by objectifying those sentences. To quote him:

> ...The law says: 'If a physical system is in state F, then the probability that it has the property P is *a*.' This tells us that for a canonical name (e.g., 32) in the *objective probability distribution corresponding to the exemplification of the antecedent* ($pr_{F\ on\ 32}$) *the probability of the exemplification of the consequent is approximately* a, *and remains approximately* a *upon further objectification* (via the sentences in the domain of resiliency).[52]

Skyrm claims that the above account gives a satisfactory explanation of the lawlikeness of statistical laws. At the same time he recognizes that the concept of physical absolute randomness is not above suspicion. In Physics there is no absolute resiliency, and 'philosophers have no business trying to lay down *a priori* standards for the scope of resiliency appropriate to physical theories. Standards for resiliency evolve along with physical theories in a big virtuous circle....'[53] One can, therefore, only expect relative resiliency. The uniformity, 'All Fs are Gs', is a law where Fs are Gs *resiliently*, that is, where the probability of Fs being Gs remains the same over suitable subclasses of F–Fs that are Hs, Js, Ks, ... , 'where the class of factors [H, J, K, ...] covers a wide range of suitable circumstances'.[54] Skyrm says:

> ... I think that it is a more faithful representation of scientific practice to bring resiliency in by the front door as a desideratum for the probabilities of laws, rather than bringing the requirement of the variety of instances in by the back door solely on the excuse that it may augment the epistemic probability of universally quantified material conditional.[55]

Ayer's interpretation of a law of nature and its distinction from a universal statement of fact may be explained in terms of the concept of resiliency. Skyrm interprets Ayer's account in probabilistic laws to mean that a single generalization 'All Fs are Gs' 'is well confirmed *qua* law if Pr (Ga given Fa & Ha) is for every H such that Ha is compatible with Ga (and also Fa, or the conditional probability would not be defined)'.[56] Thus, for Ayer, lawlikeness is the resiliency of Pr (Ga given Fa) = 1. A universal statement is expressive of a law, if it satisfies the instantial resiliency. Secondly, for Skyrm, an accidental generalization of facts is about a finite class, and the generalization is usually held to be true after a survey of all the instances that construct the finite class. The resiliency account excludes statements established by complete enumeration from the class of laws. A universal statement about a finite class established after the exhaustive examination of all its instances does not pass the resiliency test. If b, c, d are the only instances of F that has G, then, having examined that b, c, and d have G, the probability of 'Fa → Ga' would not be high. This is so, since the probability that a is something else is quite low, but it is not zero. If, on the other hand, the evidence supports the prediction of new or unobserved instances, that is, the possibility that besides b, c, and d there may be other instances of exhibiting G, then the probability that an unobserved instance of F exhibits G is quite high, '...that is, *within* the small probability that a is something other than what I have surveyed and yet an F, a large proportion of the probability will go the case where a is also a G'. Skyrm finds that the resiliency version 'shows why a generalization "about" a finite class should fail the test of instantial resiliency when based solely on what is taken to be an exhaustive survey of its instances. But it gives us no reason to believe that this is the *only* place where the resiliency can break down. Thus it leaves open the possibility that we may encounter other species of "accident" '.[57] One can never be confident that one has encountered all the instances of the class F. However, one may have reasonable confidence in the predictive force of a law. In the case of a law, the level of confidence matches with the resiliency, but it does not in the case of a non-law. Further, a law is compatible with a set of other accepted laws, and any counter-instance not only falsifies a law, but also disrupts the whole system. For this reason we are not willing to give up a law as easily as we are in the case of a non-law. Skyrm thinks

> ...the resiliency account of nomic force meshes nicely with the pragmatic factors identified by philosophers of science. But the idea that the probability of laws bears up under all sorts of evidence that would crush the probability of an accidental generalization hardly needs translation into the language of resiliency.[58]

5.5.1 The difficulties of the resiliency version

Following Armstrong, certain difficulties in the resiliency interpretation of laws may be noted. The resiliency account introduces a 'considerable arbitrary and conventional element' into the explanation of probabilistic laws. When a law is said to assign a precise probability a to Fs for being Gs, 'this conceals the fact that there will regularly be an element of decision that the facts are to be so described'.[59] This, however, is not true of Skyrm, who is honest enough not to conceal this point. Skyrm admits that absolute resiliency is impossible to achieve because there is no such thing. The only kind of physical randomness one may claim is 'randomness relative to a given set of physical properties'.[60] As a result, Skyrm had to live with 'imprecision and relativity'.[61]

Skyrm claims that his notion of resiliency holds the key to an understanding of the notion of laws and other related concepts. The notion also is believed to help in the objective test of laws. However, all that this criterion claims of a law is that the law is 'potentially resilient'. If it is to be a law that Fs have the probability *a* to be Gs, then Fs have this probability under 'every nomically possible circumstance'.[62] It is a contingent fact whether the possible circumstances are ever actualized in the real world. Some of the possible circumstances are instantiated in the real world, but some others are fabrications of our imagination and may never obtain. How can we have confirmation for laws under every variety of circumstances? Armstrong finds that Skyrm, who is a regularist, cannot handle this problem. The only kind of variation in the circumstances available to him is the actual ones, and accordingly, the laws, for him, are resilient over the actual variation of circumstances. Thus 'the spottiness of the occasions of variation accounts for the spottiness of his concept of a law'.[63] But one may conceive of laws which cannot be put to test as no resources, natural or artificially created by men, are available to produce an appropriate situation conducive to carry out such a test. If it is a law that all Fs are Gs, Gs have a certain 'limiting frequency' over Fs, and the limiting frequency is resilient over a wide range of factors. Let us suppose, for example, that Fs are Hs and Js and Ks omnitemporally. Are these factors relevant to an F for being a G? This is a question which demands an objective answer. Armstrong finds 'no evidence available which epistemically probabilified any answer'. Nevertheless, 'Skyrm would have to treat this as a case where there was no objective matter of fact to be decided'.[64]

There is a further problem of determining whether the range of factors H, J, K ... covering a wide range of suitable circumstances under which the resiliency holds is wide enough for a law. Besides, what makes the factors suitable? The circumstance that constitutes a test for a law comprises several factors. One way of putting a law to the test is, for example, trying to produce, provided it is nomically possible, a situation that would falsify the law. For example, whether 'All Fs are Gs' is a law or not may be decided by trying to produce, if nomically possible, a situation where there are Fs that are non-Gs. Armstrong, at this point, makes use of Tooley's example of Smith's garden. It has been found that all the fruit in Smith's garden are apples, since no effort to bring other kinds of fruit into Smith's garden has been successful. Oranges brought into the garden have become elephants, bananas have turned into apples, while pears, resisted by an insurmountable force, have failed to cross the boundary, and all the cherry-plants in the garden either bear apple or stand fruitless. The generalization about fruit in Smith's garden has high resiliency because it holds in a wide range of circumstances that would have falsified the generalization, if the generalization were falsifiable. But Armstrong asks: why may not there be laws which are in fact not resilient? He objects:

> ...If it is a law that all Fs are Gs then, by definition, it is *potentially* resilient. It is not physically possible that there should be a K such that, if there is an F which is a K, it is not a G. But why should nature be so obliging as to furnish us with reasons for thinking that there is no such K? Why should there be Fs accompanied by factors which are plausible, but failed, candidates for being K? Why should not Smith's garden exist in a remote country which contained no fruit but apples, yet still it be a *law* that it bears nothing but apples? It seems to me that only a vulgar positivism could make us reject such a possibility.[65]

The above consideration leads Armstrong to reject the resiliency solution. At least it is clear enough that this solution needs to incorporate many elements of the systematic version of sophistication brought upon the naïve regularity theory. The resiliency version can explain the factors that put a law to the test by infiltration of nomically significant factors from other statements. Thus it becomes important for a regularist to select amongst uniformities those that coherently constitute a system. As the resiliency version of sophistication ultimately hinges upon the systematic version, the worth of the former depends upon that of the latter. The systematic version comes to be considered next.

5.6 The Systematic Version of Sophistication

The systematic approach seeks to demarcate law-statements from statements of accidental generalization by reference to some logical relation a law-statement bears to other statements. This is suggested by J. S. Mill, C. G. Hempel, and P. Oppenheim, B. Berofsky, besides Ramsey and Lewis. Armstrong does not deny the instantaneous appeal of this version. This view as upheld by Ramsey and Lewis is considered by him to be the best one when it comes to distinguish between a law of nature and an accidental generalization within the Humean tradition. Whether, however, it succeeds in salvaging the regularity theory remains to be seen.

Ramsey points out that a universal statement of law cannot be distinguished from a universal of fact by syntactical considerations. It is not enough to say that a law is a statement where the subject-term does not mention any 'particular portion of space-time'. One can easily construct examples of statements in which the subject-term does not refer to any particular portion of space-time, and yet people may hesitate to call such statements laws. Again, there may be statements having reference to a particular point of space and time and still such that they may be recognized as laws, for example, the Kepler's law. Ramsey further points out that the distinction in question cannot be explained, as Braithwaite tries to explain it, in terms of belief. In a paper entitled 'Universals of Law and of Fact', written in 1928, Ramsey writes:

> ... even if we knew everything, we should still want to systematize our knowledge as a deductive system, and the general axioms in that system would be the fundamental laws of nature.[66]

Two types of statements, Ramsey holds, are called laws: the ultimate laws of nature and the derivative laws of nature, the general propositions derived from the ultimate laws. A law of nature is, therefore, a general statement that is either an axiom or a deduction from an axiom in the simplest possible deductively organized system. Ramsey's own exposition of this view may well be quoted here:

> As it is, we do not know everything; but what we do know we tend to organize as a deductive system and call its axioms laws, and we consider how that system would go if we knew a little more and call the further axioms or deductions there would then be, laws (we think there would be ones of a certain kind but don't know exactly what). We also think how all truth could be organized as a deductive system and call its axioms ultimate laws.
>
> The property of a universal that it *would* be an axiom in a deductive system covering everything is not really hypothetical; the concealed if is only a *spurious one*; what is asserted is simply something about the whole world, namely that the true general propositions are of such forms that they form a system of the required sort with the given proposition in the required place; it is the facts that form the system in virtue of internal relations, not people's beliefs in them in virtue of spatio-temporal ones. Of course, the system is required to be as simple as possible; but this is another vague formal property,... [67]

It is noteworthy[68] that there is here no use of the concept of omniscience made subjunctively. Only the general statements expressing regularity are selected to form a deductive system. In the system, there may be some unknown laws as well, and corresponding to each such law there is a true proposition. The deductive system is not formed, according to Ramsey, because of people's belief; for then the set becomes purely subjective and arbitrary; the system is formed because of some objective facts. True propositions possess some logical relations amongst them, and it is these relations which play a role in forming the deductive system. The standard of simplicity also is a standard which is commonly accepted. In this way, Ramsey tries to overcome the subjective element present in the epistemic version of Braithwaite.

It is, however, interesting to note that Ramsey himself rejects this theory of laws after one year on the ground that it is impossible to know everything and organize our knowledge into a deductive system. Jonathan Cohen points out that certain further constraints must be imposed on the system, if the system is to readily demarcate a natural law from an accidentally true generalization; 'for in a system that axiomatises everything we know both types of propositions would be derivable . . . . Perhaps Ramsey could have avoided this by requiring the derivation of [causal] laws to proceed without using as premisses any statements about specified individuals'.[69] Interestingly, Cohen tries to show that Ramsey's second theory of laws, which he propounds in a paper entitled 'General Propositions and Causality' written in 1929 rejecting his first theory, looks remarkably similar to the first one if 'certain *prima facie* inconsistencies and implausibilities in this second theory are ironed out'.[70] The second theory considers the causal laws to form a system with which the speaker meets the future. The laws are not judgments, but rules for judging. This version is to be dealt with later on in connection with a discussion of logical positivism. It is to be noted that Ramsey, like Hume, is interested only in particular occurrences and accepts no necessary connections in nature. He admits that we may find more than one system of generalizations explaining the observed facts. And the system which a person accepts to guide his life at present is not necessarily believed to be the system which everyone else accepts at all times. Cohen points out that not everyone is so convinced that 'intelligent life in the universe will continue long enough, under conditions of free inquiry, for a conclusive scientific consensus to emerge.... But the vicissitudes of past history - both human and geophysical - do not offer much evidence to support such convictions'.[71] Cohen suggests a possible way out of this difficulty by adopting *idealised pragmatism*[72]. The scientific system is identified as one that would be acceptable to everybody, provided 'free scientific enquiry is allowed to continue long enough'; but 'no one could be sure that free scientific enquiry continued long enough unless he already knew every fact, i.e., every observable occurrence'. Thus Ramsey's scientific system turns out to be the 'simplest acclimatization of our knowledge if we perceived everything'[73], and his second analysis of laws, reformulated in this manner, becomes not distinguishable from his first one in any significant respect. In that case, the problem of impossibility of omniscience persists in his second theory as well.

David Lewis accepts Ramsey's theory of 1928 as a 'working hypothesis'. He observes that Ramsey's theory need not be taken as a 'counterfactual about omniscience'. Whatever may be the scope of our knowledge, there exist many true deductive systems - systems of 'deductively closed, axiomatizable sets of true sentences'. Of course, some systems are simpler than others. Moreover, some may be stronger in information-content than some others. Apparently, simplicity and strength may seem to be at loggerheads; since 'simplicity without strength can be had from pure logic, strength without simplicity from (the deductive closure of) an almanac'. What is expected of the best deductive system is a balance of simplicity and strength, and combining this balance with truth. Following Ramsey, Lewis says that a law is a contingent generalization appearing as a theorem or an axiom 'in each of the true deductive systems that achieves a best combination of simplicity and strength'.[74]

Lewis points out that Ramsey's account enjoys excellence on six considerations. Firstly, it shows that lawhood is not accountable on syntactical or semantical considerations. Two statements may be equal in truth and generality, and yet only one of them, that which fits in with other true general statements to constitute the best deductive system, may be a law. The theory rightly emphasizes that the matter of lawhood is a purely contingent one. A generalization may be true as a law in one world, but may be simply a truth without being a law in some other world in so far as there are other truths in the first world with which the law constitutes a perfect system, though this may not be the case with the second world. Further, the theory rightly shows that we may exhaust all the instances coming under a generalization to exhibit that the generalization is true, and that even then the generalization could not be proved as a law. Fourthly, it clearly shows that every law is not necessarily *regarded* as a law. That is, a statement being a law is not the same as being a true statement that actually enjoys the status of a law in our knowledge-system. Besides, the theory explains why we take theorems of a well-established system provisionally as laws: 'our scientific theorizing is an attempt to approximate, as best we can, the true deductive systems with the best combination of simplicity and strength'. Finally, Lewis says that the theory rightly emphasizes that lawhood is a 'vague and difficult concept': the standard of balance between simplicity and strength expected of a system of scientific theorems is not a fixed matter. Lewis observes: 'we may hope, . . . , that our world is one where certain true deductive systems come out as the best, and certain generalizations come out as laws, by *any* remotely reasonable standards - but we might be unlucky'.[75]

For Lewis, then, the laws of a world, as generalizations fitting into the true and best deductive system, are highly informative about the world. The laws of a world hold a place of importance and determine in a significant manner the character of the world to which they belong. For Lewis the similarity (or dissimilarity) of worlds in respect of laws is extremely important. In this context, Lewis' remarks on necessity may be noted for what they are worth:

> ...Since a difference in laws would be a big difference between worlds, we can expect that worlds with the same laws as a world *i* will tend to be closer to *i* than worlds at which the laws of *i* hold only as accidental generalizations, or are violated, or - worse still - are replaced by contrary laws. In other words, the laws of *i* will hold throughout many of the spheres around *i*, and thus will tend to be co-tenable with counterfactual suppositions. That is so simply because laws

> are especially important to us, compared with particular facts or true generalizations that are not laws.[76]

Armstrong observes that on the systematic interpretation the vacuous laws do not add strength to the scientific system. Nevertheless, some of these laws, recognized as uninstantiated laws, are included in a simple deductive system along with the actual (instantiated) regularities, since they fill up the gaps adding strength to the system.

Before discussing the difficulties involved in the systematic version, a brief statement of Berofsky's view will be in order. The view has been discussed by Suchting. Berofsky has mentioned some conditions a law-statement should satisfy. Only two of them may be mentioned here. The first requirement is the *Deductive Systematization Requirement* which stipulates that a law-statement L_1 is deductively systematized if there is a sentence L_2 that 'is either higher or lower on the "scale of deductive systematization than L_1" '. A generalization is 'higher on the scale of deductive systematization' as compared to another if it is 'more general' than the latter. Suchting immediately points out that this criterion is not so important for Berofsky, 'since any generalization at all can be deductively systematized in accordance with it'[77]. The most important criterion for Berofsky is the *Comprehensiveness Requirement* (C) which lays down the following condition for a law. Suchting puts it thus:

> ... (C) states that L is a law only if (1) it appears in a deductive systematization which 'accounts for' each sentence of a set S_1, each member of which entails some sentence of the form *Px* (or *Pxy*, etc), and (2) there is no other deductive systematization that 'accounts for' (a) the members of S_1 and (b) other entailing sentences of the form *Px* (etc.).[78]

To explain the above criteria: The statement 'All men in the room are bald' explains why each member of the set S consisting of men in the room, Ma, Mb, Mc, . . . , Mn is bald. Thus it passes the first condition mentioned above. But it fails in condition (2) of (C); for another generalization, namely, 'All men with scalp condition P are bald' explains the baldness of men in the particular room plus others.

5.6.1 Difficulties of the systematic version

The first objection raised by Armstrong to this systematic version is that it leaves ample scope for the insurgence of a subjective element in the theory. A system, according to this version, must satisfy the demand for simplicity, and the standard for simplicity is the standard accepted by human beings in general. However, the theory is clueless as to what that universally accepted standard is. Granted that there is such a universally accepted standard, is it shared by other rational beings? The same problem persists in the case of the other standard of strength expected of a deductive system. Lewis's account further requires a balance between simplicity and strength. But, Armstrong asks, 'May there not be irresoluble conflicts about the exact point of balance ?'[79]

The deductive system raises problems when grue-like artificially conceived predicates are considered. Armstrong gives an example of a natural system with three fundamental laws in it, namely, 'All Fs are Gs', 'All Hs are Js', 'All Ks are Ls'. The laws are unified with the introduction of two newly conceived predicates M to mean 'Fs or Hs or Ks', and N meaning 'Gs or Js or Ls'. One may have then a single fundamental law 'All Ms are N'. Can M and N be treated as real properties having a connection by real uniformity and treat the original properties indicated by predicates F, G, etc. as artificial subdivisions of M and N? Armstrong observes that 'M-ness and N-ness cannot be ruled out by an appeal to the criterion of simplicity'[80]; for simplicity is a criterion applied to a deductive system of statements of regularities after the regularity-statements are already organized into a system. Can the criterion of strength be of any help in this matter? Is the law with predicates M and N weaker than the original generalizations? Let us analyze the situation. Given an F, in the new system, we may infer it to be N; whereas in the old system we may say that it is G, and G is a further specification of N. Does this suffice to show that the earlier law 'All Fs are Gs' is stronger in information than the M-N law? Thinkers like Armstrong do not think so. Scientific progress may bring about an improvement upon the old system of generalizations when the predicates G, J and L are considered to be theoretically identical. To say, then, that an F is a G is to say no more than it is G or J or L. The single property picked up as N may be broken up into G, J or L. And after the said improvement is achieved, we know that G = J = L. Thus the M-N law is as strong as the earlier generalizations. This would not trouble an epistemic theorist like Goodman; for, according to him, laws are generalities which we decide to choose from the class of generalities and project unto the unobserved cases. The systematic theorists cannot give such an explanation; for, compared to the epistemic theorists, they are much more realist in their theory of laws. They have to provide an objective criterion to distinguish between a genuine law and a mere uniformity. Besides, any law is applicable to a class of objects. But how is a class to be formed of objects? Are the things brought under a class-head because there is a single predicate applicable to each member of the class? Is the same predicate applied to every member of a class because the things of a certain class resemble each other? Armstrong remarks that 'the resemblance solution without universals breaks down'.[81] A systematic theorist, even if he does not accept Armstrong's theory of universals, must provide us with some objective resemblance amongst objects for this purpose. But he does not.

The systematic version does not explain the counterfactual import of laws satisfactorily. Epistemic theorists are in a better position on this particular point. A law, it is believed, would be equally effective if certain situations, which have not actually occurred, had occurred because lawfulness consists in crossing the boundary of the actual and covering the range of possible as well as actual cases. An epistemic theorist can explain it as our *preparedness to extrapolate* beyond the actual instances. But in the systematic version laws are regarded as statements of uniformity constituting the best deductive system of true generalizations. In a counterfactual situation, a new property of a particular object is imagined or a new object is introduced into the world. What would justify that such an introduction would fit into the generalizations of the best deductive system? The best deductive system is a *de facto* systematization, and it does not necessitate that the new objects or changed objects would continue to conform to that system.

One may imagine Lewis to suggest the following reply to this question. The best deductive system of general statements may be viewed as the representative of an important feature of the world, and a counterfactual seems to retain this feature as fixed as far as possible. The system in which the generalization, for example, 'All Fs are Gs' is a law may be so important to us that we should like to retain it even if this involves making a certain supposition which we are aware is false. Thus 'All Fs are Gs' may be considered to be true even if this involves making the false supposition that if *a* were F (when it is known that *a* in fact is not F). It may be contended that the truth-condition for counterfactuals is not relative. For example, the counterfactual that is implied by the law 'All Fs are Gs' is expressed as 'If *a* were F, then it *must be* G'. The necessity here is not the necessity relative to the importance we decide to attach to a certain system instead of to others. Is the importance attached to a deductive system of true generalizations a subjective matter? Or, does it reflect an objective standard adopted by people in spite of their cultural or racial backgrounds? If the systematic solution is to avoid subjectivism, it has to explain a counterfactual conditional *a la* Mackie.

Mackie considers a counterfactual conditional to be an abridged argument. Mackie's interpretation has already been discussed in the previous chapter. We have seen that that his account tries to provide a justification of inference, but in the process has to cross the limits set by the regularity theory. The process of induction cannot be fully justified from the standpoint of the regularity theory of laws. Besides, Mackie's account, as has been noted earlier, is not acceptable to every supporter of Hume. Beauchamp and Rosenberg point out that, for Mackie, what distinguishes an accidental sequence from a nomological (or causal) regularity is the 'absence of a "qualitative" persistence'[82]. However, the identification of persistence presupposes a causal determination, and, therefore, persistence cannot distinguish the causal from non-causal sequences without circularity.

But if a regularist rejects Mackie's solution, how does he then propose to defend his own position against Kneale's principal objection to the regularity theory of laws?

It may be further contended that if laws are axioms in a deductively organized system, then there would be different laws regarding the same class of objects because there may be several alternative, incompatible but internally coherent, systems of generalization. A subjectivist or conventionalist tendency of interpreting laws seems unavoidable in the systematic account.

Armstrong points out that if we follow the systematic version, then many accepted laws are so regarded quite arbitrarily. Lewis is aware of this problem. This is perhaps the reason why he calls the concept of lawhood a vague and difficult one. But it may be objected that we do distinguish between a law and a non-law with clarity and conviction, and that a theory that fuses this distinction must be abandoned. Armstrong agrees that laws may be picked up from the class of regularity-statements in the way suggested by the Ramsey-Lewis theory. At the same time, he does not accept that 'their criterion is part of our concept of a law of nature'.[83]

The systematic version demands a deductive system of generalizations in which the laws are axioms. Now many systems may be formulated out of the total set of generalizations - systems only consisting of laws, or, systems in which none of the generalizations are laws, that is, it is logically possible to choose only uniformities that are laws to form a system and the choice is so made that the complementary class of the class of generalizations forming the system are reduced to accidental generalizations. In the systematic version, the number of laws, as Armstrong points out, may be shown to vary keeping the Humean uniformities fixed, or, as Suchting points out, we may keep the number of laws fixed varying the number and distribution of their instances indefinitely. For Tooley, points made by Suchting and Armstrong mirror each other, and both aim at showing the implausibility of the systematic interpretation.

Again, we may conceive of a law that is not coherent with the system of generalizations we hold. Let us imagine some properties, namely, P, Q, R, and S. It may be conceived that wherever there is co-instantiation of P, Q, R, and S there is the emergence of a newer property E. It may be imagined that the law '(P, Q, R, S) → E' does not add simplicity or strength to the accepted system, and that there is hardly a joint instantiation of (P, Q, R and S) actually occurring in history. As a result, the resiliency requirement fails here. Let us also imagine that the law is not easily accommodated in the system; it might be a 'nomological dangler'.[84] According to the Ramsey-Lewis version of law, '(P, Q, R, S) → E' can hardly be counted as a law, yet it is a law. The systematic view, thus, seems to be insufficient.

Though science today views laws of nature as forming an integrated or well-knit system, David Stove points out (as Armstrong reports) that in the past the systems of generalizations with which science worked were not conceived as so well integrated. Armstrong's reaction in this context is worthy of notice. He says:

> Suppose that what then seemed likely enough to be the truth about the laws of nature had turned out in fact to be the case. The Systematic theorist can accept this possibility. He can say that, in that case, the true deductive system, which achieves a best combination of simplicity and strength, fails

> to achieve a very good standard of simplicity and strength. The winner is a winner out of a poor field.[85]

There remains a further difficulty. The systematic version refers to a deductively organized system of generalizations to distinguish between laws and mere generalities. General statements like 'All ravens are black' and 'All moas die before the age of fifty' are not laws because they do not constitute the axioms of the simplest and strongest system. But what will happen if our simplest and strongest system is not well equipped to eliminate such accidental generalities? Will they become laws then? It is quite unlikely. 'The patricians, lacking organization among themselves, will lack the power to exclude pushy plebeians'.[86]

Ramsey has himself rejected his systematic version to come very close to Braithwaite's epistemic version, apprehending a possible objection to his theory that however great the advancement in scientific knowledge may be, omniscience can never be achieved. Cohen, however, feels that the objection to factual omniscience is not so important. But a stronger objection to Ramsey's account is still conceivable. As Cohen states it:

> ...Why should we accept Ramsey's unargued assumption that what he calls 'the true scientific system' is uniquely determined, even by the observations of an omniscient intelligence? The universe might just be so tantalisingly niggardly with crucial data that some choices between rival scientific theories - or between rival methodologies for choosing between rival scientific theories - remain for ever undetermined...[87]

But even if we decide to ignore this objection, the systematic version of Ramsey becomes non-explanatory. It regards certain propositions as laws of nature in contradistinction from some others which are regarded as accidental generalizations. However, it is not clear why we should use the laws as rules applicable to counterfactual as well as factual situations. Cohen points out that, for Ramsey, 'generalizations are consequences of an axiomatised representation of the actual', and that however comprehensive this representation of the actual might be, what 'entitles us to assume that if we had it, it would also give us knowledge about the non-actual-knowledge of true ampliative counterfactuals ?'[88]

Berofsky's account of the systematic version also involves some difficulties. Suchting points out that there are some accidental generalities which in Berofsky's account become laws. Berofsky is himself aware that any generalization may be *trivially* systematized to make the generalization an axiom and that one may deduce lower-order generalizations from it. Hence Suchting remarks that Berofsky's account is not satisfactory for the reason that 'some systematically isolated generalizations would, we should expect, be laws, and others not. Berofsky's conditions do not allow us to make this distinction'.[89]

By now it is quite clear that the systematic version has left many problems originally facing the regularity theory unresolved. Hence the attempt to sustain the regularity theory by introducing the systematic version of sophistication has not been successful. Nevertheless, this has an undeniable appeal. The appeal may be described in the following way: there are regularities observed in the world, and the laws of nature explain the regularity of our observation. Hence there may be laws. The best explanation is generally believed to be true. However, it is to be borne in mind that the statement which constitutes the best explanation if it is true need not be actually true. Thus from the fact that uniformities are best explained if there are laws, it does not follow that there are laws in the world. At least, the systematic version does not eliminate the logical possibility of lawlessness. Further, if there are two systems of laws, then the system that is simpler and stronger is to be accepted. However, it is not ruled out that the actual system of laws has less degree of simplicity and strength compared to a false system. Therefore, the systematic version is not protected by its appealing characteristics, and the 'Systematic approach mistakes good methodology about laws for analytic truth about lawhood'.[90]

The different sophisticated versions of the regularity theory have been examined and it has been seen that all of them are unsatisfactory. The regularity theory of laws cannot, therefore, be accepted.

Notes

1 G. Molnar, 'Kneale's Argument Revisited', *The Philosophical Review*, vol. LXXVIII, 1969, pp. 80-81.

2 *Ibidem.*

3 A detailed account is available in Armstrong, '*What is a Law of Nature?*' ch. 3.

4 W. A. Suchting, 'Regularity and Law', in *Boston Studies in Philosophy of Science*, vol. 14, D. Reidel Publishing Co., Dordrecht, 1974, p. 75.

5 *Ibidem.*

6 *Ibidem.*

7 T. L. Beauchamp and A. Rosenberg, *Hume's Theory of Causal Connection*, Oxford University Press, Oxford, 1981, p.157.

8 *Ibid.*, p. 151.

9 R. B. Braithwaite, *Scientific Explanations*, Cambridge University Press, 1953, p. 302.

10 *Ibid.*, p. 301.

11 *Ibid.*, p. 302.

12 *Ibidem.*

13 *Ibid.*, pp. 302-303.

14 *Ibid.*, pp. 301-302.

15 *Ibid.*, pp. 304-305.

16 *Ibid.*, p. 305.

17 *Ibid.*, p. 303.

18 N. Goodman, *Fact, Fiction and Forecast,* The Bobbs Merrill Co., Inc., Indianapolis, 1973, p. 20.

19 *Ibid.*, p. 21.

20 *Ibid.*, pp. 20-21.

21 *Ibid.*, p. 22.

22 *Ibid.*, p. 23.

23 *Ibid.*, p. 24.

24 *Ibid.*, p. 74.

25 *Ibidem.*
26 *Ibid.*, p. 75.
27 *Ibid.*, pp. 74 - 75.
28 *Ibid.*, p. 83.
29 *Ibid.*, pp. 120 - 121.
30 *Ibid.*, p. 116.
31 P. F. Strawson, *Introduction to Logical Theory*, Methuen & Co. Ltd., 1971, p. 198.
32 *Ibidem.*
33 *Ibid.*, p. 215.
34 *Ibid.*, p. 200.
35 *Ibid.*, pp. 199 - 200 .
36 *Ibid.*, pp. 199-200.
37 *Ibid.*, p. 200.
38 Cf. Suchting, *op. cit.*, p. 77, and Armstrong, *op. cit.* p. 62.
39 A. J. Ayer, 'What is a Law of Nature?', *Revue Internationale de Philosophie*, No. 36, 1956, reprinted in B. A. Brody, ed. *Readings in the Philosophy of Science*, Prentice Hall, Englewood Cliffs, 1970, p. 51.
40 *Ibid.*, p. 53.
41 Suchting, *op. cit.*, p. 78.
42 *Ibidem.*
43 Armstrong, *op. cit.*, p. 62.
44 *Ibid*, p. 63.
45 *Ibidem.*
46 *Ibid*, p. 64.
47 *Ibidem.*
48 *Ibidem.*
49 *Ibidem.*
50 *Ibid.*, p. 81.
51 B. Skyrm, *Causal Necessity*, Yale University Press, New Haven, 1980, p. 12.
52 *Ibid.*, p. 24.
53 *Ibid.*, p. 19.
54 Armstrong, *op. cit.*, p. 65.
55 Skyrm, *op. cit.*, p. 17.
56 *Ibid.*, p. 57.
57 *Ibid.*, p. 59.
58 *Ibid.*, p. 61.

[59] Armstrong, *op. cit.*, p. 36.
[60] Skyrm, *op. cit.*, p. 15.
[61] *Ibidem.*
[62] Armstrong, *op. cit.*, p. 36.
[63] *Ibid.*, p. 37.
[64] *Ibid.*, p. 65.
[65] *Ibidem.*
[66] F. P. Ramsey, 'Universals of Law and of Fact', in D. H. Mellor, ed. *Philosophical Papers: F. P. Ramsey*, Cambridge University Press, Cambridge, 1990, p. 143.
[67] *Ibid.*, pp. 143-144.
[68] See Armstrong, *op. cit.*, p. 66.
[69] J. Cohen, 'The Problem of Natural Laws', in D. H. Mellor, ed. *Prospects for Pragmatism*, Cambridge University Press, Cambridge, 1980, p. 214 (parenthesis added).
[70] *Ibid.*, p. 214.
[71] *Ibid.*, p. 215.
[72] *Ibid.*, p. 216.
[73] *Ibidem.*
[74] Lewis, *Counterfactuals*, Basil Blackwell, Oxford 1973, p. 73.
[75] *Ibid.*, p. 74.
[76] *Ibid.*, pp. 75.
[77] Suchting, *op. cit.*, p. 83.
[78] *Ibid.*, p. 84.
[79] Armstrong, *op. cit.*, p. 67.
[80] *Ibid.*, p. 68.
[81] *Ibid.*, p. 69.
[82] Beauchamp and Rosenberg, *Hume and the Problem of Causation*, Oxford, p. 128.
[83] Armstrong, *op. cit.*, p. 71.
[84] *Ibid.*, p. 72.
[85] *Ibidem.*
[86] *Ibidem.*
[87] Cohen, *op. cit.*, p. 217.
[88] *Ibidem.*
[89] Suchting, *op. cit.*, p. 86.
[90] Armstrong, *op. cit.*, p. 73.

CHAPTER SIX

KNEALE'S CRITIQUE OF WHITEHEAD'S REGIONALISM REGARDING NATURAL LAWS

6.1 Foreword

Kneale, in his discussion of the alternative theories concerning the logical character of natural laws, refers to a view which is described in the philosophy of science as the 'Restricted Generalization'[1] theory of natural laws or as 'Regionalism'.[2] The restricted generalization theory does not mean that the statement expressing a law of nature is a restricted generalization concerning a class with restricted membership. A law speaks of an open class which includes an infinite number of objects and naturally a law-expressive statement cannot be established by summative induction. Since all the instances covered by a law cannot, in principle, be enumerated individually, many thinkers impose a stipulation on a law-statement - the stipulation that a genuine law of science should not carry the name of any particular individual.

Kneale refers to an alternative suggestion to the effect that a law is a restricted generalization though every instance coming under it is not enumerated individually. In the history of philosophy Kneale traces such a view to Aristotle, who 'maintained on *a priori* grounds that the universe is restricted in its extension'.[3] For Aristotle, one may meaningfully speak in terms of infinity in cases of possibility alone. Some astronomers also regard the world as finite in scope, but they have an altogether different reason. Eddington even went to the extent of mentioning a definite number of the actual particles which constitute the universe. If such views are accepted, then natural sciences may be taken to deal with a theoretically limited number of things. In this sense a scientific law-statement may be understood to have a restricted generality.

Kneale, however, does not accept these views. He finds nothing in the arguments of Aristotle or Eddington to prove that 'the sequence of future events must have an end'.[4] He mentions yet another version of regionalism which is advocated by Whitehead. It is Whitehead's theory which is under discussion in this Chapter.

6.2. An Exposition of Whitehead's Regionalism

Whitehead's view suggests that a thing of a particular kind may follow different behaviour-patterns and that the same thing may possess different properties at different times and places, 'although the conditions which prevail are not different except in respect of space and time'.[5] Is such a view worthy of defence? Before offering an answer to this question, an exposition of the view seems essential.

Incidentally two different interpretations of Regionalism as given by Armstrong may be noted:

(1) Regionalism may be interpreted to mean that there are different laws obtaining at different cosmic epochs. Though none of these laws are reducible to any other, all of them may be subsumed under a higher second-order law. Armstrong observes: 'this second-order law determines that, for any time t, if the laws at time t are L, then, given a time g(t) which is a certain function of t, the laws at g(t) will be a certain function, f, of L'.[6]

or,

(2) Regionalism may be interpreted to assert that there are different laws in different cosmic epochs and that there are no higher-order laws to subsume the laws of different cosmic epochs. The law of each epoch is different from that of another epoch.

The second version, according to Beauchamp, matches perfectly with a 'process and time-oriented philosophy such as Whitehead's...'[7] Beauchamp offers a schema as a 'simplification and reconstruction of Whitehead's view that it is logically possible, and not known to be empirically impossible, that relevantly similar and fully described causal items may produce dissimilar effects in different cosmic epochs'.[8] The schema is stated below:

1. 'All ag things are b & - p' is true in Cosmic Epoch 1.
2. 'All ag things are b & p' is true in Cosmic Epoch 2.
3. 'All ag things are p & - b' is true in Cosmic Epoch 3.

For Beauchamp, 1, 2, and 3, as they are stated above, cannot be true omnitemporally, since each falsifies the others. Nevertheless, there is no logical reason prohibiting their joint possibility; for such a reason would make the law of uniformity of nature logically necessary. It would also beg the question by denying the plausibility of the doctrine that laws evolve in different cosmic epochs. Whitehead, with his introduction of novelty in different natural epochs, has rejected the idea of a single law of uniformity of nature running through different cosmic epochs. Laws, according to Whitehead, are mere contingencies holding in one epoch but failing in some other. An understanding of Whitehead's metaphysics seems essential to an understanding of his theory of laws. A brief account of his metaphysics follows.

6.2.1 The metaphysical background of Whitehead's theory of laws

Whitehead has offered a unique way of understanding and interpreting the world around us. He finds that the science of today is concerned with the 'description and measurement' of real objects and that the objects are 'abstracted forcibly from the totality of things' for this purpose. Science accordingly does not represent reality in its true form - 'it is more like a blueprint'. On the other hand, '... the task of seeing wholes can belong only to philosophy'.[9]

Whitehead rejects the Newtonian idea of nature as absolute, and 'attacks the time-honoured dichotomies of sense-experience and thought...'.[10] He rejects the 'bifurcation of nature' into perceived qualities known through sense-experience and the theoretical entities of scientific theories constructed out of the sense-data. His philosophy of science seeks to analyse 'the ontological status of scientific and mathematical concepts in terms of their derivation from the elements and relations of nature as disclosed in sense-experience'.[11] In his *Science and the Modern World* and also in his *Process and Reality*, Whitehead adopts a novel point of view called by him the 'organic point of view'. He finds that the words of our common language often cannot express his unique ideas. However, this has not led him to reject metaphysics as 'nonsense'. He has gone on to enrich language by developing some special coinages which stretch the applicability of language to his novel ideas. He recommends 'a new aspect which is neither purely physical nor purely biological' for every science. True science is 'becoming the study of organisms'.[12]

A primary organism, according to Whitehead, is 'identified as the emergence of some particular pattern grasped in the unity of a real event', and 'each event involves the pattern of aspects of other events which it grasps into its own unity (its own prehension)'.[13] A real thing of the world, described by other philosophers as a substance, is called by Whitehead an 'actual entity'. Such entities, which are ordinarily described as 'subjects', are infinite in number. The subject is not anything permanent; it represents a momentary experience. A. N. Johnson mentions the following features of a Whiteheadian subject:

a) The content of a subject's experience is chiefly, though not exclusively affective;
b) It is a unity of component parts;
c) A subject has its environment active in its nature;
d) It becomes what it is as a result of its subjective reactions to the data provided by its environment;

e) A subject selects data from its environment in accordance with a conceived ideal.[14]

Whitehead propounds an evolutionary philosophy that is fundamentally different from the emergent evolutionary thought of Alexander. Whitehead, as observed by J. Martin, 'never in practice admitted finality'.[15] The actual entities, for Whitehead, are all in a process. They arise and pass away. The process by which an actual entity reacts to its environment is called 'prehension', and there are different types of prehensions. The process of development of an actual entity is guided by an ideal or abstract pattern, called by Whitehead an 'eternal object', i.e. 'any entity whose conceptual recognition does not involve a necessary reference to any definite actual entity of the temporal world'.[16] An eternal entity is often described in philosophy as a universal.

The actual entities of nature are not independent bits of existence; they are interrelated societies[17]. A group of actual entities forms a society 'when they all manifest a common eternal object...'.[18] A society, which arises from the immanence of one actual entity in others by prehension, is different from a nexus in which the entities are related with each other in the most general sense. The actual entities are transitory, but the societies 'endure, at least for a time'.[19]

Whitehead has thus jettisoned the idea of a simple location dominant in classical physics where matter is believed to exist in one particular point in the universe at a certain time without any relation to other forms of matter existing in different places and times. A particle of matter has no existence in isolation; 'it is essentially related to every other item of nature by the spatio-temporality of nature, and...has no meaning apart from this spatio-temporality'.[20] Events stand in general relation to each other. This general relation is called by him 'extension', which 'is a part and whole relation and is hence transitive'.[21] Extension gives continuity to events. Every event extends over others. The relation of extension makes the events actual matters of facts by means of properties which arise in spatial relations. Further, events are involved in the process of 'becoming of nature' by means of the properties issuing in temporal relations. Nature is thus viewed by Whitehead as 'an interrelated structure of events'. Each event here possesses volume and duration and stands in the 'part and whole relation of extension which is more general than the specific notions of space and time'.[22]

Whitehead rejects also the Newtonian concept of space and time. Things are generally believed to exist in space and time when the latter are said to be independent of things. For Whitehead, there can be no space and time apart from the actual entities. The actual entities are spatial and temporal, but space and time do not house the actual entities - they are internal relations. The nature of the actual object is determined by its spatio-temporal relations. In a different spatio-temporal relation, there is a different actual entity. Another novelty of Whitehead's theory lies in his conception of time as a continuous process, a succession of different quanta of times. It does not flow; rather it moves by taking jumps. The universe is a series of successive cosmic epochs. In each cosmic epoch, a set of laws emanates, or rises to predominance. The set has a stage of endurance, and it gradually fades away as the society undergoes change.

Whitehead maintains a holistic attitude in understanding and interpreting the world. The entities of the universe possess an internal relation amongst them, and the changes in the entities bring about certain changes in their interrelations. Whitehead observes:

> ...an individual entity, whose own life-history is a part within the life-history of some larger, deeper, more complete pattern, is liable to have aspects of that larger pattern dominating its own being, and to experience modifications of that larger pattern reflected in itself as modifications of its own being. This is the theory of organic mechanism.

> According to this theory, the evolution of laws of nature is concurrent with the evolution of enduring pattern. For the general state of the universe, as it now is, partly determines the very essences of the entities whose modes of functioning these laws express. The general principle is that in a new environment there is an evolution of the old entities into new forms.[23]

6.3 Whitehead's Theory of Natural Laws

By now it is clear that upon the Whiteheadian metaphysics some causal or natural laws arise in a definite society prevailing in a particular cosmic epoch. The society undergoes a change with the change in interrelations among actual objects. And in a different society there is a different set of laws. The laws of nature are understood not as laws running across different cosmic epochs. Recurrences or uniformities are to be expected within a single cosmic epoch. Whitehead, at the same time, recognizes the importance of the concept of natural laws. He admits that an accurate expression of the notion of law which 'has entered into the explicit consciousness of various epochs under every variety of specialization, arising from its coalescence with other components in the popular cosmology'[24] is an extremely difficult matter. He says:

> ...Let us grant that we cannot hope to be able to discern the laws of nature to be necessary. But we can hope to see that it is necessary that there should be an order in nature. The concept of order of nature is bound up with the concept of nature as the locus of organisms in process of development.[25]

That the laws are required for our understanding of the world is also insisted on by Whitehead in a different work:

> The relations of sense-objects to their situations are complex in the extreme, requiring reference to percipient events and

> transmitting events. Apart from some discovery of laws of nature regulating the associations of sense-objects, it is impossible by unintelligent unsorted perception to form any concept of the character of an event from the sense-objects which might be situated there for percipients suffering from any normal or abnormal perceptions.[26]

A paragraph from his *Adventures of Ideas* expresses the same view :

> The notion of law, that is to say, of some measure of regularity or of persistence or of recurrence, is an essential element in the urge towards technology, methodology, scholarship and speculation. Apart from a certain smoothness in the nature of things, there can be no knowledge, no useful method, no intelligent purpose. Lacking an element of Law, there remains a mere welter of details, with no foothold for comparison with any other such welter, in the past, in the future, or circumambient in the present.[27]

Whitehead accepts the doctrine of immanence of laws. According to this view, the order of nature expresses the character of real things of the natural world. To know the essential character of these things is also to know the relations obtaining amongst them. If there are certain common elements found in the essences of these real things, then that accounts for the identities found in their mutual relations. Whitehead writes: 'some partial identity of pattern in the various characters of natural things issues in some partial identity of pattern in the mutual relations of those things. These identities of pattern in the mutual relations are the Laws of Nature'.[28] This view presupposes the essential interdependence of things and rejects an 'absolute being'. This doctrine is recognized by Whitehead as a rationalistic doctrine leaving an open possibility for understanding nature.

Whitehead also points out the following features of this theory:

1. Sciences provide us with explanations and not mere descriptions of observed facts.

2. In science, exact conformation to the laws is never expected. If all the things of the world had exactly the same essence everywhere, then the laws of nature would have to be considered to be strictly universal. In actuality, though the majority of the things of a particular kind are found to have the same character, the character is, nevertheless, absent in a few. In these cases, 'the mutual relations of these things will exhibit lapses when the law fails to obtain illustration'.[29] Understood in this sense, the laws of nature may be understood to have a statistical character.

3. Again, the laws are not viewed as permanent or fixed. The laws of nature evolve concurrently with the changes of natural things which constitute the environment. There could be no eternal law.

4. The theory recommends a 'limited trust' in the processes of induction. If the world is conceived as an environment in which we do only partly know the nature of a large number of objects, then we may claim to have some knowledge of the laws of nature governing the environment. Without the doctrine of immanent law and the supposed theory of the nature of the world, 'we should then acknowledge blank ignorance, and not make pretences about probability'.[30]

5. The doctrine of immanent law becomes untenable without a plausible metaphysical doctrine, according to which the characters of the relevant natural objects are the outcome of their interconnections and 'their interconnections are the outcome of their characters'.[31] In other words, the doctrine is based on the doctrine of Internal Relations.

Whitehead, in his *Adventures of Ideas*, discusses three other theories of natural laws. They are considered below along with Whitehead's criticisms of them.

6.3.1 Whitehead's examination of the doctrine of imposition

Understandably this doctrine is based upon the doctrine of external relations between things in the natural world. Each of the existent beings may be understood in isolation from others. These ultimate beings are conceived to exist with 'private qualification', and they share no characteristic in common. Nevertheless, there is a necessity imposed on these entities for which they enter into relationships with one another. And 'these imposed behavior patterns are the laws of nature'.[32] These laws are not to be discovered by inspection of the nature of the ultimate existents of the world, nor can the nature of the things be inferred from the laws.

Deism lies at the root of this theory. Imposition implies an imposer, and the imposer, according to some such thinkers as Newton, is the transcendent imposer, i.e. God. Further, if the laws of nature are imposed by God, then they are to be exactly obeyed by all the entities of nature without exception. This is how the doctrine successfully explains the universality of laws and endorses a belief in the efficacy of laws in spheres lying beyond the range of meticulous observation. However, this theory is unacceptable to Whitehead. First, it is not compatible with his metaphysics of internal relation. Secondly, the things in nature are not exactly identical in their minute details. Nature is full of surprises, and there is no fixed law obtaining at all spaces and times. Whitehead remarks: 'the physicists in their recent researches have disclosed a novel illustration of capriciousness'.[33]

6.3.2 Whitehead's examination of the positivist theory

Whitehead mentions another theory, described by him as the positivist theory. Upon this theory, the laws of nature are 'observed persistence of pattern in the observed succession of natural things .... Thus a law says something about the things observed and nothing more'.[34] No doubt, the theory puts the right emphasis upon a fundamental truth of scientific methodology. A great scientist like Newton insists that he is neither 'speculating' nor 'explaining', he is rather 'enunciating a formula which expresses observed correlations of observed facts'.[35] Positivism has greatly influenced the Humean sort of atomism. The laws are believed to be the 'formulation of observed entities'.[36] Since Hume deals with subjective experience, he maintains that we have only a psychological expectation that the regularities or recurrences observed in the past would also recur in the future. Whitehead observes that Hume has no answer to the question whether there would be actual recurrences in the future, and, if so, why they occur at all. He has developed no metaphysics to support this expectation; he only tells that human life cannot be carried out without the 'metaphysical persuasion that the past does in fact condition the future'.[37] Now, Whitehead observes that nature is full of surprises; it does not always satisfy our anticipations.

Again, science is not satisfied with a general description of facts. It provides an 'explanatory description' that justifies the extension of laws beyond the observed actual instances. The positivists cannot appeal to statistics to justify an inductive leap from the observed to the unobserved. Whitehead's remarks in this context are noteworthy. He says:

> ...statistics tell you nothing about the future unless you make the assumption of the permanence of statistical form. For example, in order to use statistics for prediction, assumptions are wanted as to the stability of the mean, the mode, the probable error and the symmetry or skewness of the statistical expression of functional correlation. . . . There is no valid inference from mere possibility to matter of fact, or, in other words, from mere mathematics to concrete nature.[38]

Whitehead further points out that the theory is unable to explain the existence of alternative theories on the same subject. Moreover, if laws are only descriptions of what has been observed, 'we can describe what has happened, but with that description all possibility of knowledge ends'.[39] The main problem of this view is the restriction imposed by theory upon our scope of knowledge. Upon this, we may know only the facts of observation which are 'rough, inaccurate and sporadic' and 'we must not ascribe, we must not expect, one step beyond our direct knowledge'.[40] The theory is unable to justify the strong urge of the scientists to go beyond the mere descriptions of facts and offer an *explanation* of the observed facts with some speculations about the future. The bridge that has been built at present between science and metaphysics with the doctrines of metaphysics modified to provide an explanation of actual events points towards the inadequacy of positivism.

6.3.3 Whitehead's examination of the doctrine of conventional interpretation

Whitehead mentions another doctrine which explains laws as conventions. To put it in the words of Whitehead: it 'certainly expresses the procedure by which free speculation passes into an interpretation of Nature....But Nature has subsequently been interpreted in terms of .... mathematical laws. The conclusion seems to be, that Nature is patient of interpretations which happen to interest us'.[41]

Whitehead, however, thinks it erroneous to interpret natural laws in terms of mathematics and treat the laws as arbitrary conventions. Undoubtedly, convention plays an important role in the discovery or formulation of a natural law. The statements of laws are developed by human beings of a particular age. And the formulations of laws, to some extent, are dependent on abstract sciences which the scientists have chosen to develop. Nevertheless, the scientific 'convention should not be twisted to mean that any fact of nature can be interpreted as illustrating any laws that we like to assign'.[42]

6.4 The Attractiveness of Regionalism

Beauchamp observes that Whitehead's view is indeed quite acceptable to all, unless one treats it as a 'conceptual truth' that the laws of nature express unrestricted laws of uniformity without any exception. To Beauchamp, the theory of Whitehead's opponents does not possess an intuitive certainty. At least, Whitehead's view coaxes us to examine it critically. Whitehead believes that the laws neither express any omnitemporal and omnispatial truth, nor have any universal reference. As Beauchamp puts it:

> ...the most one can say about laws is that (A) no known data indicate that the examined instances of contemporary laws constitute the complete class of instances, and that (B) we have reasonable grounds for holding laws to be unrestrictedly universal within a certain spatio-temporal scope (whereas we can, by experimentation, know that accidental universals are close or subject to exceptions). The evidence for the knowledge claim in (A) coincides with the reasonable grounds of (B).[43]

6.4.1 Some reflections on regionalism *vis-à-vis* universalism

J. P. Day refers to Bondi as a supporter of Universalism. For Bondi, '...we live in a world that is homogenous at least as far as the laws of nature are concerned'.[44] He further urges: '*If* we are still able to apply our terrestrially gained knowledge in such far-flung fields (*sc.*, distant astronomical objects, the ancient geological history of the Earth etc.), then the uniformity of cosmos must be very great'.[45] But Day points out that 'the question whether there are truly universal laws, is by no means so easy to settle... .[46] Scientists have not unanimously accepted the direct applicability of the laws of our world to remote fields rendering the spatio-temporal positions as unimportant. For the regionalists, there are no constants in nature and the laws of nature vary with the spatio-temporal background.

Regionalism is certainly a convincing doctrine in social sciences. In the study of human nature and economics, certain laws are accepted as true only within a certain age and domain. When a universalist, like Hume, says that human nature in its basic character or principal operation is the same, what he means is a sort of 'weak' uniformity, i.e. the theory that human nature is *in the most part* the same. This is, in principle, the acceptance of regionalism. Regionalism may be accepted in economics, too. We all know that the laws determining the economy of a developing country are different from the economic laws of a developed country[47].

Day thinks that universalists are mistaken in taking scientific law-statements literally. As said earlier, though the law-statements are expressed in the timeless present, there is always some tacit qualification restricting the 'scope' of such generalizations. One wonders whether there exists at all an empirical law or a true universal proposition which is unconditionally true. Day contends:

> Sometimes we do indeed judge place or date to be certainly or probably inductively irrelevant, and generalize accordingly. But when we do so, we are just making a normal antecedent judgement of ... irrelevance. ... It seems to me, however, that we can never make such judgements of irrelevance in the case of future, as opposed to past or distant, things and events; and that accounts for the common sense conviction that assertions about the future are peculiarly precarious.[48]

6.4.2 Some more words on regionalism

In accordance with his philosophy of science (which Kneale calls 'a peculiar doctrine'), Whitehead considers the laws of nature to be 'local and temporary customs established among some constituents of the universe during a cosmic epoch'.[49] Since laws are established by inductive generalizations upon instances of a certain spatio-temporal zone, there is hardly any guarantee that the general propositions, so obtained, would be true at all places for all times. Certainly, it would be more rational to suggest that a law holds only under certain conditions ideal for the efficacy of the law. This ideal condition need not always be a single phenomenon; rather it may be a set of several conditions. Surely, our knowledge being limited, we are never absolutely certain of these special conditions to be able to incorporate them into our statements of laws. The law about the boiling point of water, or the law concerning the melting point of a metal, say gold, is true against a definite background. A change in the background often baffles the predictions based on the laws. Whitehead's view is surely a reasonable one, if, in maintaining a regionalist attitude, he intends to endorse the importance of the conditions under which the law holds. Understood in this sense, the scientific laws may be viewed as 'conjectures about uniformities in limited regions of space-time'.[50]

Toulmin, in his discussion of the nature of natural laws, examines Whitehead's theory. He holds that there is definitely a merit in Whitehead's contention. For 'a few hundred years' experiments on this Earth could hardly justify us in advancing generalizations of a completely unrestricted kind'.[51] A statement of a law of nature, in practice, is regarded as true within a certain region of space and time, and its trustworthiness is adjudged in reference to the size of this region. In fact, the strength of the truth of a law-statement is proportionate to the restrictions imposed upon it. Kneale expresses this view as:

> ...when a universal proposition is tacitly understood to refer only to matter within the solar system during a few centuries, it should be accepted with more confidence than when it is taken to all matter within the galaxy during several millions of years, and *a fortiori* with more confidence than when it is taken to refer to things in distant nebulae during a still longer period.[52]

Thus the greater is the scope of the law-statement the lower is the probability of the generalization. The validity of a law-statement and the magnitude of its field vary inversely.

6.5 Kneale's Criticism of Whitehead's Regionalism

It is time to turn to Kneale's criticism of Regionalism. Kneale considers the laws to be principles of necessitation. As principles they must be essentially universal. Thus Kneale is under a compulsion to reject regionalism and uphold universalism. And that may be done only if certain blemishes in regionalism may be found.

Kneale maintains that Whitehead has not clearly specified the range of the spatio-temporal epoch within which a law holds, and perhaps he has not done so because 'the limits are not to be supposed as precisely determined'.[53] This is, for Kneale, 'a peculiar theory'. As said earlier, the doctrine of immanence of laws is based on a metaphysical doctrine. But the metaphysical foundation provided by Whitehead is counter-intuitive. It is opposed to the common sense theory and is indeed difficult to understand.

If regionalism is interpreted to mean the doctrine that a statement of a law of nature is true only in a set of ideal conditions and that the truth-value of such a statement gets affected when the basic conditions vary, then certainly the theory has an appeal. Both Whitehead and Kneale refer to a common fact. It is a common fact that the scientists observe great caution and special care while applying the laws to remote cases. This caution has been construed by Whitehead to prove his regionalism. For Kneale, on the other hand, the general practice adopted by the scientists of applying laws to remote cases stands rather as evidence of the universality of laws. He observes:

> ...Indeed, the considerations which make the scientist cautious in such a case cannot be stated without an assumption that precisely formulated laws of nature have unrestricted universality.[54]

A scientific law is established after observation of some instances at a particular time and space. It is quite legitimate to doubt whether or not the recurrent feature of the observed instances is present in all unobserved cases as well. There is every possibility that the feature noticed uniformly in the observed cases is not invariably present in every sample of the class. Kneale writes:

> ...If we have found all α things in our experience to be β, we may assert that all α things without restriction are β and yet presently feel some hesitation in using this proposition as a premiss for inferences about remote instances of α-ness because we reflect that all the instances we have observed may be subject to some local or temporary condition (e.g. of temperature or atmospheric pressure) not mentioned in our statement of the supposed law.[55]

However, the recognition of local conditions does not compel us to embrace regionalism. One may still support universalism by taking law-statements as elliptical statements. They may be formulated in full by incorporating a reference to the ideal conditions. Such conditions are not generally mentioned in a statement of law because they are either obvious or overlooked. If they are overlooked, every care is taken by the scientists of the next genre to consider them and state them specifically in the formulation of the law-statement. In this manner, the law-statements become refined or reformulated in course of time. Thus, instead of saying 'All α things are β', we should rather say: 'All α things, in the presence of the condition γ, are β', i.e. 'All $\alpha\gamma$ things are β'. However, once this is accepted as a law, every time everywhere there is an α in γ, it is bound to be coupled with β. Thus the universality claim may be still retained. It is found that Kneale and Whitehead have alternative explanations of a common scientific practice. And Whitehead's theory cannot claim supremacy over Kneale's on this point.

6.5.1 The distinction between refinement and rejection of a natural law-statement

Kneale's position may be elaborated further. He seems to hold that when, in the history of science, an earlier law, e.g. 'All α things are β' is refined to 'All $\alpha\gamma$ things are β', the refinement is not to be understood as the rejection of the earlier law. Nor is the introduction of the qualification of 'γ' construed to impose a restriction on the law 'All α things are β'. In fact β-ness is considered a regular feature of α which normally has the qualification of 'γ'. The law 'All $\alpha\gamma$ things are β' is an improved version of the earlier law, 'All α things are β'. And if the refined version of the law-statement is not a rejection of the earlier law, then the universality claim, implicit in the law, is also not given up. This point is emphasized by Campbell when he explains the meaning of alteration or refinement in laws in clear terms:

> A law is not materially altered in character or simplicity if the values of the magnitudes change, so long as the nature of the relation between them is unaltered. Thus if a re-examination of the law relating the volume and mass of silver led to the belief that the density of silver is 10.9 and not... 10.5, we should not regard the law as altered materially for the primary purposes of scientific enquiry; but we should regard it as altered, if we found that the mass was not proportional to the volume and therefore there was no such thing as density.[56]

6.5.2 Laws and universality

Kneale seems to hold further that it is the universality which distinguishes a local generalization from a law. A law is true and is a universal statement. Thus the statement 'All crows are black' is not a law, since it is not true. The crows of the snowy region and the crows of Australia are white. But if we add a qualification to the above statement and say instead that 'All crows of Calcutta are black' - even though it is true, will it be considered to be a law? No one, perhaps, is ready to ascribe the title of 'law' to such generalizations that are true within a limited region. Laws are more than mere statements of facts. They provide rational justification for future prediction. And such predictions are possible because the laws are regarded as universally true.

Tooley makes use of an imaginary example where 'it seems logically possible that even a small scale local possibility could be a law or manifestation of a law'.[57] Tooley imagines a garden belonging to Smith where all the fruit are apples. Can it be viewed as a law of nature? Possibly not, according to Tooley. He says:

> ... In our world, if all fruit in Smith's garden are apples, it is only an accidentally true generalization. But if the world were different in certain ways, one might classify the generalization as nomological. If one never succeeds in getting pears into Smith's garden, if bananas changed into apples, and oranges into elephants, as they cross the boundary, etc. one might well be tempted to view the generalization as a law.[58]

A universalist might argue that there is a property P identified in Smith's garden that can explain its peculiarity. Any garden endowed with this property P would reveal the same peculiarity as Smith's garden. However, if a careful investigation does not reveal any property to differentiate Smith's garden from others and no experiment has been successful to produce such a second garden, then it is not reasonable, for practical purposes, to hold that such a property exists. The law about Smith's garden then may be viewed as a local or limited law holding only in Smith's garden.

Tooley observes that we need to examine the evidence that accounts for the critical difference between the nomological law and a mere accidental generalization. Why is some sort of event considered to be significant for this purpose? It may be suggested that 'they are events which determine which of "conflicting" generalizations are true'.[59] The generalization of our example, 'All the fruit in Smith's garden are apples', is supported by a number of positive instances and also by the absence of any counter-example. At the same time, we have certain other already accepted generalizations like 'No bananas can be apples' and 'No oranges can become elephants'. Tooley says: 'given the generalizations that (x) (Px ⊃ Rx) and that (x) (Qx ⊃ – Rx), discovery of an object b such that both Pb and Qb would be a situation of inevitable conflict'.[60] Even if both the generalizations have positive instances and there is no negative evidence against any, the discovery of b which is both P and Q would reduce the likelihood of both the generalizations as nomological. Tooley takes m as the probability of the former and n as that of the latter - 'where (m + n) must be less than or equal to one'.[61] An instance of b possessing both P and Q along with the property R would falsify the second generalization and the first one is yet to be proved as nomological.

Tooley observes:

> ...provided neither m nor n is equal to zero, the likelihood that the generalization is nomological will be greater after its survival of the conflict situation than it was before.
>
> ...Secondly, ...If the event that falsified the one generalization were one that would have been very likely if neither generalization had been nomological, one would not expect it to lend as much support to the surviving generalization as it would if it were an antecedently improbable event.
>
> Thirdly, ... This means that survival of a conflict with a well supported generalization results in a greater increase in the likelihood that a generalization is nomological than survival of a conflict with a less well supported generalization.
>
> Finally, it can be seen that the evidence provided by survival of conflict situations can quickly raise the likelihood that a generalization is nomological to quite high values.[62]

Tooley takes a natural law to express a relation between two universals. A difficulty arises if the lawhood of a generalization is considered to be due to the facts about the particulars. He observes: 'it is hard to see how one is justified in assigning any non-zero probability to a generalization'[63], where one is dealing with an infinite universe. The main reason for accepting the theory that laws of nature represent the relations between universals is to retain the infallibility of laws in varying regions of space and time.

Toulmin refers to a point of distinction between laws of nature and the results of the application of laws to some special cases or ranges of circumstances. For example, there exists a distinction between the Law of Gravitation which is a genuine law of nature and the empirical law specially applied to the conditions of our earth, for example, the law that 'Freely falling bodies accelerate by 32.2 feet / second every second'.[64] However, Toulmin admits that it is not entirely inappropriate to call the latter the Law of Gravitation, though the law, in a sense, is understood as restricted to some particular aspect of the universe. Toulmin clarifies the situation for taking the latter as the law:

> ...if it were found, e.g., that over the whole region to which we had previously had access there was a constant 'field' of a hitherto-unrecognized type; and if, on investigating the properties of this field, we found that the law of gravitation could be expressed in its present form only for so long as this field remained constant. One can imagine, say, the value of the gravitational constant, 'G', being found to depend on the strength of this field. If this happened, we should have to reformulate our law so as to take account of the new discovery, and the present formula would be dethroned. The success of our present law would then be spoken of as a local and temporary consequence of the 'true law'... [65]

Nevertheless, for Toulmin, the above consideration does not prove that the laws of nature are local or temporal regularities.

A statement is called a law, when we are ready to apply the formula irrespective of its conditions in space and time. Of course, a statement of law does not always carry with it some such labels as 'always', 'everywhere', etc. Toulmin remarks: 'these words would be out of place within a law...' [66]. Such words are suitable not for 'laws', but for 'applications of a law or principle to certain individual cases'. They are required to speak 'about the circumstances in which any particular law has been found to hold'.[67]

Toulmin finds that Whitehead confuses laws and other generalizations. He says:

> ...Nor, for that matter, is the fact that it makes sense to say, 'Perhaps our so-called Law of Gravitation is only a local affair', any reason for despondency: there is not the slightest reason at the moment to suppose the existence of the undiscovered field which would force us to this conclusion. Of course it *makes sense* to say, 'Perhaps we have not got the law right'. Nevertheless, we shall need to have good reasons before we can abandon our present formulation of the law for another.[68]

Kneale says that when a law is stated as 'Every F thing is G', it is not a '*de facto* generalization of the kind logicians express by writing "(x) [Fx ⊃ Gx]" '.[69] It would not be proper to express a law-statement with the help of "⊃", a symbol used to stand for material implication. A material implication may be vacuously true, but it would be meaningless to assert that a law-statement is true merely because it is about a null class. A law-statement has not only a universal application, but also a counterfactual import. In the case of the said law, it would be true to say of any thing which is not in fact F that if it were F then it would have been G. This is the feature that distinguishes a law from a local generalization, e.g. 'All coins in my purse are silver-coins'. The latter is not a law, since it does not allow us to say that if one puts a 10p. coin in the purse, it would be that of silver. Even if it be somebody's practice to put only silver-coins in his purse, the statement about his habit is not a law, and it does not hold of necessity. It is always possible to put a nickel-coin in the purse by mistake, assuming it to be a silver-coin. Further, if a non-silver coin is put in the purse, there is nothing to throw it out of the purse; the coin may very well co-exist there with the silver-coins. This proves that the purse of the said person has no specifiable property by which it may prevent any non-silver coin from existing there or turn it into silver to match the owner's choice. A law of nature, on the other hand, refers to an essential property. If it is a law of nature that 'sugar dissolves in water', then we are justified in saying that 'Had a piece of stone been a sugar-cube, it would have dissolved in water'. This is because sugar has this dispositional property essentially. And sugar, irrespective of its historical or geographical position, possesses this property.

Instances covered by a law must resemble in some important respects. The uranium of Australia may behave in a manner slightly different from the uranium of other countries. Nevertheless, there is no radical difference between the law-statement about the uranium of Australia and the law-statement about the uranium found elsewhere. Hence it is unnecessary to maintain that the law about uranium has an essential reference to space.

6.5.3 Meanings of the universality claim of laws

John Earman, in his article, *The Universality of Laws*, distinguishes four different senses of the universality claim of laws. To him, they are the conditions which claim to 'capture or at least to delimit'[70] the essential meaning of universality. The object of his paper is to discuss the mutual relations holding amongst these senses in order to determine the primacy of the meaning of universality. He also wishes to find out the justification of the universality claim of laws. To say that laws of nature are universal in space and time may mean, to put it in Earman's words, the following:

1. Laws do not make reference to specific spatio-temporal locations.
2. Laws have an unrestricted range in space and time.
3. Laws do not contain explicitly space or time coordinates.
4. Laws are invariant under spatio-temporal translations.[71]

Earman takes up each of the above interpretations. In the course of his discussion, *M* is taken to stand for the entire set of models of language in which the law-statements are expressed. For the sake of simplicity, the space-time background is assumed to be absolute in the sense that all the members of *M* are given in a fixed single space and time. Further, for the sake of simplicity of the treatment of *time translation invariance*, simultaneity is assumed as absolute - meaning that that the partition of events is unique. Later on, of course, such restrictions are removed to elucidate the notion of universality fully.

He begins with the second meaning indicated above. He tries to bring out the negative significance of 'universality' by determining the condition under which a law, L, falls short of universality. It would then be necessary to presume that there is a certain region 'R_o of space-time such that, as far as L is concerned, "anything goes" in R_o'.[72] This condition of universality is described by Earman as (U) in the following manner:

> (U) There is no non-empty proper sub-region R_o of space time such that for any $M \in M$, there is a $M' \in M$, where $M' \models L$ and $M' |_{Ro} \approx M |_{Ro}$.
>
> The symbol $\approx$ stands for model isomorphism and $M |_R$ denotes the restriction of M to R.[73]

He points out that many familiar laws of physics may be interpreted to fulfil this condition. However, he concedes that in the cases of many laws, the notion of the restriction of a model to a particular region R is not understood to possess any simple and natural interpretation. Thus he comments that 'the notion of the universality of laws has no simple and natural interpretation'. There are many laws which fail to satisfy (U). For example, the condition (U) fails in the case of the law (L_1), viz. (R) [R = N_o → D(R)] where the consequent D(R) is considered non-trivial and N_o is a constant standing for a restricted region of space-time. (U) also fails in the case of (L_2): (R) [C(R) → D(R)], where C(R) is expressed in purely spatio-temporal terms. Some might urge, Earman reflects, that 'it is the fault of (L_1) itself, but not of (L_2), itself, that it fails to exhibit universality'. It may be said that (L_2) is more universal than (L_1), since the proof from the latter must 'make use of the interpretation of the constant N_o'[74]. However, this is not clear at all. Thus Earman concludes that the notion of universality of laws ultimately is reduced to a problem of the philosophy of language and that it is a matter of debate whether reducing the problem of lawfulness to a problem of philosophy of language is any better or worse. The point remains that the meaning of universality as a condition of (U) lacks clarity and precision.

With this Earman turns his attention to the first meaning of universality. The main interest in this meaning, Earman contends, comes from a belief that 'this sense provides necessary and sufficient conditions for unrestricted range in space and time'. Nevertheless, '(1) has yet to be formulated in a precise manner'. It is not enough to say that a law-statement should not contain any name of a particular space-time region. In fact, many law-statements (e.g. 'All planets move round the sun') may be found to carry such references and there are others which overtly do not carry such a reference, but they are ultimately interpreted by reference to some specified region of space-time. An additional stipulation seems essential - the stipulation, viz. that a law should not contain any predicate which may be interpreted by using names or definite descriptions of particular regions. This is called by him the 'no-reference' or NR condition. Earman next argues that 'NR is not a desirable requirement on law sentences',[75] for it is easy to see that there are laws that are applicable to all space-time even though they do not comply with the NR condition.

The third sense, according to Earman, suffers from a greater imprecision. To him: 'A law sentence may be formulated with the help of coordinate systems (...) and yet may be invariant under space-time translations'.[76] And conversely, non-translation invariant laws may be formulated in a completely coordinate-free form with the help of differential geometry.

Earman contends that neither is the fourth sense of universality mentioned above a necessary condition for lawfulness. The time translation invariance (TTI) recommends that events occur in a lawlike schedule without reference to any particular point in time. This TTI is formulated by Earman thus:

> (TTI) For any $M \in \mathcal{M}$, such that $M \vDash L$ and for any $\Delta \in /R$ there is an $M' \in \mathcal{M}$ such that $M' \vDash L$ and $M'|_{t=\lambda+\Delta} \approx M|_{t=\lambda}\, \mathcal{M}$ for all $\lambda \in /R$
>
> In English, the time translation invariance of L requires that for any M which verifies L, there is an M′ which also verifies L and which is just like M except that everything is shifted in time by an amount Δ.[77]

Regarding the relation between U and TTI, Earman observes that the latter does not entail the former and that the converse implication also does not hold in every case. And when we remove the assumption of the fixed space-time background, 'the notion of the universality range of laws becomes much trickier to formulate and to evaluate'.[78] One is then faced with two notions of the 'universality' of range - viz., (i) the notion of unrestricted applicability to all physically possible space-time regions and (ii) the notion of unrestricted applicability over a given space-time region, S, i.e. 'universality in the sense of unrestricted range over S'. In Earman's words:

> As for (1), it can be held that lawfulness requires only that the range include the subset of physically possible space-times and not the entire set of all mathematically possible space-times of the intended sort.[79]

However, this subset is not given *a priori*, it is to be determined by reference to the law of nature. There is a circularity arising here, as one has to first possess the knowledge of the law in order to apply it to the notion of universality in the first sense. And the circularity is not prevented from viciousness by claiming that not all laws of nature need to be known at the outset; all that is required is to know only those laws which determine the space-time structure. For, upon the relativity theory of space and time, the laws determining the space-time structure are internally connected with all other laws. Hence Earman acknowledges that the criterion of 'universality' in the first sense, stated above, is not applicable to isolated law-statements, but to a total system of laws, α which is truly universal when it ranges over all mathematically possible space and time. And it is also difficult to formulate an appropriate version of universality in the second sense. The notion thus is quite problematic.

Earman accepts the Ramsey-Lewis account of law where a law is an axiom or a theorem in a deductively closed axiomatizable set of true sentences. This version of the nature of natural laws, Earman thinks, has a better explanation for the 'universality demand' of laws. The aim of science is to achieve simplicity and strength of scientific theory. But often the two are at loggerheads; the increase in the one results in the decrease of the other. According to Earman, the criterion of universality offers reconciliation between these two criteria: 'increasing the range of the axioms tends to increase simplicity in a way that does not sap strength, for it tends to reduce the number of independent axioms needed to achieve the same informativeness'.[80] Earman finds that the Ramsey-Lewis account that regards a law as an axiom in the best available deductive system rightly points out that the criterion of universality 'is not a condition *sine qua non* for laws...'[81].

It may be remarked here that Earman gives a good analysis of the different meanings of the 'universality' criterion of laws. But the meanings stand separate and exclusive of one another. And the source of his claimed vagueness of the universality criterion lies here. If these senses are taken to be equivalent, or a relation of implication is seen to hold amongst them, then Earman's problem would not be as inevitable as it seems to him. Kneale's theory has a solution to the problems referred to by Earman. Kneale recommends that the laws, prima facie found without any reference to spatio-temporal locations, are to be construed as elliptical statements. They are supposed to be true in every space and time, that is, in every possible world which possesses certain basic common conditions. And, under the identical basic or initial conditions, the laws are believed to be invariant under spatio-temporal variations. Further, a scientist, in his prediction, takes the laws to be universal, and to him there is no vagueness in the universality claim of laws. A logician like Earman finds difficulty in comprehending the meaning of the universality of laws; yet he is logically compelled to accept its importance for preserving the strength and simplicity of a good deductive system of scientific laws. Thus it is somewhat useless to complain about the vagueness of the criterion. If, in the case of natural laws, we fail to understand the meaning of 'universality' clearly enough, can we ever meaningfully make this claim in the case of laws?

6.6 An Examination of Kneale's Criticism of Whitehead

Beauchamp, in a paper entitled 'Cosmic Epoch and the Scope of Scientific Laws', interprets Whitehead's theory as an 'extension of Hume's polemic against induction'.[82] Beauchamp observes that Hume 'had a strong faith in induction beyond the immediate environment but could not rationally justify it'.[83] Whitehead is more skeptical than Hume of the abilities of scientists to predict things or events of remote space and time. For him, 'the laws should be construed as spatially and temporally restricted'. Hence the scientific predictions made on the basis of such laws 'must be confined to a particular space-time region where there is a traceable continuity'. Beauchamp quotes a passage where Whitehead makes this recommendation:

> In every inductive judgment, there is therefore contained a presupposition of the maintenance of a general order of the immediate environment, so far as concerns actual entities within the scope of induction.... The anticipations are devoid of meaning apart from the cosmic order which they presuppose... Thus the completely unknown environment never enters into an inductive judgment.[84]

Beauchamp finds that this challenge to the principle of uniformity is in perfect compatibility with a 'process and time-oriented philosophy'[85] as propounded by Whitehead. For Whitehead, the uniformity of a law is restricted to a certain epoch. The law fails when we transcend the boundary of that epoch.

Now, with regard to Kneale, Beauchamp finds that Kneale's philosophical standpoint is committed to accepting the uniformity principle as fundamental. Accordingly, Beauchamp contends that Kneale's argument against Whitehead is guilty of question-begging. Kneale is confident that, in every case, where there is an exception found to the law of unrestricted generality 'All α things are β', a condition 'g' remains overlooked. And when this hidden or overlooked 'g' is taken into account and the law is modified to 'All αg things are β', the law becomes actually exceptionless. But what makes Kneale so sure that a 'g' is to be found everywhere the law is apparently found to have an exception? The only justification for Kneale's belief in the existence of 'g' is the law of the Uniformity of Nature. To express the same point in different words: Kneale holds that when the antecedent in the law-statement,

'All α things are β', is further determined as 'ag', the consequent 'β' follows surely. This claim can be made only on the presupposition of the law of Uniformity of Nature as fundamental. For Whitehead, on the other hand, this uniformity, or, 'maintenance of the general order' may be presupposed only of the immediate environment. The uniformity principle cannot be stretched over all spatio-temporal epochs. Thus Kneale in presupposing the principle of uniformity which 'Whitehead is...directly challenging' is, according to Beauchamp, guilty of question-begging.

Beauchamp's criticism of Kneale does not seem to be appropriate. Kneale says: 'It must be admitted that scientists do in fact show special caution when using some of their supposed laws of nature for the making of inferences to events which are very remote in space or time; but their caution can be explained and justified without reference to... Whitehead's theory that laws of nature have only restricted universality'.[86] To say this, however, is not to beg the issue against Whitehead. Kneale's only contention is that the fact under reference, which can be explained by Whitehead's theory, can also be explained without reference to this theory. If Beauchamp were to score a point over Kneale, he was required to argue either that the fact in question could not be explained at all by the theory accepted by Kneale or that this fact could not be explained as well by it as it was explained by Whitehead's theory. But he has made no serious attempt to argue in this way. His criticism therefore is not convincing. If Kneale is to defend his own theory, he must defend it along with its presupposition, and if this presupposition has been challenged by Whitehead, then Kneale, in setting aside Whitehead's theory and explaining the entire matter that needs explaining in terms of his own theory, has done nothing that can be called unnatural and unsatisfactory.

Whitehead has rejected a single law of uniformity of nature prevalent all over nature and accepted smaller or local uniformities. Kneale, on the other hand, accepts the general uniformity principle and holds the laws of nature as manifestations of this general uniformity. When a law, for Kneale, fails to hold in a cosmic epoch, he refers to the scientific practice to look for a hidden factor and incorporate that in the revised statement of law. Thus the law 'All α are β' or its revised version, 'All αg things are β', are considered to be *particular uniformities*. The general principle of uniformity and the particular uniformities, i.e. the laws of nature, belong to different levels, and supposing the former to prove the latter is certainly not committing the fallacy of question-begging.

With regard to Kneale, Beauchamp says:

> Kneale is contending that the concepts ordinarily used to describe universally connected features in nomological generalizations may differ radically from those which always could be mentioned and which would be contained in a complete formulation of the law.[87]

Where does Kneale say precisely that 'α' and 'αg' are *radically different* concepts? It is intuitively evident that they are not so. The law 'All αg things are β' is only an improvement upon the law 'All α are β', and the former does not contradict the latter. In fact, laws are accepted in a group and when any particular law is rejected, what is rejected is the conjunction of the law with the accepted set of laws in a particular scientific era. In a *revision*, however, the entire set of accepted scientific laws is not rejected. If the concepts of 'All α are β' and 'All αg are β' were *radically* different, then in accepting the latter, one must reject the entire set of previously accepted laws. However, that is not done. Beauchamp is unnecessarily harsh on Kneale when he takes the concepts involved in 'All α are β' and 'All αg are β' as radically different.

Gary Gutting's interpretation of Whitehead also demands our attention. Gutting observes that Whitehead introduces his theory of internal relations to solve the riddle of induction. Gutting quotes the following passage from Whitehead's *Process and Reality*:

> Another way of stating this explanation of the validity of induction is, that in every forecast there is a presupposition of a certain type of actual entities, and that the question then asked is, under what circumstances will these entities find themselves? The reason that an answer can be given is that the presupposed type of entities requires a presupposed type of data for the primary phases of these actual entities; and that a presupposed type of data requires a presupposed type of social environment. Hence when we have presupposed a type of actual occasions, we have already some information as to the laws of nature in operation throughout the environment.[88]

Gutting clarifies Whitehead's position thus:

> What any given actual entity is, depends to a large extent, on what the actual entities in its past were .... Since on this view an actual entity is, to a great extent, itself a projection of the past, it would seem that we are justified in projecting its future behavior on the basis of the known behavior of past actual entities.[89]

In his paper entitled 'Metaphysics and Induction', Gutting argues that the problem of induction is an epistemological problem which cannot be solved by any metaphysical theory. To infer that the future would be like the past, e.g. that in future bread will nourish as it did in the past, one has to be convinced that the future example is a regular piece of bread, like B_1 and B_2, sharing the common essential property of producing nourishment (N). But how can we be sure that the future and the past instances do not differ in any important respect? Gutting apprehends that there may be objects like y, that is, a loaf of bread 'laced with arsenic' or 'a clever synthetic product which simulates all external properties of bread but has no nutritional value'.[90] We must be sure that what we take as bread in our inference is really a piece of bread and not the kind of an object like 'y'. The problem of the scientist is not whether there is uniformity in nature;'... the problem is rather, *which* of these laws apply to y'.[91] Gutting finds that the doctrine of internal relations is neither necessary nor sufficient to solve the problem of induction. Further, internal relations between entities, even if they exist, must be known by some non-inductive method. They cannot furnish the ground of validity for inductive reasoning without being circular. To infer that the future bread would be like the past bread in producing nourishment is already to *know* the law of nature that bread nourishes. As Gutting says:

> ...according to the Whiteheadian doctrine of internal relations, to be a loaf of bread means to have incorporated a certain kind of structure from things in one's past.... But this, in turn, means that to be a loaf of bread is to be a part of a certain kind of environment - i.e., to have certain types of entities in one's immediate past. Consequently, as soon as we talk about 'a loaf of bread', we are necessarily talking about a certain kind of physical environment. But part of being 'a certain kind of physical environment' is being governed by certain kinds of physical laws (....). As a result, when we talk about today's loaf of bread, we are necessarily discussing something that obeys the same laws of nature as did yesterday's loaf of bread. Since nutrition follows the eating of bread in virtue of laws of nature, we can justifiably conclude that today's bread, like yesterday's, will produce nutrition.[92]

Gutting refers to two special assumptions Whitehead had to make to justify inductive inference:

> Each actual occasion objectifies the other actual occasions in its environment. This environment can be limited to the relevant portion of the cosmic epoch. *It is a finite region of*

> *the extensive continuum, so far as adequate importance is concerned in respect to individual differences among actual occasions.* Also, in respect to the importance of individual differences, we may assume that *there is a lower limit to the extension of each relevant occasion within this region.* (PR 313, italics added)[93]

Obviously, this reading of the Whiteheadian philosophy is not in accord with Beauchamp's interpretation of Whitehead's Regionalism. To Beauchamp, Whitehead has propagated an undiluted form of regionalism where it is not only logically but also empirically possible that 'relevantly similar and fully described causal items may produce dissimilar effects in different cosmic epochs'.[94] The trouble with Beauchamp is that he wants to treat Whitehead's epistemology independently of his metaphysics. In fact, Whitehead himself remarks that his theory of law may be understood upon the foundation of his metaphysics. Further, no branch of a *system* may be understood in isolation from its other branches. Whitehead himself seeks to justify our inference about the future and for this purpose he introduces his metaphysical doctrine that any real entity is historically determined by its past, and that its future is to a great extent determined by its present state. Is this not a kind of general regularity? If so, then this is a return of the principle of Uniformity of Nature in a new garb.

Notes

1 A phrase taken from S. Toulmin, *The Philosophy of Science*, Hutchinson University Press, London, 1955, p. 98.

2 J. P. Day, *Inductive Probability*, Routledge and Kegan Paul, London, 1961, p. 186.

3 W. C. Kneale, *Probability and Induction*, 1966, p. 72.

4 *Ibidem*.

5 Armstrong, *What Is a Law of Nature?*, 1983, p. 24.

6 *Ibid.*, p. 25.

7 T. L. Beauchamp, 'Cosmic Epochs and the Scope of Scientific Laws', *Process Studies*, vol. 2, 1972, p. 298.

8 *Ibid.*, p. 299.

9 J. Martin, *New Shapes of Reality*, George Allen and Unwin, London, 1968, p. 17.

10 *Ibid.*, p. 144.

11 J. Bradley, *Routledge Encyclopedia of Philosophy*, vol. 9, Routledge and Kegan Paul, London, 1998, p. 715.

12 W. Mays, *Whitehead's Philosophy of Science & Metaphysics*, 1977, Martinus Nijhoff, The Hague, Netherlands, 1977, p. 60.

13 *Ibid.*, p. 61.

14 A. H. Johnson, *Whitehead's Theory of Reality*, Dover Publications Inc., New York, 1962, p. 17.

15 Martin, *op. cit.*, p. 15.

16 Quoted from Johnson, *op. cit.*, 1962, p. 19.

17 Whitehead speaks of 'society' in *Process and Reality* and *Adventure of Ideas*; but, in *Science and the Modern World,* he uses the term 'organism'.

18 Johnson, *op. cit.*, p. 51.

19 *Ibid*, p. 19.

20 A. N. Whitehead, *The Interpretation of Science*, The library of Liberal Arts, The Bobbs-Merrill Co. Inc., New York, 1961, p. 140.

21 Mays, *op. cit.*, p. 52.

22 *Ibid.*, p. 53.

23 A. N. Whitehead, *Science and the Modern World*, Cambridge, 1927, p. 134.

24 A. N. Whitehead, *Adventure of Ideas,* Penguin Books, London, 1933, p. 130.

25 Whitehead, *Science and the Modern World*, p. 92.

26 A. N. Whitehead, *An Enquiry Concerning the Principles of Natural Knowledge*, Cambridge University Press, Cambridge, 1955, p. 186.

27 Whitehead, *Adventure of Ideas,* p.130.

28 *Ibid.*, p. 133.

29 *Ibid.*, p. 134.

30 *Ibidem.*

31 *Ibid.*, pp. 134 -135.

32 *Ibid.*, p. 135.

33 *Ibid.*, p. 137.

34 *Ibid.*, pp. 137 -138.

35 *Ibid.*, p. 139.

36 *Ibid.*, p. 149.

37 *Ibid.*, p. 150.

38 *Ibidem.*

39 *Ibid.*, p.147.

40 *Ibid.*, p.148.

41 *Ibid.*, pp. 161 - 162.

42 *Ibid.*, p.165.

43 Beauchamp, *op. cit.*, p. 299.

44 Day, *op. cit.*, p. 186.

45 *Ibidem.*

46 *Ibidem.*

47 Day on pp. 187-188 refers to the British classical school of economics, followed by Smith and others, where the economic laws are prevalent universally and to the German historical school for which different laws are true of different countries at different point of history. Mill tries to arrive at a compromise by distinguishing between Pure and Applied Economics. Universalism is true in the former and Regionalism is true in the latter. Mill tries to develop a new science called 'Political Ethology' to determine what important features are to be taken into consideration when the laws of economics are applied to a particular country.

48 *Ibid.*, p. 252.

49 Kneale, *op. cit.*, p. 72.

50 Ibid., p. 73.

51 S. Toulmin, *The Philosophy of Science*, pp. 98 - 99.

52 Kneale, *op. cit.* [italics added].

53 *Ibid.*, p. 73.

54 *Ibidem.*

55 *Ibidem.*

56 N. R. Campbell, *Relativity*, Cambridge University Press, Cambridge, 1923, p. 38.

57 Armstrong, *op. cit.*, p. 26.

58 M. Tooley, 'The Nature of Laws', *Canadian Journal of Philosophy*, vol. 7, 1977, p. 689.

59 *Ibidem.*

60 *Ibid.*, p. 690.

61 *Ibidem.*

62 *Ibid.*, p. 692.

63 *Ibidem.*

64 Toulmin, *op. cit.*, p. 99.

65 *Ibid.*, pp. 99 -100.

66 *Ibid.*, p. 100.

67 *Ibidem.*

68 *Ibidem.*

69 W. Kneale, 'Universality and Necessity', *The British Journal for the Philosophy of Science*, vol. 12, 1961, p. 89.

70 J. Earman, 'The Universality of Laws', *Philosophy of Science*, vol. 45, 1978, p. 173.

71 *Ibidem.*

72 *Ibid.*, p. 174.

73 *Ibidem.*

74 *Ibid.*, p. 175.

75 *Ibid.*, p. 176.

76 *Ibidem.*

77 *Ibidem.*

78 *Ibid.*, p. 177.

79 *Ibidem.*

80 *Ibid.*, p. 180.

81 *Ibidem.*

82 Beauchamp, *op. cit.*, p. 297.

83 *Ibidem.*

84 Whitehead, *Process and Reality*, pp. 311f.

85 Beauchamp, *op. cit.*, p. 298.

86 Kneale, *op. cit.*, p. 73.

[87] Beauchamp, *op. cit.*, p. 298.

[88] A. N. Whitehead, *Process and Reality,* Social Sciences Book Store, New York, 1941, p. 311.

[89] G. Gutting, 'Metaphysics and Induction', *Process Studies,* vol. 1, 1971, p. 174.

[90] *Ibid.*, p. 176.

[91] *Ibidem.*

[92] *Ibid.*, p. 175.

[93] *Ibid.*, p. 176.

[94] Beauchamp, *op. cit.*, p. 299.

[95] A detailed account of *"Whitehead's metaphysics and his regionalism concerning natural laws"* by the author may be found in the *Journal of the Department of Philosophy, Vol-X,* 2010-2011 of University of Calcutta, under Appendix II p. 327-350.

CHAPTER SEVEN

KNEALE'S CRITIQUE OF THE PRESCRIPTION THEORY OF NATURAL LAWS

7.1 Foreword

Kneale discusses the prescription theory of natural laws advanced by the early logical positivists of the Vienna Circle as another alternative to the theory of natural necessity. He rejects it finally. In this Chapter the prescription theory is explained, and Kneale's criticism of it is considered, in detail.

The early positivists' theory of natural laws is based on their criterion of *meaning*. According to this criterion, a sentence is empirically significant (meaningful) if the statement expressed by it is (being non-analytic) completely verifiable in experience. As for statements of natural laws, they are unrestrictedly general and so not completely verifiable in experience. They are not accordingly genuine (i.e. true or false) empirical statements representing any empirical fact or event: they rather stand for something else.

It is, indeed, hard to defend such an extreme position. The conclusion of the Vienna Circle has led the later positivists to modify the theory of meaning radically. It is very difficult to see whether there is at all any common element of thought serving as the continuing link between early positivism as advocated by the members of the Vienna Circle and later Positivism. Edward Mackinnon's comment in this connection is worthy of notice:

> ... If there is any doctrinal core linking present positivism with the goals of the Vienna Circle and distinguishing them from other philosophical interpretations of science, it is surely

> to be found in the cluster of ideas surrounding Carl Hempel's model of scientific explanation...[1]

Hempel tries to show that a scientific explanation ultimately aims at the 'subsumption of its subject-matter under general regularities; ...it seeks to provide a systematic understanding of empirical phenomena by showing that they fit into a nomic nexus'.[2]

For a later positivist, like van Fraassen, a scientific theory does not represent the natural world in an apt and accurate manner. To accept a theory is not to accept it as *literally* true. He observes that a theory is empirically adequate for 'prediction, control, research...'.[3] Mention may be made of yet another positivist writer, Nancy Cartwright. She finds that the laws are not *true* propositions. The laws of Quantum Mechanics, for example, do not describe any actual state of affairs. They are intellectual tools for successful experimentation, explanation, and understanding of the world. The laws of nature do not indicate any *exact uniformity*. They are rather our *ways of thinking* about the things of the world[4]. Thus the early and the later version of logical positivism have tried to emphasize one point in particular, namely, that a law of nature is nothing but a tool that acts as a guide for our actions.

Kneale, in his discussion of the prescription theory of natural laws, cites a passage from Schlick's work entitled 'Causality in Contemporary Physics'. This, for Kneale, expresses the quintessence of the prescription theory. The passage is quoted below in order to identify the main points of the prescription theory and also the hidden pillars on which it rests:

> Natural laws do not have the character of propositions which are true or false, but rather set forth instructions for formation of such propositions... Natural laws are not universal implications, because they cannot be verified in all cases; they are rather *directions*, rules of behaviour for the investigator to find his way about in reality, to anticipate

> certain events... The relations between reality and ourselves are frequently expressed in sentences which have the grammatical form of assertions but whose essential sense consists of the fact that they are directions for possible acts.[5]

Kneale's exposition of Schlick's view may be outlined in the form of an argument with the following axioms used as premises:

1. Laws of nature are expressed by statements of *unrestricted generality*.
2. Any genuine empirical statement is completely verifiable in experience.

From the above, it is concluded that a statement of law, as it is commonly called, is not a statement or proposition in the true sense of the term, as it is not completely verifiable in experience.

7.2 The Logical Positivist Theory of Natural Laws

The refusal of the Vienna Circle philosophers to take the so-called law-statements as genuine (i.e. true or false) statements is not to be understood as their rejection of the two-valued traditional logic in favour of a many-valued system. The statements of law, as they are commonly called, are, for them, not endowed with any truth-value. Although they bear an affinity to propositions, this affinity is no indication of their real status. (In this exposition the common expression 'law-statements' or 'statements of laws' will no doubt sometimes be used, but it should be understood that, for positivists, law-sentences do not express genuine statements or propositions.)

Schlick's philosophy treats a natural law as an utter nonsense; nevertheless a law is believed to provide practical guidance in great many spheres of life. For Schlick, then, the laws cannot be robbed of their practical importance. This realization has led Schlick to call natural laws 'prescriptions of our own making'.[6] To understand Schlick fully, it will be well to turn to the historical background of his view. For this purpose, reference to the works of Ludwig Wittgenstein, a very important philosopher of Schlick's time, is necessary to some extent. Schlick himself acknowledges to have borrowed his terminology from Wittgenstein[7]. Kneale refers to Ramsey as the forerunner of Schlick, and so a brief sketch of Ramsey's view of natural laws would not be out of place. We have historical evidence that Wittgenstein had several discussions with Ramsey during his stay at Cambridge, and Wittgenstein himself acknowledges his obligations to Ramsey in his *Philosophical Investigations.* Before proceeding to evaluate Kneale's criticism of logical positivism, the theories held by Ramsey, Wittgenstein, and Schlick have to be stated and explained.

7.2.1 The prescription theory of Ramsey

Ramsey has given a special dimension to the prescription theory of natural laws. Kneale considers Ramsey to be the harbinger of this theory of natural laws. In one of his philosophical papers, Ramsey writes:

> As opposed to a purely *descriptive theory* of science, mine may be called a *forecasting* theory. To regard a law as a summary of certain facts seems to me inadequate; it is also an attitude of expectation for the future.[8]

Ramsey calls a statement of law, e.g. 'All men are mortal', a *variable hypothetical.* Perhaps he may be interpreted to mean that the subject-term 'man' here does not stand for any constant individual value. It is rather a variable, a place-indicator, where one may put individual constants, e.g. Aristotle, Plato, Hume, etc. to obtain sentences representing truths of facts that Aristotle is mortal and Plato is mortal and so on. To quote Ramsey: 'It expresses an inference we are at any time prepared to make...'[9] The statement, in this sense, may be understood to indicate that, for any x whatsoever, if x is a man then x is mortal (i.e. a rule for making an infinite number of inferences). Thus, a statement of law is reduced to a formula of deriving a proposition and, strictly speaking, is not a proposition itself.

In this connection, Ramsey distinguishes between what is called a statement of restricted generality and a universal statement that differs from such a generalization. The former is a set of conjunctions. To take the example cited by Ramsey: 'Everyone in Cambridge voted'. The variable here, according to him, is not the persons residing at Cambridge, but the limited part of space varying according to the 'definiteness of the speaker's idea of "Cambridge" '[10] as a town of England. Such a statement differs from a law or a variable hypothetical. A law, e.g. 'All men are mortal', is not to be identified with a mere conjunction of individual facts, such as Aristotle is mortal, Plato is mortal, Hume is mortal, etc. Ramsey clearly distinguishes between a variable hypothetical and a general statement obtained by summative induction. He puts up a question: 'What do they have in common with conjunctions and in what do they differ from them?'[11] He offers an answer himself. A variable hypothetical and a general statement obtained through summative induction look alike; for both begin with the word 'all', or, as Ramsey says: 'when we look at them objectively, i.e. at the conditions of their truth and falsity, they appear to be the same'.[12] Any statement '(x)[ϕx]', be it a statement obtained by summative induction or a statement of law, is true when all xs have ϕ. Yet there are important differences between the two. Ramsey mentions four points of difference between them. They are:

(i) A law 'cannot be written' as a conjunction. A law ranges over the entire class. The individual constants, which may be written in place of a variable, are infinite. Hence the entire range of a law can never be exhaustibly represented by a set of conjunctions.

(ii) 'Its constitution as a conjunction is never used'. As the range of law is not restricted to a finite group, 'we never use it in class-thinking except in its application to a finite class, i.e. we use only the applicative rule'.[13]

(iii) A general statement or a law always talks about something beyond the range of actually observed cases. If it be a law that 'All men are mortal', we are justified in asserting the mortality of every man at any place and time. In this sense, a law extends to infinity. A law thus differs from what may be called 'a belief of the primary sort', or, 'a map of neighbouring space by which we steer'. A map remains a map even if we decide to complicate it by filling in every intricate detail. But if we stretch the map to infinity, it is no more a map; for we can no longer steer by it - 'our journey is over before we need its remoter parts'.[14]

(iv) The relevant degree of certainty for a law is the certainty of a particular case, or of a finite set of such cases. We can never know an infinite range with certainty. Nor is it correct to claim that the truth of each subclass quantitatively contributes to the certainty of the general statement. However, in the case of the conclusion of a summative induction, the certainty with which each individual case is known adds to the certainty of the conjunction.

To summarize, a statement of law, like 'All men are mortal', is never used 'in class-thinking except in its application to a finite class'.[15] It is only a rule for such application. A universal statement $(x)[\phi x]$ is accepted as true if and only if every x has ϕ. The truth or falsity of a law-statement would have been completely determined only if the statement were equal to a conjunction of actual statements of facts. Since a law subsumes under it all cases, actual and possible, it is impossible to determine the truth-value of a so-called law-statement by reference to the actual states of affairs. Thus the question of its truth or falsity can never be settled in a determinate manner. Consequently, to take a putative statement of law as a proposition is to take it as a conjunction and 'to have a theory of conjunctions which we cannot express for lack of symbolic power. [But what we can't say we can't say, and we can't whistle it either.]'[16]

A variable hypothetical or a causal law of the form, 'All ϕ things are ψ', Ramsey says, 'is not a judgment but a rule for judging "if ϕ is found, one must regard it as a ψ" '[17]. Only propositions can carry the labels 'true' and 'false'. The so-called law-statements do not carry such labels. They are *rules* which are important for the purpose of application. The sum-total of evidence on the basis of which we adopt laws is, for Ramsey, such that 'we trust it to guide us in a new instance'.[18]

But why cannot we take a law as a proposition, true or false? Ramsey points out that there are two different senses in which a proposition may be true or false. A proposition may be true or false when the user of the expression 'makes a truth function of it, i.e., argues disjunctively about the cases of its truth and falsity'.[19] But this is not true in the case of a variable hypothetical. This point needs further clarification. We seem to argue disjunctively when we take into account different theories obtainable by combination of different proposed laws of nature. But in fact we never do so (this practice in mathematics has been shown to involve fallacies). In natural science if 'p' is proposed as a statement of a natural law, then we do not judge the alternatives, 'p', i.e. $(x)[\phi x]$, and '~p', i.e. $\sim(x)[\phi x]$. Rather we choose between having 'p' or not having 'p'. Again, not having 'p' does not imply the falsity of 'p'. Not having 'p' as a law in no way implies that '~p' is a law.

The second sense of truth or falsity of a proposition is found in connection with an onlooker who regards a man's belief in the proposition as right or wrong, that is, true or false. But if what is considered to be true or false is a matter of the onlooker's belief, it becomes a purely subjective matter. Ordinarily a proposition is considered by one to be true if it is identical with one's own belief; otherwise it is considered false. In other words, a proposition p is regarded as true or false in the sense of its agreement or disagreement with the onlooker's belief. However, every agreement or disagreement is not a mutually exhaustive, exclusive alternative like true or false. To put it in the words of Ramsey:

> In fact agreement and disagreement is (*sic*) possible in regard to any aspect of a man's view and need not take the simple form of 'p', '$\overline{\text{p}}$'.
>
> Many sentences express cognitive attitudes without being propositions; and the difference between saying yes or no to them is not the difference between saying yes or no to a proposition. This is even true of ordinary hypothetical . . . and much more of the variable hypothetical.[20]

Now what does the belief in the law mean? According to Ramsey, the general belief consists in (i) a general enunciation, and (ii) a habit of singular belief. These two elements are of course interconnected - the habit arises from the enunciation according to the psychological law governing the meaning of 'all'. Variable hypotheticals 'form a system with which the speaker meets the future'.[21] Thus a variable hypothetical is not subjectively true or false. If two persons enunciate differently then they are actually endorsing their beliefs in two different systems to deal with the future. Thus a law cannot be '*negated* but can be *disagreed* with one who does not adopt it'.[22]

Ramsey adds that the ground for the efficacy of a law in prediction of an event or 'expectation about the future' does not lie in any form of necessity embedded in the law-statement. He says:

> ...causal necessity is not a fact; when we assert a causal law we are asserting not a fact, not an infinite conjunction, nor a connection of universals, but a variable hypothetical which is not strictly a proposition at all, but a formula from which we derive propositions.[23]

Ramsey thinks it inappropriate to preserve the necessity of

a law by taking the law as a relation between universals[24]. He says that the meaning of any such doctrine is not clear to him. Accordingly he admits his inability to either affirm or deny it.

Although Ramsey denies that a putative law-statement is a *proposition* proper, he at the same time admits that laws are indispensable in our system of knowledge. Even though the law-statements, as they are called, are not propositions proper which are either true or false, they play a pivotal role in our deliberation about the future.

Ramsey proposes to explain the counterfactual import of laws within the framework of his prescription theory. He does not deny that one may derive an unfulfilled hypothetical from a supposed statement of law. Belief in an unfulfilled hypothetical does not rest on the consideration whether the antecedent of the statement in fact obtains or not. The unfulfilled hypothetical like 'if this stone had been a man, then it would have been mortal' is only our expectation of a certain event if the things of the present had been otherwise. This is explained only if the law, supporting the counterfactual or the unfulfilled hypothetical, is taken not as a description of fact, but as a system adopted by us to arrange the facts. The unfulfilled conditional is not a fact itself; for in that case we must have a clear method to determine its truth or falsity. However, there is no available theory by following which an unfulfilled conditional may be determined to be true or false in a definite manner. An unfulfilled hypothetical is obtainable from the system we have chosen to adopt. The system, however, can never be true or false.

It seems that Ramsey, in his view that a law-sentence does not express a proposition proper, is referring to the criterion of significance or meaning adopted by Schlick and other positivists. If Ramsey's view is in this respect identical with that of Schlick, then, of course, both the views must be open to the same criticism that is made by Kneale. The views of Wittgenstein and Schlick have to be considered next before proceeding to consider Kneale's objections to the logical positivist theory of natural laws.

7.2.2 Wittgenstein's account of propositions and laws

G. P. Baker and P. M. S. Hacker, in the Preface to the second volume of their illustrious work on Wittgenstein entitled *Wittgenstein: Rules, Grammar and Necessity: An Analytic Commentary on the 'Philosophical Investigations'*, remark that understanding Wittgenstein is an extremely difficult task:

> ...The articulation of the text was difficult to fathom; the individual remarks were more problematic than anything we had hitherto tackled. Looking around for skilful guides, we saw others floundering, or firmly wedged in various canvasses. The only safe recourse was to map the terrain by reference to the underlying writings in Wittgenstein's *Nachlass* and then to trace his footsteps slowly and carefully, avoiding the pitfall of jumping to a conclusion on the basis of a single remark or sentence.[25]

The problem is nothing special to the *Philosophical Investigations*; it prevails through the entire work of Wittgenstein. It is mainly due to his style of expression. He is emphatic but extremely cryptic in his statements, and this style hinders the comprehension of his main points. G. E. Moore in his notes on 'Wittgenstein's Lectures in 1930–1933'[26] points out that Wittgenstein at times uses common phrases in a special sense. So the understanding of Wittgenstein involves a careful determination of the intended sense of his words. It would not be out of context to mention here that very often he was misunderstood by the members of the Vienna Circle: in fact many ideas, which Wittgenstein himself never claimed to be his own, were attributed to him.

In the *Tractatus* Wittgenstein speaks of a single propositional form exemplified in every proposition. A proposition is characterized by him as 'a picture of reality',[27] and sometimes as the 'description of a fact'. Moore comments that his characterization of a proposition as a 'picture' is apt to be misunderstood. Propositions are not pictures in any ordinary sense. To say that propositions are pictures is merely to stress that 'our uses of the words "propositions" and "picture" follow similar rules'.[28] At one time Wittgenstein recognized only experiential propositions as significant (i.e. genuine). For him, every significant proposition is completely verifiable. This view, according to Carnap[29], is the result of the influences of Russell and Mach on him. Moore refers to 'the famous statement' made by Wittgenstein in a lecture in 1930: 'The sense of a proposition is the way in which it is verified'.[30] This verification principle occupies a central position in the general theory accepted by the Vienna Circle. Surprisingly, there is no mention of the verification principle in the *Tractatus.* Historically the principle made its first appearance in print in Waismann, and there are other pieces of historical evidence attributing the principle to Wittgenstein[31]. If a proposition does not have the sense according to Wittgenstein's stipulations, then it is declared to be 'nonsense'. The term 'nonsense' is explained by Moore in the following way:

> ...where we say that 'This makes no sense' we always mean that 'This is nonsense *in this particular game*'; and in answer to the question 'Why do we call it a "nonsense"?' Wittgenstein said that when we call a sentence 'nonsense', it is 'because of some similarity to sentences which have sense' and that 'nonsense always arises from forming symbols analogous to certain uses, where they have no use'.[32]

On this point Wittgenstein's view is similar to that of Schlick. To both of them not every semblance of a propositional expression represents a significant proposition. Upon the verification principle [construed as the principle according to which *sense* consists in *verifiability*], all the rules of logic, all tautologies and contradictions, besides the laws of nature, e.g. the principle of causation etc., are declared meaningless. A few sentences may be quoted from the *Tractatus* in this connection:

> ...Laws of inference, which - as in Frege and Russell - are to justify the conclusions, are senseless and would be superfluous.
>
> In no way can an inference be made from the existence of one state of affairs to the existence of another entirely different from it.
>
> There is no causal nexus which justifies such an inference.
>
> Superstition is the belief in the causal nexus.[33]

On the verification principle [construed in the way indicated] both a tautology and a contradiction turn out to be nonsensical. Wittgenstein does not consider a tautology or a contradiction a picture of reality; for 'a tautology follows from all propositions',[34] and any proposition whatsoever is implied by a contradiction. Therefore, 'they present no possible state of affairs'.[35] Let us take a tautology, 'Either it is raining or it is not raining'. This does not say any thing about the world, about the weather of any time and place. Neither is it verifiable by any event in the world, since neither actual rain nor its absence can serve to verify the proposition. Further, the real state of affairs is in no way affected by the assertion of a tautology or its rejection (which is equivalent to embracing a self-contradiction, that is, an absurdity). The only form of necessity that is admissible to Wittgenstein is the logical necessity. He writes in the *Tractatus*:

> The necessity for one thing to happen because another has happened does not exist.
>
> There is only logical necessity.

> At the basis of the whole modern view of the world lies the illusion that the so-called laws of nature are the explanations of natural phenomena. [36]

What, then, is a law for Wittgenstein? A law is considered by him to be an *instrument* which is altogether different in nature from an empirical or contingent statement. A law is neither true nor false. For example, a law of grammar does not fall within the bipolarity of truth and falsehood. It only allows certain usages and prohibits certain others. The laws themselves are not descriptive of any real state of affairs. They are the tools required for adequate description, harmonization, and understanding of the matters of facts. In the *Tractatus* Wittgenstein observes that the Newtonian Mechanics 'asserts nothing about the world'[37]; it only shows us the way in which the things of the world may be described. Mechanical axioms determine the form of describing the world. All descriptions of the world are to be deduced from these axioms in a stipulated manner in the way the bricks are used to construct a building.

However, it may be noted that later on Wittgenstein has shifted from the *Tractatus* theory of meaning to an altogether different theory in his *Philosophical Investigations.* There he recognizes three types of proposition. Modern scholars, like Donald Gillies, find this later theory 'preferable'[38] to his earlier one. In Moore's notes on Wittgenstein's Lectures one finds the following classification of propositions:

1. Genuine propositions, which are completely determined as true or false in reference to reality. These are sense-datum statements describing immediate experience.

2. Hypotheses, which are not completely verifiable by experience. Wittgenstein is aware of the problems involved in the complete verification criterion. The criterion makes statements about the past and the future, statements about the mental states of other persons, and all universal statements including the laws of nature meaningless. But Wittgenstein does not intend to deny the importance of laws in our life. Wittgenstein calls the laws 'hypotheses' which are neither true nor false. Obviously, the hypotheses are different in logical structure from genuine propositions which are completely verifiable in experience. Hacker points out that the impossibility of complete verification in the case of a hypothesis is not, for Wittgenstein, due to any human limitation. Wittgenstein thinks that a hypothesis has a 'different formal relation to reality from that of a completely verifiable proposition'.[39] A hypothesis is a law that provides a guideline for the construction of a genuine proposition. The relation between a hypothesis and a genuine proposition is an *a priori* one. A proposition, as a 'symptom', gives support to a hypothesis. And a hypothesis is a rule for deriving a symptom or a law for forming expectations.

3. Mathematical propositions, which cannot be compared in any way to reality. They do not represent truths about the world. They are rather grammatical constructions or rules of representation.

Even though it is Wittgenstein who has introduced the principle of verification to the Vienna Circle, he himself holds the principle in high esteem only for a short period of time. Wittgenstein soon realizes that even genuine propositions, earlier conceived by him to be completely verifiable in experience, are not really so; neither are they comparable to reality. Hacker observes:

> ... But how can his later insistence that he had never advanced verificationism as a theory of meaning, but only as 'one way of getting clear about the use of a word or sentence' be explained? It was not ...wholly ingenuous. It is doubtful whether even in 1929-30 he would have thought of his verificationism as a *theory* of meaning[40].

Hacker further refers to the *Philosophical Investigations*, where Wittgenstein maintains that the question of 'whether and how a proposition can be verified is only a particular way of asking "How d'you mean?"'[41] The central idea of Wittgenstein's theory of law is the doctrine that rules - all of them - are instruments. Further, unlike physical objects, which may be used or may remain unused, a rule or law cannot remain unused. As has been aptly observed by Baker and Hacker:

> Something is a rule only dynamically, only in so far as it is *used* in a certain way...... . A lever, Wittgenstein emphasized, is a lever only in use, disconnected it is just a rod.[42]

Thus there can never be any idle rule, i.e. a rule that exists but does not play its role in future prediction, in justification, explanation or systematization of our action, 'in teaching and correcting, evaluating and criticizing'.[43] Consequently, Wittgenstein has rejected the idea of an unknown or 'hidden' rule. The question of the discovery of a rule can never arise; for 'something is a rule only if it is used as a standard by participants in practice - there is no such thing with which one is unacquainted as a standard of correctness for one's behavior'.[44] Wittgenstein has recommended that both mathematical propositions and some metaphysical statements are to be taken as 'rules'.

In the *Tractatus* Wittgenstein speaks only of logical necessity. He is not, however, unaware of other types of necessity. What he means is that logical necessity is the only form of expressible necessity. He has given examples of mathematical and metaphysical necessity, and reduced both to grammatical rules. A grammatical rule is different from an empirical proposition. An empirical proposition may be identified as true or false. One may specify the situation in which an empirical proposition is true and may also indicate the condition in which it would turn out to be false. In other words, an empirical proposition is contingently true or false. A necessary proposition or a rule, on the other hand, has no meaningful negation - such a proposition as well as its negation says nothing about the world. In an article contributed to the *Philosophical Review,* Max Black observes that Wittgenstein 'clearly treats them [necessary propositions] as limiting or degenerate cases of statements proper'.[45] Black has spelled out three possible reasons[46] owing to which a necessary statement is claimed to be included in the list of statements proper, though Black himself would like to do away with the expression 'necessary statement'. They are:

1. A necessary statement, e.g. a tautology, is a well-formed sentence and not 'nonsense' in the pejorative sense of the term.
2. It has cognitive uses.
3. It can be inserted into a series of sentences according to its 'strength' or 'logical priority'.

Although these may be some reasons for regarding necessary statements as statements proper, yet there are enough reasons, Black says, to regard such statements as '*limiting* cases of statements proper'.[47] We speak of 'validity' of necessary statements instead of their 'truth', and of their 'certification' instead of their 'verification'.[48] Necessary statements are unfailingly true, and 'they do not convey any differential information'.[49] They are 'empty commands that make *no* demands upon their recipients'.[50] In fact they are 'dummy assertions' used as 'surrogates for rules, formulae resembling (and yet, also not resembling) contingent statements, that serve the purpose of simplifying the patterns of valid inference'.[51] Similarly, a statement of a law of nature is not to be construed as a proper statement, significant and descriptive of reality. A law is believed to be necessary in so far as it is certainly true in every case. Its negation is not only 'false', but 'impossible'. An example of a mathematical proposition may serve to elucidate the matter further. The proposition, for example, '2 + 2 = 4', according to Wittgenstein, talks about the concept of adding 2 and 2 and that of 4. The concepts are internally related, and in our conceptual scheme we do not use the concept of '2 + 2' in a way that licenses us to say that it is *not* 4. To deny a tautology, in other words, is to reject our system of thought and expression, and this rejection is, at times, loosely called an absurdity. A tautology and its negation do not belong to the same system, while an empirical statement and its negation may both do. Hence a tautology cannot be considered true or false in the sense in which an empirical statement is true or false. The statement '2 + 2 ≠ 4' has no place in our arithmetic; for it would falsify the inferences permissible in our arithmetical system. Hence it is not a proposition in our arithmetic. It is indeed true that a necessary statement and an empirical statement look alike in form. Yet they are significantly different. An empirical statement, e.g. 'This table is round in shape' is about a particular object, and it is true or false depending on its correspondence or non-correspondence with reality. But what is the statement '2 + 2 = 4' about? Is it a statement about numbers? Wittgenstein points out that even if in common sense it is regarded as a statement about numbers, it is not a statement in the same sense in which the first statement is a statement about a particular object. Baker and Hacker observe:

> ... He [Wittgenstein] suggested that we are again misled by the superficial analogies of form. Statements about lions tell us facts about lions, but what we call 'statements about numbers' have the role of rules for the use of number-words or numerals.[52]

Similarly, the statement '2 + 2 = 4' tells us about the way of using numbers just as the statement 'All bachelors are unmarried' is a rule for the use of the word 'bachelor'. The modality of a necessary statement is the indication of the norm of expression. They are metalinguistic statements; 'they fix concepts'.[53] A necessary statement, like 'All bachelors are unmarried', or, '2 + 2 = 4', expresses an internal relation between concepts which are used to describe truths about the world. Empirical statements are descriptive; necessary statements, on the other hand, are rules that describe no empirical or trans-empirical reality. The rules serve as our guides for the application of concepts, while empirical statements are applications. A rule is, so to say, a 'part of the apparatus of language, not uses of the apparatus'.[54] Similarly Black says:

> The distinctive use of the rules of language is to inculcate, reinforce and preserve the meaning of statements in that language.[55]

A rule simply allows us to pass from one statement to another; it is a permission and not a statement, just as the rule in the game of chess permits us to move pieces, but is not itself identical with any of the pieces. Since necessary statements indicate a relation between concepts, Wittgenstein believes that they permit us to pass from one concept to another. This relation seems to be a necessary, unfailing, one, but its modality 'corresponds to the inexorability of our attitude towards our techniques of representation'.[56] Necessary statements do not set any boundary for empirical possibilities; for they are said to lie at the limits of experience, being the norms of representation that form the scope of speaking sense. 'They [the rules] fence us in only from the void'.[57] The rules are the norms of representation delimiting the description of reality. Any description not conforming to the norms is not simply false, it is nonsense.

Whatever is said of logical, mathematical, or metaphysical necessity may be extended unaltered to natural necessity. A law of nature differs radically from an ordinary empirical statement. It is no description of the world. It may be viewed as a norm of representation or an expression of an internal conceptual relation. It stands as a rule to use one concept in such a way that every time we use this concept we have the license to use or infer another concept. In other words, nowhere the former concept may be used without also signifying the latter. For Wittgenstein, 'Necessities in the world are merely shadows cast on the world by grammar'.[58] The reduction of natural necessity to conceptual necessity leads to the rejection of the theory of unknown necessity. If necessity is a rule of use, it is inappropriate to imagine that someone uses a rule without being aware of it. Anyone who uses the rule must know the rule and use it consciously.

Wittgenstein has no doubt paved a new path in the history of philosophical thought by rightly enunciating the difference between an ordinary descriptive statement and a law-statement. But in his enthusiasm to distinguish a law from a contingent statement, Wittgenstein has committed the fallacy of 'putting the cart before the horse'. A few legitimate questions may be asked at this point: How are the concepts formed? Why has a particular concept an internal or inseparable relation to some specific concept, but not to others? In fact, concepts are not formed arbitrarily. In the process of forming concepts to describe the reality, we are guided by our experience of the objective world. We form the concept of 'man', for example, initially with some ideas as to man's general physical traits. The progress of knowledge gradually reveals a relation between manness and mortality for which the concept of 'man' and that of 'mortal' are considered to have an intimate relation so that in every case the concept of 'man' is used, there is a license to infer mortality. However, there is no such license available justifying the inference from the concept of a man to the colour of his eyes.

Besides, the doctrine that there can be no unknown law of nature is too strong a view to be rationally accepted. The analogy between the world-show and the game of chess need not be pressed too far. The game of chess has a specific arena, and one cannot play the game unless one is well conversant with the rules of the game. The scenario is quite different in the case of natural science. History shows that human knowledge is in constant progress, and that many truths, previously unknown, have been revealed through great efforts. The progress of knowledge often replenishes the old conceptual scheme. Instead of taking objective necessity as the result of grammar or conceptual scheme, it is plausible to take grammar and linguistic conventions as reflections of the connections in objective reality. Further, the laws of nature bear a close resemblance to the ways of using the language. The natural laws play an important part in our forming the conventions related to the meanings of words. However, as has been rightly pointed out by Musgrave, the laws of nature are not about 'linguistic items':

> ... the law of inertia does not talk about *linguistic items*, and contains no names of *linguistic* entities. Statements of (putative) laws of nature do of course *use* words, but they do not *mention* them.[59]

Musgrave believes that Wittgenstein in his *Tractatus* was not aware of the use-mention distinction, and all the problems of the Wittgensteinian theory, according to Musgrave, arise because of this non-discrimination. Further, the facets of resemblance between map-making and laws do not prove that the laws of nature are laws about our ways of representing nature, or that the laws 'do not govern the way we experience the world, but the way we talk about it'.[60]

7.2.3 Schlick's theory of natural laws

In his *Philosophy of Nature* Schlick writes:

> ...The function of laws (the meaning of laws) is to *de*-scribe and not to *pre*-scribe. They relate what actually occurs, and not what ought to occur. And when necessity is ascribed to the laws of nature, this means that they are *universally valid*, and not that they exert force.[61]

Do the lines quoted above indicate that Schlick has at one time held a descriptive theory of laws of nature? Hacking observes that natural laws are, for Schlick, 'accounts of regularities only'.[62]

Elsewhere Schlick himself explains how a law of nature is to be treated functionally. In an essay entitled 'Causality in Everyday Life', he writes:

> It is the object of science to discover Order in the world. This is done by finding and formulating Laws of Nature.[63]

In 'Causality in Contemporary Physics', Schlick refers to the relation between causality and laws of nature. The principle of causality, according to him, states that every natural event is subject to a certain law of nature. A law of nature indicates, for him, a sort of causal relation; he says, 'causality is just another word for the existence of a law'.[64] He emphasizes that natural laws do not involve *force* or *compulsion* in the sense that the laws of a country involve force or compulsion. A law of nature does not compel nature to behave in a definite manner in the way that a law of a country imposes restriction upon the citizens to follow a certain behaviour-pattern. He writes:

> ...Laws of nature do not *pre*-scribe a certain order *to* the world, but simply *de*-scribe the order *of* the world; they do not command what must happen, but simply formulate what does happen. The 'necessity' which we attribute to them must not be misunderstood as a kind of compulsion (this term would imply the possibility of 'obedience' and 'disobedience'), but it means only that there is *no exception* to the laws, that they hold in all cases.[65]

Schlick agrees with Hume that there is no objective necessity involved in the laws of nature. Further, for both of them, laws represent only regularities of event-patterns in nature. Schlick thinks that the necessity ascribed to natural laws is a misnomer on account of the misleading term 'law'. The term 'law' is borrowed from its usage in human society. The usage signifies a command of the ruler who wishes to compel and control the behaviour of his subjects. By the necessity of the concept of causality and that of natural laws we are to understand only *regularity* (as opposed to lawlessness) and *universal validity.*

But if Hacking is right, is Kneale then justified in offering Schlick's view as an alternative to the regularity view? Shortly passages from Schlick will be cited to show that he is no mere supporter of the regularity view of natural laws. It will be seen that Kneale has rightly understood Schlick and accredited him with what he calls a prescription theory of natural laws.

Schlick's view, Kneale points out, is anchored on the foundational theory peculiar to the early version of logical positivism. The burden of the prescription theory is the criterion of meaning adopted by Schlick equally with other contemporary positivists. This criterion is the litmus paper used for testing whether a statement (or, if one prefers to say, a sentence) has significance or not. Laws of nature and metaphysical statements fail in this test. Schlick's view is explained below.

7.2.3.1 Schlick's criterion of meaning

Schlick believes that the meaning of a sentence is to be found in the *rules of its proper usage.* In his famous essay entitled 'Meaning and Verification' he elaborates this concept of meaning:

> ... whenever we ask about a sentence 'What does it mean?' what we expect is instruction as to the circumstances in which the sentence is to be used...
>
> Stating the meaning of a sentence amounts to stating the rules according to which the sentence is to be used and this is the same as stating the way in which it can be verified (or falsified). The meaning of a proposition is the method of its verification.[66]

According to Schlick - who, by the by, is not fastidious about distinguishing between a sentence and a proposition,- a meaningful sentence need not be actually verified to prove its significance. All that is required for a sentence to be meaningful is its *verifiability*. If the significance of a sentence consists in its actual verification, all sentences speaking about the future would cease to have any meaning, because the things referred to by them are not actual objects of experience. Here arises an absurdity. A sentence would then remain meaningless before its actual verification, and meaning would come to adorn it as soon as it is actually verified. Hence, not *actual verification*, but *verifiability*, is the criterion of meaning.

Certain sentences, again, may not be verifiable owing to the dearth of apposite techniques. But that is not the ground for calling them 'meaningless'. A sentence is meaningless only if it is logically impossible to verify it, that is, if the process of its verification leads to the violation of any fundamental rule of logic. Verifiability, therefore, is to be understood as the *logical possibility of verification*[67] which differs from the *empirical* possibility of verification. Empirical possibility, Schlick says, 'is determined by the laws of nature but meaning and verifiability are entirely independent of them'.[68] Schlick cites the example of a false proposition: 'River flows uphill'. According to him, this is a meaningful sentence even though it stands opposed to the actual state of affairs in nature. The state of affairs described by this sentence is not empirically possible. Schlick considers it a matter of 'tremendous philosophical importance'[69] that logical possibility or impossibility of verification is always *self-imposed*. He seeks to clarify this point in the following passage:

> The possibility of verification does not rest on any experiential truth, or a law or any other true general proposition, but is determined solely by our definitions, by the rules which have been fixed for our language, or which we can fix arbitrarily at any moment... . No rule of expression presupposes any law or regularity in the world... . The rules of language are rules of application of language; so there must be something to which it can be applied.[70]

Ayer observes that the verifiability criterion, if taken in a 'strong sense',[71] would lead to an extreme position. To follow the criterion strictly, a proposition is verifiable if its truth (or falsity) is conclusively established by experience. Evidently no general proposition can satisfy this requirement. A general proposition has an infinite scope of application, since it has infinite spatio-temporal points of reference. It ranges over the actual and the possible with equal force. No experience can cover the future empirically or logically. An individual future fact or event may be verified only 'by waiting for it to happen'.[72] But no experience can ever exhaust all the future individual cases. The 'waiting' goes on and on. For this reason, no universal proposition which ranges over an infinite number of future cases is completely verified. Consequently, all general propositions being in principle non-verifiable, the sentences expressing them cease to be meaningful. They are nonsense, though Schlick regards them as '*important nonsense*'. Laws of nature or general propositions, that is, propositions with 'universal validity', like metaphysical statements, are, according to this position, supposed to have only an *emotive value*. They set forth instructions for the formation of actual propositions which carry truth-values.

7.2.3.2 Schlick's view as to natural laws

Speaking about a natural law, Schlick says:

> ...If there is *in principle* no possibility of testing it, and the proposition is therefore compatible with any possible experience, it must be vacuous, and can contain no knowledge of nature. If, on assuming the proposition to be false, there were to be anything in the experienceable world that differed from when the proposition was true, then it could indeed be tested; hence untestability by experience means that the appearance of the world is wholly independent of the proposition's truth or falsity, so that it says nothing at all about the world.[73]

Schlick in 'Causality in Contemporary Physics' refers to two senses in which an expression may be vacuous: (i) an expression is considered to be vacuous when it is empty, or (ii) it is vacuous if logically it is not a proposition at all. Now, in which sense can one take the laws of nature to be meaningless? Are they mere tautologies? They are not. Natural sciences are not interested in anything that is in no way connected with the world. Schlick is aware of this fact; for he writes himself: 'Science has essentially no interest in a tautological proposition'.[74] But if a law of nature is not a tautology, what actually is the status of such a law? Can a prescriptionist ignore the fact that such sentences are widely used in our ordinary as well as scientific discourse? No philosophy which moves away from the common sense interpretation of the world and deviates from the normal usage of words can be sustained in the long run. The task of a philosopher is not to reject the natural world and the language of common people, but to interpret them in the light of truth and accuracy. Thus Schlick was psychologically impelled to grant some sort of status to the laws, even though they do not satisfy his criterion of meaning. If they cannot be regarded as propositions and do not indicate the facts of the world, what then are they? Schlick thinks that they are *instructions* by following which the facts of the world may be discovered and described. It is interesting to note here that even if an expression is not technically a genuine proposition, Schlick does not reject it on that ground as 'a meaningless, incoherent string of words'. He states this clearly :

> ...We have to remember, however, that there are strings of words, which are not statements and convey no state-of-affairs, and yet fulfill extraordinary significant functions in life: the so-called *question* and *imperative* utterances.[75]

As Schlick cannot speak of *complete verification* of natural laws, sentences expressing natural laws are not significant sentences upon his theory of meaning. He remarks:

> ...at bottom a natural law does not essentially possess the logical character of an 'assertion', but rather a 'prescription for the making of assertions'. (I owe this idea and terminology to Ludwig Wittgenstein.).... As we know, it is possible to test only the individual statements that are derived from a law of nature.[76]

7.3 Kneale's Criticism of Logical Positivism: A Critique of Schlick

Kneale's chief objective is to bring to light certain difficulties or defects of the prescription theory of natural laws. These are as follows:

7.3.1 Inadequacy of the verification criterion

Both Kneale and the prescriptionists agree that the statements of laws of nature are not analytic. According to the prescription theory, if a statement is not analytic, then it may be regarded as a true or false (and hence a proper) statement or proposition about a matter of fact, provided it is susceptible of complete verification. In this sense all particular propositions are propositions proper; for the question as to their truth or falsehood is empirically settled. Besides the particular propositions, propositions of restricted generality which begin with the quantifier 'all' may also be taken as true or false phenomenologically. This, however, does not mean that at least some general propositions, being completely verifiable, are significant. A proposition of restricted generality is an abridged form of conjunction comprised of several particular propositions as its components. And each of the constituent conjuncts is individually verifiable. A law of nature is essentially different from such a proposition. A law is a statement of unrestricted generality. It is, for that reason, non-verifiable in principle. No universal statement with unrestricted generality, therefore, may be at the same time contingent (i.e. not analytic) and significant.

Kneale's rejection of the prescription theory begins with the rejection of the criterion of meaning which reduces the laws to nonsense. He considers it 'somewhat high-handed'[77] to adopt a theory of meaning which compels us to sacrifice a large part of our ordinary language. We are facing a dilemma here. Either one has to accept Schlick's criterion of meaning and consequently reject a large part of our ordinary language as non-significant and be content with a rather restrictive language-system (as proposed by Carnap in 'Testability and Meaning'). Or, one would retain the glory of common language, thereby sacrificing the early positivists' criterion of meaning. Kneale opts for the second.

Is Kneale's decision irrational at all? It does not seem so. Reasons may be offered to support Kneale's decision. First of all, there is no plausible reason offered by the prescriptionist to accept a somewhat artificial, empirically restricted language-system at the cost of the significance of general propositions which are perfectly understood and interpreted for all practical purposes both ordinarily and in scientific enterprise. It is idiosyncratic on the part of the prescriptionist 'to say that sentences which are commonly treated in all respects as though they were statements cannot be such because they do not satisfy the test of being verifiable in experience...'.[78]

Besides, the criterion of meaning proposed by the early logical positivists is not generally accepted. The weakness of this criterion has been recognized even by scholars sympathetic to the basic tenets of logical positivism. The problems inherent in the criterion have led to several attempts to modify it. This amply proves that Kneale is not, after all, overbearing in rejecting the positivists' criterion of meaning. And if this criterion may be rejected without any violence to the fundamental rules of logic, then there is no compulsion to adhere to it.

It would be interesting to take note of Popper's criticism of the verification criterion here. As shown earlier, Popper's view of natural laws differs widely from Kneale's, yet he agrees with Kneale in rejecting the verification criterion of meaning as unsatisfactory. The criterion, Popper shows, not only fails to exclude metaphysical statements as intended by the logical positivists, but also excludes what Popper calls 'the most important and interesting of all scientific statements', i.e. 'the universal laws of nature'.[79]

7.3.2 Some further unhappy consequences of the verification criterion

Kneale points out another strange consequence of the criterion of complete verifiability. Following the square of opposition, it may be said that the denial of a particular proposition ('I' or 'O') is equivalent to an assertion of a universal proposition ('E' or 'A') and that the denial of a universal proposition ('A' or 'E') is equivalent to an affirmation of a particular proposition ('O' or 'I'). Logically the following equivalences hold:

1. $(x)[\phi x] \equiv \sim(\exists x)[\sim \phi x]$, i.e. $A \equiv \sim O$.
2. $(x)[\sim \phi x] \equiv \sim(\exists x)[\phi x]$, i.e. $E \equiv \sim I$.
3. $(\exists x)[\phi x] \equiv \sim(x)[\sim \phi x]$, i.e. $I \equiv \sim E$.
4. $(\exists x)[\sim \phi x] \equiv \sim(x)[\phi x]$, i.e. $O \equiv \sim A$.

Evidently, a particular statement is significant, according to the logical positivists' criterion of meaning. Now, if a sentence is significant, its denial also must be significant. The original statement and its denial are both possessed of truth-values, and for that reason, both are to be regarded as statements or propositions in the strict sense of the term.

Kneale explicates the point in this way. Any proposition of the form of 'A' is logically equivalent to the negation of 'O'-form, according to the logical rule of contradiction. To assert 'All αs are β' is to deny that there exists an α, which is not β. Now, if the proposition 'All αs are β' is a law of nature, it is neither analytic, nor is it a summation of particular propositions. Further it is not completely verifiable by experience. Hence it is devoid of any meaning or truth-value, and the same is expected to be the status of its contradictory. But the contradictory here speaks of an empirical fact and is therefore both contingent and significant. Here arises the anomaly. Logically when a contingent proposition is true, its negation must be false, and vice versa. But to assign a truth-value to an expression is to accept it as a proposition. According to Kneale, it is *strange* to say that a contingent proposition 'has no significant negation'.[80]

In a paper entitled 'Problems and Changes in the Empiricist Criterion of Meaning' published in 1950, Hempel endorses Kneale's point. Hempel finds the verifiability requirement 'overtly restrictive'. The law-statements form an integral part of science, and they cannot be rejected as nonsensical simply because they are not 'conclusively verified by any set of observational data'.[81] The following paragraph from Hempel will serve to highlight the similarity between Kneale and Hempel on this point:

> ...Let 'P' be an observation predicate. Then the purely existential sentence '$(\exists x)P(x)$' ... is completely verifiable, for it follows from any observation sentence asserting of some particular object that it has the property P. But its denial, being equivalent to a universal sentence '$(x) \sim P(x)$' ... is clearly not completely verifiable.... Hence... the denials of certain empirically–and thus cognitively–significant sentences are empirically meaningless; and as they are neither analytic nor contradictory they are cognitively meaningless. But however we may delimit the domain of significant discourse, we shall have to insist that if a sentence falls within that domain, then so must its denial.[82]

The import of this passage is clear enough. Hempel has pointed out some other unhappy consequences of the complete verification criterion. It may be as well to recall them here. The criterion of complete verifiability disqualifies such important sentences as 'For any substance, there exists some solvent' (containing a universal and an existential quantifier) on account of the fact that such sentences are not logically deducible from any 'finite set of observation sentences'.

Again, Hempel considers a sentence S which is meaningful according to Schlick's criterion and another sentence N which has no significance on that criterion. Logically then, as one of the disjuncts S, is considered to be meaningful, the disjunction S v N is to be considered meaningful, although its other component is meaningless. Thus Hempel finds the complete verifiability criterion 'too inclusive', because the 'empiricist criterion of meaning is not intended to countenance sentences of this sort'.[83]

7.3.3 Kneale's other criticisms

Kneale draws our attention to another important point. He considers the following sentence: 'Any Dodo has a white feather in its tail'. Even if the expression is not to be regarded as a proposition proper according to the verification principle, but as a prescription, it is still to be regarded as a prescription with a universal scope: 'Whenever you find a dodo assume that it has a white feather in its tail'.[84] In what way, then, is the initial problem besetting a general proposition avoided by the prescriptive analysis? If, according to the principle of the early logical positivists, a general proposition, as it is commonly called, ceases to be a proposition proper, for a similar reason a prescription which is universal in scope cannot be allowed. A prescriptionist would be unfaithful to his own principle if he resolves to apply a prescription omnitemporally and omnispatially. Such a prescription virtually amounts to a law 'which the prescription is intended to replace'. For to say that we make a general rule of this kind for the guidance of our expectations 'is to state a law, that is, a proposition of unrestricted universality, about human behaviour'.[85]

The prescriptionist may here make a merely modest claim in order to get rid of the difficulty which has been mentioned. He may say that he is not making a statement of unrestricted universality about human behaviour, but only a statement about the behaviour of those scientists whose methods of procedure he has studied. Those scientists - he may say - have in fact behaved, while formulating natural laws, in such a way as to suggest that they are making rules for the guidance of their own expectations. But even this modest claim is, according to Kneale, inadmissible. He says that, in formulating a law of nature, scientists not only think that they can make predictions about unobserved matters of fact from observed matters of fact, but also that they can assert unfulfilled hypothetical statements which are implied by the law. This counterfactual import of the law can by no means be explained in terms of rules to expect something. He writes:

> ...If the sentence which purports to formulate a law gives only a general rule, what is derived from it can be no more than a command or injunction. It is absurd, however, to treat an unfulfilled hypothetical statement as an injunction to expect something. I can, of course, advise someone to believe that if a certain thing had been α it would have been β, but then I assume that it is possible to believe in an unfulfilled hypothetical proposition, i.e. something which is not a mere matter of fact.[86]

C. D. Broad in his critical review of Kneale's *Probability and Induction* has endorsed the latter's rejection of the prescription theory. His reasons for doing so are as follows.[87]

A prescription can be either a command or an admonition. A law of nature cannot be a command. A command always refers to an authority who issues it, and there is some fixed punitive measure in case a command is violated. In the case of a law of nature, however, none of these are found, nor is any such question ever asked. Can one, then, regard the law as an admonition? In that case one is justified in asking questions regarding the advantages of complying with a law and the disadvantages faced in its violation. However, no satisfactory answer may be provided on this matter. If effective prediction is mentioned as an advantage of obeying the prescription of laws, then, Broad thinks, one is 'enunciating a law of nature in a non-prescriptive sense'.[88] Prediction is possible, provided the present and the future are bound by laws, and such binding is not an accidental one. The question arises: Is a law considered to be a prescription simply because it is a pattern of behaviour followed so far by the scientists? Or, is it enunciated in a non-prescriptive sense as referring to the behavior of a certain class of human beings? Broad says:

> ...whichever answer is given to this question, one can then ask: 'What is the relevance of your answer to the question, why I should follow your advice in this matter?' To put it shortly, is there any reasonable ground for following the advice to act as if S were P whenever you meet an instance of S except that there is reason to believe that 'All S is P' is a law of nature in a non-prescriptive sense?[89]

In a paper entitled 'Rules and Commands' (in *Mind)* van Loon presents a distinction between rules and commands which is worth referring to here.[90]

7.4 An Examination of Kneale's Criticism of the Prescription Theory

Toulmin finds some flaws in Kneale's criticism of the prescription theory. He fastens upon the following observation made by Kneale (as occurring in a passage quoted before):

> If the sentence which purports to formulate a law gives only a general rule, what is derived from it can be no more than a command or injunction.

Toulmin thinks that Kneale intends to make two points:

1. A law, taken as a command, is a generalized command.
2. Only a command may be derived from a command.

Toulmin's criticism of Kneale covers both these points. He (the former) points out that both Ramsey and Schlick 'use unduly imperatival words such as "instructions", "directions", and "rules" instead of some rather less exciting word such as "principles" '[91]. The reason for this choice of vocabulary on their part, Toulmin believes, is their overemphasis on the practical aspect of laws. Kneale's objections would lose all their force, Toulmin contends, if Schlick's words were not taken 'too strictly'. He says:

> ... Schlick and Ramsey are not claiming that laws of nature are generalized commands; the point of describing laws of nature in their way is to remind us of their use as inference-licenses entitling us to argue from known facts about a situation to the phenomena we may expect in that situation;....[92]

Toulmin's contention is, however, far from satisfactory. A general sentence, e.g. 'All P is Q', according to Schlick and others, means that 'P' is the license-ticket for inferring 'Q'. The only role of such a statement in our life is the instruction it imparts in connection with the application of our knowledge. But is it not the case that once such a license is permitted, the license remains valid for all Ps - observed or unobserved? In other words, are we not justified in interpreting 'All P is Q' as a command which is effective for all times? Certainly it would be an assault to our vocabulary (in ordinary as well as scientific discourse) to deprive laws of their universal character. Toulmin's point rather strengthens Kneale's view.

Besides, if a command, 'C', is not imperative for all times, then there must be some circumstance 'R' in which 'C' becomes obligatory. This is to tacitly presume, however, a general law behind its effectiveness - namely, the law that 'Whenever one finds "R", one is justified in taking "C" as a command or injunction'. Thus Toulmin is led into the very situation he sought to avoid.

Further, to contend that an injunction is not what is derived from a law, but is identical with it, is to misrepresent the nature of both a law and a prescription equally. The law 'All P is Q' speaks of a relation between P and Q, and this relation is the justification behind the injunction to infer 'Q' from 'P'. Without the law, the command becomes a baseless one.

Toulmin's second point is trivial. He urges:

> ...It is only if one takes Schlick's phrase 'rules of behavior' too seriously that Kneale's objection carries weight.[93]

But if Schlick never intends to use his terminology quite 'seriously', then, surely, he is guilty of speaking loosely, and his view is not worthy of philosophical discussion.

Attention may be drawn to another point in Toulmin's criticism. Toulmin retorts that a valid syllogistic conclusion is 'loosely speaking'[94] derived from the principles of syllogism; but it does not mean that the syllogistic conclusion itself is always a rule or a principle. The phrase 'derived from the principle' hides a distinction between a conclusion deduced *from* the principle and a conclusion derived *in accordance with* the principle. Toulmin agrees that Schlick's thesis appears to project a separation between the natural laws and the world. But this is just an appearance. A physicist forms his laws to speak about the world in a precise and accurate manner. In Toulmin's words:

> ...the fact that some inferences rather than others come to be licensed usually tells us much more about the world than about the physicist and his methods.[95]

The link between the law and the world is sought to be preserved by Toulmin by treating the scientific law statements about the world not as statements derived *from* the principle, but as statements derived *in accordance with* the principle. On this interpretation, it is not necessary that what is derived from an injunction has to be another injunction. The rules provide guidelines for obtaining empirical propositions. Correctly speaking, the rules are *applied* to get significant propositions about the world.

The supporters of the prescription theory are not totally unaware of the problem that arises if a law is taken as entirely separated from the world. If a term in a theory does not correspond to any fact in the observable world, then such a term is taken as a variable, and correspondingly the expression containing such a term is not a proposition proper, but a proposition-form. Ramsey has sought to show a formal device for deducing a proposition from a proposition-form. The device consists in interpolating an existential quantifier before the proposition-form. Comments on this will be made soon.

Nagel refers to William Craig's attempt[96] to retain the empirical content of any natural language L in an artificial language L^P where there occurs no theoretical term. Nagel believes that even though such a language may be formally constructed, Craig's method would be so cumbersome that no effective logical use may be made of it. The same charge of artificiality may be brought against Ramsey and all others aiming at any such formal deduction. Even if a logical language may be devised to fulfil the prescriptive criterion of meaning, such a language would be a purely arbitrary one. Kneale's argument against the prescription theory is: if a theory is viewed as a command, then it can entail no statement about facts of observation. Nagel does not reject it as baseless. Nagel tries to work out the inherent reasons of Kneale as in the following manner:

> ...The claim is obviously sound if a theory is construed to be a leading principle, since a rule of inference is not a premise in factual inquiries and is not the sort of thing of which one can say that it entails factual conclusions. The claim is also sound if it is understood to assert that, even if a theory is used

> as premise, no instantial conclusions follow from the theory alone, but only when appropriate rules of correspondence are supplied for the theory and when suitable statements of initial conditions are added as premises. On the other hand, the claim is plainly mistaken if it maintains that no statements about matters of observable fact are implied by a theory even when this proviso is satisfied. For such a contention is contradicted every time a theory is used...[97].

Ramsey's device to add an existential quantifier before a statement-form obviously functions through the introduction of empirical data to an injunction to obtain a real statement from the statement-form. Kneale has never said that actual statements are not obtainable from an injunction; he only intends to emphasize the impossibility of deriving a statement about reality from an injunction *alone.*

It may be remarked here that an application of a law to the actual world is possible, provided the law says something about the world. Behind every application there is some assertion. For example, in case one wishes to follow the ethical rules of the society and practises non-violence or abstains from stealing, one has to be aware of an ethical rule descriptive of an ideal and accept it (voluntarily or involuntarily) as a standard of behaviour. For example, one must know and accept non-violence as a principle of life for some reason whatever. Since the laws of natural sciences are applied in order to achieve practical success, the laws must be understood to describe objective connections amongst natural phenomena. Schlick's view, or positivism in general, is unable to represent the true nature of natural laws.

The literature of logical positivism has witnessed a journey from sentences to systems. Empirical meaningfulness also traverses the path from verification via confirmation to expressibility in principle in an empiricist language. However, the endeavour of the logical positivists - their search for a proper language of philosophy and science - has never been successful. In the absence of any final solution available within the scheme of the prescription theory, we are compelled to reject the theory and the logical consequences issuing from it.

NOTES

1 E. MacKinnon, 'Epistemological Problems in the Philosophy of Science', *The Review of Metaphysics*, vol. 22, 1968, pp. 113f.

2 C. Hempel, *Aspects of Scientific Explanation and Other Essays in the Philosophy of Science*, New York, 1965, p. 488.

3 B. van Fraassen, *The Scientific Image*, Clarendon Press, Oxford, 1980, p. 51.

4 Nancy Cartwright, *How the Laws of Physics Lie* ? Clarendon Press, Oxford, 1983.

5 Kneale, *Probability and Induction*, 1966, p. 76. [Italics added]

6 *Ibidem.*

7 Moritz Schlick says: '... at bottom a natural law does not essentially possess the Logical character of an "assertion", but rather a 'prescription for the making of assertions' (I owe this idea and terminology to Ludwig Wittgenstein.).' See his 'Causality in Contemporary Physics' ('Die Kausalitat in der gegenwartigen Physik') in *Die Naturewissenschaften*, 19, 1931, trans. Peter Heath, in H. Mulder and Barbara F.B. van de Velde-Schlick, eds., *Philosophical Papers*, vol. 2, D. Reidel Publishing Company, Dodrecht, Holland, 1979, p. 188.

8 F. P. Ramsey, *Philosophical Papers*, D. H. Mellor, ed. Cambridge University Press, Cambridge, 1990, p. 163.

9 *Ibid.*, p. 146.

10 *Ibidem.*

11 *Ibid.*, p. 145.

12 *Ibidem.*

13 *Ibidem.*

14 *Ibid.*, p. 146.

15 *Ibid.*, p. 145.

16 *Ibid.*, p. 146.

17 *Ibid.*, p. 149.
18 *Ibid.*, p. 150.
19 *Ibid.*, p. 146.
20 *Ibid.*, pp.147f.
21 *Ibid.*, p. 149.
22 *Ibidem.*
23 *Ibid.*, p. 159.
24 *Cf.* Armstrong and others.
25 G. P. Baker, and P. M. S. Hacker, *Wittgenstein: Rules, Grammar and Necessity–An Analytic Commentary on the 'Philosophical Investigations*', vol. 2, Basil Blackwell, Oxford, 1985, preface, p. X.
26 G. E. Moore, 'Wittgenstein's Lectures in 1930–1933', (1955, reprinted) in R. R. Ammerman, ed. *Classics of Analytic Philosophy*, Tata McGraw-Hill Publishing Ltd, India, 1965, p. 234-284.
27 L. Wittgenstein, *Tractatus Logico-Philosophicus*, Routledge and Keegan Paul, London, 1958, no. 4.01, p. 63.
28 Moore, *op. cit.*, p. 242.
29 R. Carnap, 'Testability and Meaning', *Philosophy of Science,* vols. 2 & 3, 1936–1937, reprinted in Ammerman, *op. cit.*, p. 178.
30 Moore, *op. cit.*, p. 244.
31 A valuable discussion on this point is available in P. M. S. Hacker's *Wittgenstein's Place in Twentieth-Century Analytic Philosophy,* Blackwell Publishers Ltd, Oxford, 1996, pp. 50-59.
32 Moore, *op. cit.*, p. 249.
33 Wittgenstein, *op. cit.*, nos. 5.132, 5.135, 5.136, 5.136-I, p. 109.
34 *Ibid.*, no. 5.142, p. 111.
35 *Ibid.*, no. 4. 462, p. 99.
36 *Ibid.*, nos. 6. 37, 6. 371, p. 181.
37 *Ibid.*, no. 6. 342, p. 177.
38 D. Gillies, *Philosophy of Science in the Twentieth Century: Four Central Themes*, Blackwell, Oxford, 1993, p. 166.
39 Hacker, *op. cit.*, p. 56.
40 *Ibid.*, p. 57.
41 *Ibid.*, p. 59.
42 Baker and Hacker, *op. cit.*, p. 47.
43 *Ibidem.*
44 Hacker, *op. cit.*, p. 127.

45 M. Black, 'Necessary Statements and Rules', *Philosophical Review*, 1958, reprinted in H. Feigl, W. Sellars & P. Lehrer, eds. *New Readings in Philosophical Analysis*, Appleton Century Crofts, New York, 1972, p. 154.

46 *Ibidem.*

47 *Ibidem.*

48 *Ibid.*, p. 143.

49 *Ibid.*, p. 154.

50 *Ibidem.*

51 *Ibid.*, p. 155.

52 Baker and Hacker, *op. cit.*, p. 281.

53 *Ibid.*, p. 269.

54 *Ibid.*, p. 283.

55 Black, *op. cit.*, p. 150.

56 Baker and Hacker, *op. cit.*, p. 269.

57 *Ibid* , p. 271.

58 *Ibid.*, p. 192.

59 A. Musgrave, 'Wittgensteinian Instrumentalism', *Theoria*, vol. 2-3, 1980, p. 67.

60 *Ibid.*, p. 70.

61 M. Schlick, *Philosophy of Nature*, Philosophical Library, New York, 1949, p. 20. [Italics added]

62 Hacking, *op. cit.*, p. 48.

63 M. Schlick, 'Causality in Everyday Life and in Recent Science', *University of California Publications in Philosophy*, vol. XV, Berkeley, California, 1932, reprinted in H. Mulder and Barbara F.B. van de Velde-Schlick, eds. *Moritz Schlick: Philosophical Papers*, vol. 2, D. Reidel Publishing Co., Dodrecht: Holland, p. 188.

64 M. Schlick, 'Causality in Contemporary Physics', in H. Mulder and Barbara F. B. van de Velde-Schlick, eds. *Moritz Schlick: Philosophical Papers*, p. 177.

65 *Ibid.*, pp. 246 - 247.

66 M. Schlick, 'Meaning and Verification', in H. Feigl and W. Sellars, eds. *Readings in Philosophical Analysis*, New York, Appleton Century Crofts, 1949, p. 30.

67 *Ibid.*, p. 36.

68 *Ibid.*, p. 37.

69 *Ibidem.*

70 *Ibid.*, p. 39.

71 A. J. Ayer, 'The Elimination of Metaphysics', *Language, Truth and Logic*, Victor Gollancz Ltd., London, 1967, p.10.

72 'Waiting is a perfectly legitimate method of verification' - Schlick, 'Meaning and Verification', in H. Feigl and W. Sellars, eds. *Readings in Philosophical Analysis*, p. 34.

73 Schlick, 'Causality in Contemporary Physics', *op. cit.*, pp. 192 - 193.

74 *Ibid.*, p. 193.

75 *Ibid.*, p. 193.

76 *Ibid.*, p. 188.

77 Kneale, *op. cit.*, p. 76.

78 *Ibidem.*

79 K. R. Popper, *Conjectures and Refutations. The Growth of Scientific Knowledge*, Routledge & Kegan Paul, 1963, p. 281.

80 Kneale, *op. cit.*, p. 74.

81 C. Hempel, 'Problems and Changes in the Empiricist Criterion of Meaning', (1950, reprinted) in Ammerman, *op. cit.*, p. 218.

82 *Ibid.*, 218 f.

83 *Ibid.*, p. 218.

84 Kneale, *op. cit.*, p. 77.

85 *Ibidem.*

86 *Ibidem.*

87 See C. D. Broad's CRITICAL NOTICE of Kneale's 'Probability and Induction', *Mind*, vol. 59, 1950, pp. 94 - 115.

88 *Ibid.*, p. 113.

89 *Ibid.*, pp. 113f.

90 J. F. G. van Loon, 'Rules and Commands', *Mind*, vol. 61, 1952, pp. 514 - 521.

91 S. Toulmin, *Philosophy of Science: An Introduction*, Hutchinson University Library, London, 1955, p.101.

92 *Ibid.*, pp. 101f.

93 *Ibid.*, p. 102.

94 *Ibidem.*

95 *Ibid.*, pp. 102f.

96 E. Nagel, *The Structure of Science: Problems in the Logic of Scientific Explanations*, Macmillan India Ltd, New Delhi, 1979, pp. 134 - 137.

97 *Ibid.*, p. 140.

CHAPTER EIGHT

SOME VERSIONS OF 'INSTRUMENTALISM' EXAMINED (Some Additional Discussion)

8.1 Foreword

About natural laws, or rather scientific theories, there are some views which need to be considered. [The differences between laws and theories may be ignored for purposes of the present discussion] Now these views (to be mentioned shortly) are not considered specifically by Kneale, but they are no less important than Schlick's prescription theory. It is customary to subsume these views under the general heading of 'instrumentalism'. According to instrumentalism, natural laws are not descriptive but tools to systematize our empirical knowledge of the natural world or essentially rules of inference or instructions for finding true statements.

An instrumentalist emphasizes the utility of a scientific theory. Such theories are said to be important only if 'they serve as guides for all actions undertaken to satisfy our non-cognitive needs'.[1] Thus instrumentalism is a kind of pragmatism, where the importance of *truth* is replaced by that of *utility*. Following Morgenbesser, one may distinguish between a noncognitivist and a contextualist Instrumentalist. A noncognitivist denies the reality of theoretical entities. He takes the scientific law-statements, ordinarily so called, as rules of inference in contradistinction from a staunch and strong noncognitivist who rejects the scientific laws that refer to theoretical entities as nonsense. A contextualist instrumentalist is cautious about the interpretation of scientific theories. He abandons the literal interpretation of the terms and contention of a theory. For him, a scientific theory is justified, provided it can solve the particular problem for the solution of which it has been devised. The theories of noncognitivists and contextualists are both brought under the umbrella of instrumentalism, since both the theories are, as Morgenbesser observes, 'disposed to take a naturalistic approach to language, to view such linguistic entities ... as tools constructed by men to cope with their environment and to examine the various interconnections between knowledge and action'.[2] Instrumentalism interprets the theoretical terms to have no reference to anything in reality. The theories are equipments for 'predicting the behavior of familiar objects'. The instrumentalists, therefore, have a 'deflationary approach to the ontological commitments of scientific theories'.[3]

Realists like John Bigelow and Robert Pargetter[4] endorse this interpretation when they interpret instrumentalism as the doctrine that although scientific theories are useful, one should not infer that the claims they make are true, or that the various words or symbols they employ refer to anything in the actual world. Musgrave's analysis[5] of the instrumentalists' contention is worthy of notice. Following Musgrave, the instrumentalist's argument may be put in the following way:

Instrumentalists find the following set of three assertions to be inconsistent :

1. Scientific theories are used as premises for future prediction.
2. Laws of science are statements, true or else.
3. In logic, we use statements as premises, and they are true or false. In fact, any argument with a true premise and a false conclusion is declared to be invalid. That shows that both the premise and the conclusion are statements.

The instrumentalists try to remove the inconsistency by rejecting the first of the above set, i.e. by maintaining that the laws are not premises of inference, but are rather inference-rules in accordance with which scientific arguments are formulated.

In this Chapter three versions of instrumentalism are considered. First of all, the three theories are explained one after another. Then some general criticisms of instrumentalism are offered in the light of Kneale's position. Thereafter the three theories are, each in turn, examined in detail. The three theories considered are Dewey's, Ryle's, and Nancy Cartwright's theories.

8.1.1 An exposition of Dewey's theory

In *The Quest for Certainty* Dewey clearly advocates instrumentalism. The main purpose of his instrumentalism is to confer on man the honorific title 'the ruler of nature'. Dewey is almost obsessed with this desire, and he is ready to pay any price for buying that name. For Dewey, all misunderstandings about the nature of scientific knowledge occur because the objects of knowledge are wrongly regarded as *independent* of knowledge. He observes that Epistemological Realism which regards 'the true and valid object of knowledge' as 'having a being prior to and independent of the operations of knowing'[6] separates science from its practical activity. This view dominating Greek metaphysics and the Newtonian philosophy regards human knowledge as just 'beholding of reality' over which the knower has no control. A knower is a passive spectator; he can only perceive the world within the range of his perception. He cannot bring any change in it. According to Newton, reality has a fixed form. The things in reality stand in fixed and definite spatio-temporal relations. Newton propagates a doctrine of unchanging and untouched reality.

Dewey, however, takes human knowledge, not as the operation of an 'outside spectator', but as that of 'a participator inside the natural and social scene'. Upon this idealistic sort of view, 'the true object of knowledge resides in the consequences of directed action'.[7] Knowledge has its meaning only in relation to a particular problem which it is its aim to solve. And as there are varieties of problems, there may be various ways of solving the problem. Thus there need not be a single theory on a particular issue. No knowledge in this sense is final. There is a constant search for further precision and accuracy. When an object is perceived passively, the resultant perception is not knowledge proper; it is an experience, so to speak, and this experience may lead to various inquiries. These inquiries allow mental interactions with the physical, and as a result of this intellectual process, which Dewey calls 'intelligence', further meaning of the natural objects may be understood. Objects, then, are not lying in nature independent of the mind; they derive their meaning from mind.

According to epistemological realism, sciences aim at ascertaining laws which describe objects, and these objects are ontically real, independent of the knowing mind. Conceived as descriptions of objective mind-independent phenomena, natural laws are only to be *discovered*, and not *made*. According to the theory advocated by Dewey, on the other hand, the laws 'are *formulae for the prediction of probability of an observable occurrence*'.[8] Natural laws, in this sense, are to be *formulated*, and in any formulation there is undoubtedly a role of an agent and his intellect. Dewey claims that the merit of his view is enormous. If the laws of nature are regarded as descriptions of objective reality, then once the laws are discovered, one can do nothing but obey them. The laws of nature being inherently *fixed*, the scope of knowledge must be finite. Consequently, it may be imagined that one day, when all the fixed laws are actually discovered, there will remain nothing more for further discovery. On the other hand, if laws are viewed as formulae for predictions of phenomena, then there is an endless possibility of bringing precision or accuracy to human knowledge, thereby increasing the probability of prediction. Probability always falls short of certainty, and absolute certainty is never reached; consequently, man's quest for certainty remains an unending process.

With regard to some physical laws, namely, those exemplified by formulae regarding relations of heat, pressure and motion, Dewey observes in his *Logic: The Theory of Inquiry*:

> They are not descriptive but instrumental. They are operatively applied, in the first place, in deciding the special sort of data to be observationally procured - the particular occurrences that are to be discriminated out of the total welter of events actually occurring, and, in the second place, in the interpretations of what the recorded events signify.[9]

The expression 'operatively applied' is important. Operations here are such operations as are 'performed upon and with existential material - as in experimental observation'.[10] The following passage will serve to give us some idea of what Dewey means:

> Operations involve both material and instrumentalities, including in the latter tools and techniques. The more material and instrumentalities are shaped in advance with a view to their operating in conjunction with each other as means to consequences, the better the operations performed are controlled. Refined steel, which is a matter of the operations by which a watch-spring is formed, is itself the product of a number of preparatory operations executed with reference to getting the material into the state that fits it to be the material of the final operation. The material is thus as instrumental, from an operational point of view, as are the tools and techniques by which it is brought into a required condition.[11]

The example in the above passage is no doubt taken from the operations of industrial arts. But the principle has, according to Dewey, general applicability.[12]

It is clear that Dewey's instrumentalism is better describable as operationalism.

8.1.2 Ryle's version of instrumentalism explained

Ryle's account of natural laws as 'inference licences' suggests that he is in a sense an advocate of instrumentalism. For to say that laws are essentially inference licences or rules of inference is to say that they are not themselves observation statements, but are devices whereby certain observation statements can be inferred from certain other observation statements. The essentially functional and non-descriptive character of laws in this way comes to be suggested and emphasized.

Laws, for Ryle, are *open* hypothetical sentences, where the antecedents contain expressions like 'any', 'whenever', etc. Because of this 'openness', laws are applicable to all instances (unobserved as well as observed) of a certain kind. A law asserts neither the truth of the antecedent nor the truth of the consequent. All it asserts is a justified inference from the antecedent to the consequent, such that wherever something fulfils the condition laid down in the antecedent, one is bound to find the consequent. For Ryle, an 'if-then' sentence has a theoretical as well as a non-theoretical usage. In this connection, Ryle draws our attention to the distinction between our theoretical usage of sentences containing the phrase 'if-then' or a word like 'because', on the one hand, and sentences with words like 'so', 'therefore', etc., on the other. Sentences with 'if-then' and 'because' are assertions, while the ones with 'so' or 'therefore' are arguments. Obviously, an assertion is true or false. However, it is queer to speak of an argument as true or false. An argument may be valid or invalid. An assertion or a statement has another very important function. Statements have a '*premissory job*' - they may function as the premise or the conclusion of an argument. A statement differs from a mere conglomeration of words - 'Commands, reproaches, questions, laments, exhortations and plaudits are not constructed for incorporation as they stand into arguments, either as premises or conclusions. By "a statement" we mean, at least *inter alia*, a sentence that is constructed for such incorporation'.[13]

An argument, for Ryle, is an operation with statements. Even though we may formulate a hypothetical statement corresponding to every argument, the validity of the argument and the truth of the hypothetical are two different things. Further, the principle of inference cannot be a premise of the inference or any part of it without involving a logical fallacy. Ryle compares our knowing an 'if-then' sentence to our knowledge of a cooking recipe that is essential to prepare a dish, or knowing the rules of a bridge convention in order to play the game. One is expected to perform in certain ways - nothing more is expected. Given any 'if-then' sentence, e.g. 'If "p" then q" ', one is justified in inferring 'q' from 'p'. Thus knowing a hypothetical sentence is, for Ryle, 'rather like being in possession of a railway ticket. It is having *a licence or warrant* to make a journey from London to Oxford'.[14]

Ryle distinguishes between an argument and an explanation. An explanation is an answer to a question, and it may be true or false. It involves statements, which are used as premises and the conclusion of an argument. An argument, on the other hand, may be valid or invalid. Ryle argues that '*p, so q*' and '*q because p*' express two entirely different things. In the latter 'we are not just asserting but *using* what is expressed by "*if p then q*"; we are putting it to work or applying it; we are attaching "*q*" to "*p*" in accordance with the licence conveyed by "*if p then q*"'.[15] Explanations are neither categorical nor hypothetical statements, 'nor are they 'conflations of categorical with hypothetical statements.' Ryle says: 'The dichotomy "either categorical or hypothetical", though initially clarifying, is finally muddling. Is the umpire a player or a spectator? He is neither a player nor a spectator nor both a player and a spectator.'[16]

A hypothetical statement differs from both an inference and an explanation in terms of its application. A hypothetical statement may be a variable one, but there cannot be any variable inference or a variable explanation. A variable statement is not a statement at all; the clauses of a variable hypothetical statement are 'statement indents - bills for statements that statements could fill',[17] but the constituents of an actual inference or an explanation are always statements proper. Ryle does not deny that often a causal relation between the antecedent and the consequent governs our inferences from the antecedent to the consequent. But the law should not be interpreted as anything more than an 'inference ticket' allowing the inference from the antecedent to the consequent. To maintain that laws describe an 'unobservable existence' is, for Ryle, 'to simply fall back into the old habit of construing open hypothetical statements as singular categorical statements', or 'like saying that a rule of grammar is a sort of extra but unspoken noun or verb', or 'assuming that all sorts of sentences do the same sort of job, the job, namely, of ascribing a predicate to a mentioned object'.[18] The laws, for Ryle, are not formulated in order to *describe* a relation between matters of fact; they give us the rules *in accordance with* which an inference is made. This view may be traced back to J. S. Mill. To quote a passage from his book, *A System of Logic*:

> ... All inference is from particulars to particulars: general propositions are merely registers of such inferences already made and short formulae for making more. The major premise of a syllogism, consequently, is a formula of this description; the conclusion is not an inference drawn *from* the formula, but an inference drawn *according to* the formula...[19]

Ryle calls a law an *inference ticket* and compares it to a railway ticket. An inference from one fact to another is like a journey by rail from one destination to another, where a valid ticket *permits* or *legalizes* the journey. The ticket is not to be identified with the place of origin of the journey or the place at which the journey terminates. Analogously, a law which is a general proposition is a licence to pass from one particular proposition to another. For example, from the particular proposition, e.g. 'Jim is a raven', one may draw the conclusion 'Jim is black' with the help of the law: 'All ravens are black'. This inference is not to be understood as an enthymeme where the law 'All ravens are black' serves as the missing major premise. The inference is directly made from one particular truth to another in accordance with the rule of inference, 'All ravens are black', which permits us to traverse from the knowledge of a particular thing as a raven to the knowledge of its black plumage. Further, when a ticket is issued, there is an implicit supposition of a railway track connecting the two stations. But the ticket is not to be identified with the track. Nor does the ticket indicate whether there is any journey actually undertaken or not. The ticket simply offers the licence of a legitimate journey. Without the ticket, the journey becomes illegal, and the traveller is liable to punishment. Analogously, an inference ticket does not assert the existence of anything corresponding to the description of the antecedent or that of the consequent. It simply warrants the inference from the antecedent to the consequent. From one matter of a fact follows another; the inference is made not *from* the inference-rule taken as a premise, but *in accordance with* this rule. For example, the expression, 'Salt dissolves in water', for the instrumentalists, does not indicate any relation of natural or physical necessity between being a specimen of salt and the dispositional property, namely, solubility in water. The said law does not state whether there is, in the actual world, any actual specimen of salt with the property of solubility in water. It only permits us to infer the property in every case where any salt may be found.

Further, a law is considered by Ryle to be an open or a season ticket. An open ticket permits its holder to make a journey on any day within the period of its validity. Analogously, a rule of inference permits the inference from the antecedent to the consequent at any time. Thus a law is distinct from a real statement, just as 'no journey can be a seasonal journey . . . Permits can be open, but permitted actions cannot be open'.[20] Because a law is an open hypothetical, actual statements may be substituted in place of its antecedent and consequent. Of course, 'that something is an eligible filling for (or satisfies) an open specification is part of what is meant by saying that the statement, rule, or warrant (etc.) incorporating the specification "applies" to that something'.[21] A variable hypothetical often appears to satisfy the vocabulary and syntactical requirements of a statement. However, it is only a schema in which the antecedent and the consequent are statement-variables.

Again, just as one may possess a ticket without undertaking any actual journey, so one may have the inference ticket without ever making any inference at all. Possessing a ticket and showing the ticket to an authority are two entirely different things. Possessing a ticket makes one equipped for a journey, showing the ticket to the ticket-checker proves his authenticity as a passenger. But 'neither buying a ticket, nor owning a ticket, nor showing or transferring a ticket is travelling'.[22]

Ryle observes that predicting one event from another does not necessarily imply a bond between the two. A prediction is not to be identified with an inference; for a prediction is successful when what it predicts turns out to be true. An inference is successful when three conditions are fulfilled, namely, (i) the conclusion is true, (ii) the premise is true, and (iii) the process of inference is a valid one. A true prediction is regarded as a 'happy' one, while a successful inference, for Ryle, is 'scoring'. Ryle maintains that a happy prediction proves the workability of a theory, but is insufficient to prove its truth. Ryle says: '... the maker of the theory ... does not *argue* from the scoring of the grounded inferences to the conclusion that the theory which generated them works. He *shows* that it works by showing it working, and he shows it working by showing inference-scores being made'.[23] In the process of showing the workability, the person who makes the experiment does not frame any inference of the form: 'p (a particular event), because T (a particular theory)'. In such cases, Ryle thinks: 'He had *shown* it working, not *inferred to* its working'.[24] And in this respect a single-score is enough for accepting the workability of a theory. We need not have to organize for repetition or multiplication of inference-scores. Further, a theory cannot act as a premise. The prediction is not deduced *from* the theory, simply because the theory in itself is not a proposition.

It is clear from the above that the empirical laws are not about gross empirical objects. Laws often speak about things which are not phenomenologically real. For example, Newton's First Law of Motion, which says 'All bodies not acted upon by any external force will persevere in their state of rest or of uniform motion in a straight line', does not assert the existence of anything corresponding to the subject of the above statement. The law is a hypothetical statement hiding its face under the veil of a categorical format. It only allows us to draw a conclusion under certain specified conditions.

8.1.3 Nancy Cartwright's instrumentalism explained

Some recent writers on instrumentalism insist that the main purpose served by a scientific law consists in providing an 'explanatory scheme' into which the explanandum fits, that is, a scheme of simplifying and organizing phenomenologically different phenomena. And in order to fulfil this purpose, the law need not be true. Nancy Cartwright in her *How the Laws of Physics Lie?* has added an interesting dimension to instrumentalism. She points out that there are two types of laws in science - (i) phenomenological laws which describe reality and often do so 'reasonably well'; and (ii) theoretical laws that explain the objects of reality, but are not true. That the theoretical laws have an explanatory power proves their falsehood. Ms Cartwright puts this point quite clearly:

> ... What is important to realize is that if the theory is to have considerable explanatory power, most of its fundamental claims will not state truths, and that this will in general

> include the bulk of our most highly prized laws and equations.[25]

The theoretical laws of science have a 'peculiar' nature. They do not describe. They only serve the purpose of organization, explanation, and simplification. Ms Cartwright points out two different ways of explanation: (i) causal explanation in which a fact is explained by tracing its cause, and (ii) theoretical explanation where 'one can set the phenomenon in a general theoretical network'.[26] Of the two types of explanation, only the former is true for Cartwright, but not the latter. For her, 'to count the basic explanatory laws as true is to fail to take seriously how physics succeeds in giving explanations',[27] 'they are simply false, not only false but deemed false by the very theory that maintains them'.[28]

Ms Cartwright rejects the view that laws of nature describe facts about reality - a view considered by her a 'pedestrian view, that . . . any scientific realist will hold'.[29] She calls this the 'Facticity View' of laws. Realists, she thinks, are wrong in ascribing both explanatory power and truth to laws at the same time. In fact, the laws are not true. The laws of Biology, the thumb rule of Engineering, and the laws of Physics are not descriptions of reality. They are not to be construed as statements about the behaviour of natural objects, or about how they must behave. No laws are exceptionless. Physical laws, for Ms Cartwright, unlike the laws of Biology, are not even approximately true.

It is commonly urged that the laws describe the facts of nature, and describe them truly. Precisely this descriptive capacity of a law enables a law to explain certain phenomena and predict the future events successfully. Ms Cartwright calls this way of arguing the 'argument from coincidence' - a powerful argument speaking against her position. She construes the opponents' argument in the following manner:

> ...the fact that a law *explains* provides evidence that the law is true. The more diverse the phenomena that it explains,

> the more likely it is to be true. It would be an absurd coincidence if a wide variety of different kinds of phenomena were all explained by a particular law, and yet were not in reality consequent from the law. Thus the argument from coincidence supports a good many of the inferences we make to best explanations.[30]

Van Fraassen puts the realists' claim in the form of an argument as stated below:

> A law-statement 'P' explains 'Q' which is a statement about a phenomenon.
>
> 'Q' is true.
>
> ∴ 'P' is true.

Duhem and van Fraassen believe that the argument above does not 'wear its validity on its sleeve'. Truth is an external characteristic of explanation. In fact, an explanation may be sufficient for the explanandum, even if it may not be true. For example, the Ptolemaic theory could successfully explain certain celestial occurrences, even though the theory fails to be true. There is nothing in the explanation relation to guarantee the truth of the explanans when the explanandum is true: 'explanation has truth going along with it only as an extra ingredient'.[31] Ms Cartwright hastens to add that, for van Fraassen and Duhem, no explanation is accepted as genuine unless it is *also* true. Causal explanations 'have truth built into them', and 'an explanation of an effect by a cause has an existential component, not just as an optional extra ingredient'.[32] The theoretical laws, however, widely differ from causal laws. The theoretical laws have a great explanatory and predictive power. But since they explain, they cannot be true.

Nancy Cartwright declares a 'trade-off between factual content and explanatory power' of laws. Often in science a complex phenomenon is explained in terms of its simpler components. Mill calls this 'explanation by composition of causes'. Ms Cartwright goes on to show that such explanations often use laws that do not fulfil the 'facticity' requirement. She observes:

> ...To play the role in explanation we demand of them [laws], these laws must have the same form when they act together as when they act singly. In the simplest case, the consequences that the laws prescribe must be exactly the same in interaction, as the consequences that would obtain if the law were operating alone. But then, what the law states cannot literally be true, for the consequences that would occur if it acted alone are not the consequences that actually occur when it acts in combination.[33]

A simple example may be offered to prove the point. According to the law of science, if a body is pulled by force from a particular direction of space, it moves towards it, that is, when a force from the left of a body pulls it, the body acted upon moves leftward. But this rule becomes nonfunctional when there are alternative forces, all at work together. In that case, the result would be quite different. The body, if pulled with equal force from opposite directions, would not budge from its original position. Evidently, the natural phenomena are results of several simple laws in combination, and not of any one of the laws taken separately. This leads Ms Cartwright to remark:

> ...In order to be true in the composite case, the law must describe one effect (the effect that actually happens); but to be explanatory, it must describe another. There is a trade-off here between truth and explanatory power.[34]

Most of the explanations in science are derived from *ceteris paribus* generalizations. These generalizations are true only under certain ideal conditions. Their expressions begin with the phrase 'other things being right' or 'other things being equal'. The problem with the *ceteris paribus* laws is this: if the law is taken minus the *ceteris paribus* modifier, then it is false; on the other hand, if the law is taken along with the modifier, then the law, even if true, has a very small range of explanation. Only a few cases which satisfy the condition will come under it. Thus, for most cases, we have either laws that are true but cannot explain or false laws with reasonably good explanatory power. '[T]he cost of explanatory power is descriptive adequacy'.[35]

Against the Facticity doctrine, Ms Cartwright along with Pierre Duhem and Hilary Putnam cites a counter-argument. The counter-argument is advanced from the 'requirement of non-redundancy'. The crux of the counter-argument is this: if laws are regarded as true, then there must be one and only one explanation for a particular notion. In other words, if explanation is the consequence, and not a part of the description that a law offers, then there can be only one explanation of an event 'p' from a true description 'd'. Thus if a law is true, then there is a single law covering a sort of event, and only one explanation in compliance with the law is possible. However, it is a fact that in science we find alternative explanations of the same phenomena. We have equally effective, different explanations of a particular phenomenon, and they are incompatible with one another. This shows that the theoretical explanations are redundant. Because the explanatory laws cannot meet the non-redundancy criterion, the laws cannot be regarded as true. The laws organize and unify different natural phenomena, but there 'is no reason to think that the principles that best organize will be true...'.[36] In fact, ' ... organizing power has nothing to do with truth'.

8.2 Some General Criticisms of Instrumentalism along Kneale's Line

Some general criticisms of instrumentalism will now be in order.

Advocates of instrumentalism fail to describe adequately the practice of scientists. In the words of Dudley Shapere it may be said that they 'fail to show how the alleged realistic aspects of scientific concepts play an actual functioning role in scientific reasoning'.[37] In point of fact, theoretical entities play a very important role in 'rational processes of science'.[38] Shapere maintains:

> Not only does science make existence-claims about electrons and other 'theoretical entities', to use the positivistic jargon, but those claims are made as an integral part of the scientific reasoning process ....Finally the conceptual devices of science ...are parasitic, in the logic of their employment, on existence-claims.[39]

It is necessary to point out that Shapere's criticism is very well along Kneale's line. Kneale does not believe that laws involving theoretical terms are merely tools for explanation. These sophisticated laws, or rather, theories, of science, are, according to him, transcendent hypotheses; for they are about things unobservable in nature. He observes:

> ...the statements made by physical scientists in the formulation of transcendent hypotheses are to be taken at their face value, namely, as assertions of the existence of imperceptible objects with certain specified structures. No other account seems to me to do justice to the facts; and I think that, when philosophers and scientists feel difficulty in admitting that transcendent hypotheses are what they seem to be, that is only because, like Berkeley, they have adopted an unduly narrow view of the possibilities of thinking.[40]

Any theory may be called a kind of instrumentalism in so far as it holds that sentences in which natural laws are formulated are not descriptive of reality, but prescriptive, as giving only rules of inference or tools of organization. As such, instrumentalism is subject to the following criticism urged by Kneale against some positivists' prescription theory of natural laws (a criticism already taken note of in the last Chapter but repeated here for its equal relevance to instrumentalism in its negative and positive aspects):

> If the sentences in which we formulate natural laws are to be construed as prescriptions, they must still be supposed universal in scope, e.g. 'Whenever you find a dodo assume that it has a white feather in its tail'. Now the positivists have no reason at all to give why we should adopt such general rules. It is not permissible for them to say that a rule of this kind will enable us to make successful predictions, for such a remark is itself a universal statement about the world and contains all the difficulties they find in those formulations of natural laws which purport to be universal statements.[41]

It is now time to proceed to a detailed examination of each of the three versions of instrumentalism presented above.

8.2.1 Critique of Dewey's theory

Dewey's view of natural laws has doubtless its own merits. Nevertheless, it is open to the charge of *one-story dwelling.* He seems to be mesmerized with the role a man plays in the natural world, and, in a way, overstates the glory of man. The role of human intelligence is by no means minimized if the laws of nature are viewed as descriptions of some fixed, or objective, relations between physical objects. Such relations are not all open to public perception. Obviously, in every case of perceiving an object, e.g. a physical object like a table, there is some beholder endowed with the power of vision and the presence of the proper conditions of perception, such as the presence of sufficient light, etc. The conditions of knowing a natural law stating an objective connection between two natural phenomena are even more stringent. A physicist ought to possess an appropriate tool for identification of the phenomenon involved, and for this he has to isolate the phenomenon which comes entangled with many others in the physical world. In order to do the needful, one must be well conversant with the sophistications of scientific knowledge. Though theories are considered to be appropriate or sufficient for all practical purposes, there is ample scope for further modifications and improvements. Dewey need not fear that a day will come when human knowledge has exhausted all the details of the entire universe, thereby stalling further advancement in knowledge. The mysteries of the universe will always provide men with scope for further precision in our knowledge. With the progress of science, there arise newer problems not previously encountered. In this way, man's aspiration to reach perfection will always persuade him to go further and further, even though he knows that the goal is a mirage and will never be reached.

The descriptive theory does not make man a passive, helpless spectator. Man does not merely discover laws of nature to control nature to his liking; he may add things of his choice to the already existing set of natural things. These new things may be called artificial, but their artificiality is a proof of man's power to control and change the natural phenomena. Dewey is right in recognizing man's superiority in the natural world. But he over-emphasizes the role of man, delimiting thereby the grandiosity of the natural world. To know a law of nature does not mean the ability to predict the future correctly every time. Often nature acts contrary to our expectations, and these surprises provide the incentive to search for clues to the solution of the mysteries of nature. The solution of the mystery at times leads to a revision of the existing law; on some other occasions, it leads man to discover certain hitherto unobserved phenomena. To take a very simple example: It is common knowledge that glass is brittle in nature: brittleness is taken as the defining character of glass. This knowledge is an integral part of our epistemic system such that whenever a piece of glass is found, its dispositions and its possible changes in certain specified situations are also known. It is known, for example, that if the glass is hit hard, it will break into pieces. Yet this knowledge does not prevent one from making any further discovery. One may always aim at discovering an article that will flex all the other properties of glass except brittleness. A new name may be given to such an entity. This shows that even if natural laws be regarded as descriptive and objective, they do not pose any threat to future discoveries.

8.2.2 Critique of Ryle's theory

Kneale argues that a law is a proposition and may be used as a premise of a scientific inference. This seems to be a very important criticism of any theory that refuses to regard laws as statements or propositions proper. Ryle's comparison of a law to an inference ticket is justified only up to a certain point. It should not be pressed too far. Like a ticket, a law-statement allows us to travel from one particular point to another. Tickets are valid or invalid; so are the laws. But the fact that a law is not usually referred to as true or false does not imply that it is not a genuine proposition which is true or false. Laws are referred to as valid or invalid rather than as true or false because of the preference for a certain terminology over others. This preference is perhaps due to the importance attached to the application of laws. Even then a law may be considered to be true or false. It may be accepted as true when it leads to successful experimentations and correct predictions. It may be believed to be false otherwise. As Nagel says:

> ...There is ... no necessary incompatibility between saying that a theory is true and maintaining that the theory performs important functions in inquiry. ...In brief, it does not follow that theories cannot be regarded as 'genuine statements' and cannot therefore be investigated for their truth or falsity, merely because theories have indispensable functions in inquiry.[42]

He adds a little later:

> ...there is on the whole only a verbal difference between

> asking whether a theory is satisfactory (as a technique of inference) and asking whether a theory is true (as a premise).[43]

It is strange to maintain that a law is not a proposition proper just as it is strange to regard an umpire as neither a spectator nor a player. A law may well be viewed as a statement with a predictive power, just as an umpire is a spectator and a special spectator who has the power to give rulings in the game-proceedings. The mistake of Ryle, Schlick, Wittgenstein, and other instrumentalists consists in holding that being a premise of an argument and being an inference-rule are contrary properties, which cannot both be true at the same time. However, there is no clear line of demarcation between a premise and a rule of inference, so to speak. Even though the two functions are, strictly speaking, different, they are often overlapping, and the entry of one into the territory of the other is certainly not trespassing. We may arrive at the same conclusion in regard to a law, taking it either as a premise of inference or as a rule of inference. As Nagel observes:

> ... It is clearly a matter of convenience in which of these alternate ways an argument is constructed. Accordingly, though the distinction between premises and rules of inference is both sound and important, a given statement may function as a premise in one context but may in effect be used as a leading principle in another context and vice versa.[44]

If it is a rule of inference, that given any individual man, one is to infer that the individual is mortal, then having known that Socrates is a man, one may safely conclude that he is mortal. The very same conclusion may be established validly when the rule of inference is expressed in the form of a categorical proposition, universal in quantity, and used as the major premise of a syllogism. The syllogism takes on the form of BARBARA:

All men are mortal.

Socrates is a man.

∴ Socrates is mortal.

Of course, a formal rule of syllogism cannot serve as a premise. For example, it is a rule of syllogism that the middle term must be distributed at least once in the premises. No conclusion is drawn from this premise, though the conclusion of a syllogism is drawn in accordance with the rule. A law of nature, however, is not such a formal rule. The law is about the world, and if it is at all a rule of inference, then it is a material rule quite different from the formal one. This material rule may act in two ways in our life. It may be taken as a general truth from which a truth about a particular may be deduced. This process may be expressed in the form of a deductive argument, where the general truth acts as the major premise. When the law is very well known, we seem to pass from one particular truth to another, making use of the law as a premise of an inference implicitly. Perhaps this is what is meant by the instrumentalists when they emphasize that laws are rules, and not premises of inference. But the process of reasoning in these cases can also be presented in the form of a deductive argument, where the law serves as the major premise. In fact, one has to proceed in this manner when one is to demonstrate to others, or convince them of the truth of, the conclusion.

A very important point of criticism against instrumentalism is: In what circumstances is an order issued and what makes an instruction worth while? Analysis reveals that every instruction presupposes a description of states of affairs. The law, e.g. 'All men are mortal' instructs us to make inferences from manness to mortality. But what makes this inference permissible? Certainly the invariant relation between manness and mortality. Thus the law may serve as a *rule or tool* of inference only on the basis of some objective relation between two features in the outside world. The statement of a relation between states of affairs is, therefore, part of the meaning of a law. Similarly, no tickets are issued if there is no connecting rail-line between the origin and the destination of the journey. Even though we may not be thinking of the 'rail' at the time of travel, yet it cannot be denied that a journey is possible provided there is such a 'rail'. In fact, these rails serve as the necessary condition of our train-journey. And the application of a law, or rule of application, is not to be identified with the meaning of the law-statement. The rule or principle of application is derivable from the meaning of a law. To take a law as an inference ticket, then, is already to accept an objective relation warranting the inference. That a law is regarded as an 'open ticket' that allows inferences about the future means the relation described by the law is not accidentally or occasionally true. The relation described by a law is a non-accidental objective one.

For criticisms of Ryle, references should also be made to Peter Achinstein's 'From Success to Truth' in *Analysis* 21, (1960-61)[45] and H. V. Stope-Roe's piece in the same volume of *Analysis*[46].

8.2.3 Critique of Nancy Cartwright's instrumentalism

Ms Cartwright rightly holds that a proper explanation is capable of explaining a true event. But the truth of the explanandum cannot guarantee the truth of the explanans. A confusion is made here between a material implication and other forms of implication. An explanation may be rewritten in the form of an inference. If 'E' explains 'P', then corresponding to this explanation, we may construct an inference with 'E' as the premise and 'P' as the conclusion. In material implication the truth of the consequent does not prove the truth of the antecedent. A *true* consequent may be materially implied by any antecedent whatever. Material implication is a purely formal relation pertaining to the realm of deductive logic. In scientific enterprise, we are not concerned with formal validity. The relation of explanation is not exactly like the relation of material implication. In *some* sense, an explaining fact implies the fact to be explained. But this implication is not material implication. Science, in order to explain and preserve uniformity, searches for causes, and sometimes even non-causal laws function like the causal ones in assuring us of the cogency of prediction and unification.

Further, it may be pointed out that a law forms a part of a system and that within a particular system only one explanation is possible. Alternative explanations are given from the standpoints of alternative systems. It is necessary to bear in mind that alternative systems are not all accepted at a time. Both the Ptolemaic and the Copernican theory are known to explain certain phenomena. But not both are believed to be true at the same time. With the advent of the Copernican theory, the then prevalent Ptolemaic theory was discarded. And this shows that the two theories are contrary statements, both of which cannot be true at the same time. If, for some reasons, the Copernican theory is accepted as true, the Ptolemaic theory must be dropped as false. If laws were mere tools, then both of them could be preserved with equal enthusiasm. Usually, if we come upon a tool which is more sophisticated than the one we normally use, the latter is not instantaneously thrown away. Unless there is a severe dearth of place, both may be kept for future use. Since, now, alternative scientific theories cannot both be maintained at the same time, then they are not instruments; they are propositions each with a definite truth-value. In fact, when Nancy Cartwright says that the laws of Physics 'are simply false', she is ascribing a truth-value to the laws, thereby virtually admitting that the explanatory laws are also statements.

We may conclude this Chapter with the following remarks: The Instrumentalists' view of natural laws rightly emphasizes the predictive and explanatory power of natural laws. At the same time, this takes away some other important role played by the natural laws in our edifice of knowledge. Man from time immemorial goes in search of knowledge to quench his insatiable thirst for knowing the world around him. The result of his endeavour is the *discovery* of the laws of nature.

Notes

1 S. Morgenbesser, 'The Realist-Instrumentalist Controversy', in S. Morgenbesser, S. Patrick and M. G. White, eds. *Philosophy, Science and Method*, St. Martin Press, New York, 1969, p. 201.

2 *Ibid.*, p. 203.

3 *Ibid.*, p. 206.

4 J. Bigelow and R. Pargetter, 'From Extroverted Realism to Correspondence: A Modest Proposal', *Philosophical and Phenomenological Research*, vol. L.,1990, pp. 437- 438.

5 A. Musgrave, 'Wittgensteinian Instrumentalism', *Theoria*, vol. 47, 1981, p. 70.

6 J. Dewey, *The Quest for Certainty: A Study of the Relation of Knowledge and Action*, George Allen & Unwin, London, 1930, p. 188.

7 *Ibidem.*

8 *Ibid.*, pp. 197 - 198.

9 John Dewey, *Logic: The Theory of Inquiry*, Henry Wolt and Company, New York, 1938, p. 473.

10 *Ibid.*, p. 15.

11 *Ibidem.*

12 Cf. pp. 15 - 16 of the same book.

13 G. Ryle, ' "If", "So" and "Because" ', in Max Black. ed. *Philosophical Analysis*, Cornell University Press, Ithaca, 1950, reprinted in Ryle: *Collected Papers*, v. 2, *Collected Essays (1929 -1968)*, vol. 2, Hutchinson of London, 1971, p. 236.

14 *Ibid.*, p. 239 [Italics added].

15 *Ibid.*, p. 241.

16 *Ibidem.*

17 *Ibid.*, p. 245.

18 G. Ryle, *The Concept of Mind*, Penguin Books Ltd, England, 1976, p. 118.

19 J. S. Mill, *A System of Logic*, Longman, London, 1970, Bk II, Ch. III, Sec. 4, p. 126.

20 Ryle, ' "If", "So" and "Because" ', p. 242.

21 *Ibidem.*

22 *Ibid.*, p. 240.

23 G. Ryle, 'Predicting and Inferring', *Collected Papers*, p. 377.

24 *Ibid.*, p. 378.

25 Nancy Cartwright, *How the Laws of Physics Lie*, Clarendon Press, Oxford, 1983, p. 78.

26 *Ibid.*, p. 75.

27 *Ibid.*, p. 77.

28 *Ibid.*, p. 55.

29 *Ibidem.*

30 *Ibid.*, p. 75.

31 *Ibid.*, p. 91.

32 *Ibidem.*

33 *Ibid.*, p. 72.

34 *Ibid.*, p. 59.

35 *Ibid.*, p. 3.

36 *Ibid.*, p. 53.

37 D. Shapere, 'Natural Science and the Future of Metaphysics', *Boston Studies in the Philosophy of Science*, vol. 14, D. Reidel Publishing Co., Dodrecht, Holland, 1974, p. 162.

38 *Ibid.*, p. 163.

39 *Ibid.*, pp. 168 - 169.

40 Kneale, *Probability and Induction*, p. 103.

41 *Ibid.*, p.77.

42 E. Nagel, *The Structure of Science*, Routledge and Kegan Paul, London, 1961, p. 137f.

43 *Ibid.*, p. 139.

44 *Ibid.*, p. 138.

45 See *Analysis*, v. 21, pp. 6 - 9.
Ryle, however, has made a reply to Achinstein; see *ibid.*, pp. 9 - 11.

46 *Ibid.*, pp. 115 - 20.

CHAPTER NINE

A FINAL ESTIMATE OF KNEALE'S THEORY OF NATURAL NECESSITY

9.1 Foreword

The main alternatives to Kneale's theory of natural necessity have been found to be unsatisfactory. The question arises whether this theory in its turn can then be considered to be satisfactory.

Kneale has indeed dealt with 'one of the hardest and weightiest of the problems of philosophy' (as C. D. Broad has aptly put it)[1]. This, however, serves only to highlight the difficulty and the importance of Kneale's theory. But the difficulty, on the other side, in the way of finally saying that his theory is satisfactory enough is no less great. For two major claims are associated with this theory, and nothing has been done so far to show in any convincing manner that the two claims are justified.

One is the claim that there are *objective* necessities, in so far as Kneale's theory of natural necessity claims to be a theory of *objective* necessity[2] (objective in the sense of being no mere product of man-made linguistic convention). This claim cannot be substantiated indeed except through rejection of the conventionalist theory of necessity, which was so influential when Kneale chose to advocate a theory of natural necessity. As is to be expected, Kneale has duly examined the conventionalist view that all necessary truths are true by convention in many of his writings[3].

As for the other claim, an idea of it has already been given in the Introductory Chapter. It is that the notion of *a posteriori* necessity is not inconceivable. Kneale's theory of natural necessity involves this claim, in that laws of nature, which are formulated and accepted *a posteriori* by scientists, are considered by him to be principles of necessity. Although some examination of the notion of *a posteriori* necessity has already been made before (in the Introductory Chapter)[4], something more may be needed to remove, or at least to minimize, any feeling of dissatisfaction that may have persisted.

It is also worth mentioning here that Kneale, who owes his theory of natural necessity in its essentials to Locke, owes Kant no less significantly for this, paradoxical though it may seem. This additional source of inspiration for his theory is usually neglected, but it deserves to be considered nevertheless in this final chapter. Some other matters also are to be considered.

It is now time to proceed to consider Kneale's critique of the conventionalist theory of necessity.

9.2 Kneale's Critique of the Conventionalist Theory of Necessity

9.2.1 Kneale on the failure of conventionalists to account for necessity and impossibility in terms of linguistic rules alone

Conventionalism as regards necessary truths is a view to the effect that all necessary truths are true by linguistic convention. This view is associated with the name of Hobbes. In its sophisticated form it is advocated by Carnap in his *Logical Syntax of Language*, and is summarized by Kneale in his paper on 'Truths of Logic' as follows. [The page-references used by Kneale are to the pages of Carnap's book just mentioned.]

> The word 'syntax' is ordinarily used to mean the study of the rules which govern the combination of signs in a given language. According to Carnap pure syntax is concerned with the possible forms of sentences without regard either to the designs of the words of which the sentences are composed or to the question whether any of the sentences has been

> uttered or written (p. 7). It is formal in the sense that it abstracts from the meanings of symbols and deals only with their combinations according to rules (p. 3) . . . . For the systematic development of a language we must suppose that rules of consequence or entailment are given. These determine everything that can be said about logical connexions within this language, and by reference to entailment all the most important concepts of syntax can be defined (p. 168). It must not be supposed however that rules of entailment are given in the sense of being imposed upon us by some external necessity. All statements of logic are relative to a particular language and we can construct languages as we please (p. 52). The rules of a language are only basic conventions to be adopted or rejected according to our convenience and all the truths commonly called necessary are truths established by these conventions.[5]

Kneale in this paper has explained the Carnapian position at some length and offered his own criticism of it. It is not necessary for the present purpose to enter into the details of his criticism, and it will only suffice to point out his basic contention. He argues that the words composing a necessarily true statement are, if they are considered in themselves, mere marks or sounds[6]. Mere marks are, however, as good as nonsense syllables. This indeed has to be said because the meanings of symbols are abstracted from. Now sets of mere marks are not even sentences. They cannot be turned into sentences by means of any further *syntactical* rules like a rule of substitution and a rule corresponding to *modus ponens*[7]. Conventionalism holds that the linguistic rules which make the marks occurring in a necessarily true statement into a significant expression are also sufficient to determine its truth. Kneale admits that truisms are indeed a by-product of rules of entailment, but points out that rules of entailment alone cannot make any mere marks into significant expressions and that, unless the marks occurring in truisms are significant expressions, they do not even deserve to be called sentences. A language constructed by mere syntactical conventions can produce an abstract calculus only. Carnap's system of logical syntax produces no more than an abstract calculus. Kneale says: 'In a genuine object language some at least of the rules of entailment are determined by more fundamental rules of usage and the only place for arbitrary syntactical convention is in the introduction of new signs by reference to old signs'.[8] But even there, he holds, mere syntactical convention cannot make anything true.[9] Syntactical convention alone cannot make anything into a significant expression and does not therefore serve to determine the truth of anything.

It may be better, for purposes of the present work, to explain the conventionalist view in clear general terms, and then to examine it first along the line taken by Kneale in his *Probability and Induction.*

It is indisputable that language is something conventional. A language consists of a vocabulary and a syntax. The vocabulary of a language consists of the sum-total of the words used in it. The words are merely symbols, and when written, they are mere shapes. These are conventional in the sense that these might have been different. In English the words 'red' and 'green', for example, are used to mean red and green features of things respectively. Instead of these words, some other words might have been used to signify the same. If these words are used, as in fact they are, it is just a matter of convention.

The syntax of a language consists of the rules which govern the combination of words in certain permissible ways for formation of sentences. Thus in English the signs 'The', 'on', 'the', 'is', 'mat', 'cat' cannot be combined as 'The on the cat is mat' to give a permissible sentence; these have to be combined as 'The cat is on the mat' to give a sentence. Now, a distinction is to be made between the grammatical syntax and the logical syntax of a language. The former consists of those rules which are explicitly stated in the books of grammar of the language. There are, however, rules not explicitly stated in any books of grammar of the language, but which are still implicitly conformed to by the users of the language in question in so far as they use the language in a correct (i.e. permissible) way. One such rule is, for example, the rule that forbids us to use two colour words together in certain ways [i.e. for one and the same uniformly coloured object]. To violate this rule is to violate the logical syntax of the language concerned.

Now the statement 'Nothing which is red can be also green all over at the same time' is, for Kneale, a principle of modality, which is in common parlance a necessary truth. For the conventionalist, however, the truth of this necessarily true statement is governed by a linguistic rule, such as the aforementioned rule that forbids us to use two colour words together in certain ways.

Kneale in his criticism of this Carnapian[10] view says:

> ...We may readily admit that the truth of the printed statement 'It is impossible for anything to be both red and green' is guaranteed by our rules for the use of the shapes 'red' and 'green', and we may admit also that we could, if wished, use these shapes differently .... It is, no doubt, arbitrary that we should forbid ourselves to use the shapes 'red' and 'green' together in a certain way, but only because it is arbitrary that we should use these shapes to mean red and green respectively. It is not arbitrary that we should forbid ourselves to use together in that way those shapes, whatever they may be, which are to mean red and green. If we decided to use the shape 'green' in such a way that 'x is red and x is green' was a permissible sentence form, then the shape 'green' would not mean what it does now in English but something else, e.g. crimson or coloured or square, according to the rules of the new language. If,

> however, we are to be able to refer to those characters which we now signify by the shapes 'red' and 'green', we must have in our language two shapes which obey a rule similar to that now holding in English for the shapes 'red' and 'green'. The rule is not something which has been introduced by an unmotivated convention and without regard to the use of the shapes in the statement of empirical facts, ...[11]

Kneale goes on developing his criticism. One cannot afford to miss, however, the central point of his criticism, which is as follows.

The necessarily true statement 'Nothing which is red can be also green all over' expresses an objective incompatibility between the features of redness and greenness. Now, a grasp of an objective incompatibility between these features lies at the back of the linguistic rule that forbids us to use the two colour words together in a certain way; for otherwise the rule could not have been framed. So it comes to be the case that the necessarily true statement is not determined by the linguistic rule, but itself goes to determine the rule, which has been introduced, not arbitrarily, but in conformity to the necessary statement which express an objective incompatibility of features.

Chisholm makes virtually the same point, in a slightly different way and with a slightly different example, when he says:

> ...But let us consider what conditions must obtain if the English sentence 'Being red excludes being blue' is to be true. One such condition is indicated by the following sentence which we may call *T* :
>
> The English sentence 'Being blue excludes being red' is true if, and only if, being blue excludes being red.[12]
>
> Clearly, the final part of *T*, the part following the second 'if', formulates a necessary condition for the truth of the English sentence 'Being red excludes being blue'; but it refers to a relationship among properties and not to rules of

> language or ways in which we use words (to suppose otherwise would be to make the mistake ... of confusing use and mention in language). Hence, we cannot say that the only conditions that need to obtain in order for 'Being red excludes being blue' to be true is that we use words in certain ways or that there be certain rules pertaining to the ways words are to be used; ...[13]

It is noteworthy that, like Kneale, Chisholm also has laid an emphasis on a relation of objective incompatibility between (extra-linguistic) features or properties[14] in his attempt to show the failure of conventionalism or linguisticism to account for the truth of a necessarily true statement in terms of mere linguistic rules.

9.2.2 Kneale on certain confusions involved in conventionalism

In *The Development of Logic* Kneale (along with Martha Kneale) says that modern conventionalism involves a confusion between logical and linguistic rules.[15] An example of such confusion is given by reference to a quotation from Carnap's *Logical Syntax of Language* (English trans., 1937, §17):

> *In Logic there are no morals.* Everyone is at liberty to build up his own logic, i.e. his own form of language, as he wishes. All that is required of him is that, if he wishes to discuss it, he must state his methods clearly, and give syntactical rules instead of philosophical arguments. ...[16]

This tendency to confuse logical and linguistic rules is noticeable in other philosophers also who are influenced by conventionalism. Conventionalists in general say that necessarily true statements are true by linguistic convention. They have come to hold this view as a result of their notion, derived from Wittgenstein's *Tractatus*, that the world consists of facts which are independent and contingent, and that necessity belongs to language. For them, to say that certain truths are necessary (i.e. true without alternatives) is only to express the speaker's determination to stand by a certain form of words in all circumstances. 'There are, they say, no alternatives to a necessary truth *within the speaker's language*, but only because he has limited his language in that way'.[17] So much about their view that all necessity is linguistic. They have also taken the Wittgensteinian view that all necessity is logical. As a result of their two views that all necessity is linguistic and that all necessity is logical, they have come to adopt ultimately the view that logical statements are linguistic statements of a certain sort - such linguistic statements as statements about linguistic inconsistency or about what is definable by reference to linguistic inconsistency. To obviate the objection that logic is not concerned with any particular language, the provision is sometimes made that the linguistic statements in question are fully translatable from one language to another. Thus Strawson writes:

> The important thing is to see that when you draw the boundaries of the applicability of words in one language and then connect the words of that language with those of another by translation rules, there is no need to draw the boundaries again for the second language. They are already drawn. [...] This is why (or partly why) logical statements framed in one language are not just about that language.[18]

W. and Martha Kneale here observe:

> If this means that logical rules are rules for all possible languages, it amounts in effect to an admission that they are not conventional and therefore not linguistic in any ordinary sense of the word but rather requirements to be satisfied in the making of what we ordinarily call linguistic rules.[19]

Modern conventionalism involves, according to W. and Martha Kneale, not only the confusion pointed out just now, but also the confusion consisting in the blurring of certain important distinctions.

Thus the philosophers who adopt the conventionalist view assume that the terms 'analytic', '*a priori*', and 'necessary' are coextensive. This assumption is, however, seriously questionable. First, there are philosophers who admit propositions, such as that nothing can be both red and green all over at the same time, which are, for them, known *a priori*, and yet not analytic.[20] These philosophers, obviously, do not regard the terms '*a priori*' and 'analytic' as coextensive. Secondly, the terms '*a priori*' and 'necessary' in their turn do not appear to be coextensive, because 'it is at least conceivable' that there are truths which are necessary and yet not known *a priori*. 'We commonly admit that there are truths of mathematics which no one in fact knows, ...'.[21] Truths of mathematics are commonly admitted to be necessary truths, and if it is admitted that some truths of mathematics are not known, it is at the same time admitted that some truths of mathematics are not known *a priori*. There are, then, some necessary truths which are not known *a priori*. The terms '*a priori*' and 'necessary', therefore, do not appear to be coextensive.

Some philosophers assume not only that the terms 'analytic', '*a priori*', and 'necessary' are coextensive, but also that they are synonymous, so that any one of these terms may be taken as contradictory to any one of the corresponding terms 'synthetic', 'empirical', and 'contingent'.[22] As an example, Kneale and Kneale refer to A. J. Ayer's definitions of analytic and synthetic propositions:[23]

> ...a proposition is analytic when its validity depends solely on the definitions of the symbols it contains, and synthetic when its validity is determined by the facts of experience.

Here Ayer is taking 'synthetic' as definitionally equivalent to 'empirical'. This appears to be a fusion of two important distinctions. W. and M. Kneale accordingly observe: 'Obviously such confusion makes Kant's notion of synthetic *a priori* truths seem completely absurd, though this notion has been accepted in recent times by mathematicians as great as Frege, Poincare, Brouwer, and Hilbert.'[24] Kneale and Kneale go on to make further criticisms of Ayer's view.[25]

Thus, on Ayer's view, the Fregean thesis that arithmetical truths are analytic turns out to be the triviality that such truths are *a priori*. If 'synthetic' and 'empirical' be definitionally equivalent - and if, for that matter, 'analytic' and '*a priori*' be such, then the thesis that arithmetical truths are analytic, which Frege regards as a substantive one, reduces to the tautology that arithmetical truths which are analytic are analytic - i.e. that arithmetical truths which are *a priori* are *a priori*.

Again, on similar considerations, the positivist view that all *a priori* truths are analytic becomes indistinguishable from the tautology that all *a priori* truths are *a priori*, or that all analytic truths are analytic. Positivists, however, do not behave as if their main doctrine were a mere tautology.

It is clear that the conventionalist theory of necessity is not satisfactory, in so far as it has not succeeded in showing that all necessity - all impossibility - belongs to language alone and in so far as it has led to some extremely unhappy consequences. Such a theory cannot, therefore, be used satisfactorily as a basis of objection to a theory of objective necessity.

9.3 On the Notion of the Necessary *A Posteriori* Once Again

To turn now to the notion of the necessary *a posteriori* once more : something has already been said about it in the Introductory Chapter. It has been shown that the notion is not inconceivable. But no example of a proposition which is accepted *a posteriori* (not *a priori*) and is yet necessary has been given. Kripke says: 'More important than any particular example of something which is alleged to be necessary and not *a priori* ... is to see that the notions are different, ...'.[26] That the notions are different has already been shown; [27] an example is nevertheless needed in order to see whether any fresh problem arises in regard to laws of nature. What has been done so far indicates only that the notion of the necessary *a posteriori* is not absurd.

Chisholm says:

> A possible example of a proposition that is known *a posteriori* and is yet necessary might be a logical theorem which one accepts on the ground that reputed logicians assert it to be true.[28]

If a man accepts a theorem on the basis of authority, he depends on testimonial evidence, and if such evidence be sufficient for knowledge, then, in view of the fact that a theorem is a necessary proposition, acceptance of the theorem on the strength of testimonial evidence (which is *a posteriori* evidence) becomes a case of *a posteriori* knowledge of a necessary proposition.

But the following observation made by Chisholm may raise a difficulty in regard to what the present work is concerned with, namely, laws of nature:

> If a man knows ... *a posteriori* that a certain necessary proposition is true, then s*omeone* knows *a priori* that some necessary proposition is true. If the first man bases his knowledge on the testimony of authority, and if this authority in turn bases his knowledge upon the testimony of some other authority, then sooner or later there will be an 'ultimate authority' who knows some proposition *a priori.*[29]

To come now to laws of nature to see what difficulty arises. Laws of nature are one and all established *a posteriori* by man. If a man knows *a posteriori* what is necessary then there must be at least *someone* who knows it *a priori.* Hence if a law of nature be necessary, and if a man knows it *a posteriori*, then at least *someone* among men is required to know it *a priori.* But admittedly, no *man* knows any law of nature *a priori.* What, then, is the source of the idea that empirical laws of nature are, or may be, necessary?

The question ultimately turns out to be one about the evidence or proof showing that empirical laws of nature are necessary. But then Kneale's answer to it is clear-cut. It would be appropriate here to let him speak for himself:

> It is evident from the nature of the case that no one can produce an unquestionable example of a truth of principle which he does not know *a priori.* For, although we may suggest that some hypotheses of natural science are such truths, the inductive method on which we rely when we accept these hypotheses does not allow us to claim knowledge of them. But it should not be supposed that this consideration is a strong objection to the theory put forward here. In order to show that ampliative induction, whether primary or secondary, is a rational policy it is not necessary to prove that there *are* truths of principle [which are not known *a priori*]. It is sufficient to establish that there *may be,* i.e. that the suggestion is not absurd.[30]

That the suggestion is not absurd has already been shown in the Introductory Chapter by way of arguing, although in a general way, that the notion of empirical necessary truths is not absurd. In the specific case under consideration Kneale's argument or observation is as follows:

> When they are engaged in their ordinary concerns, inductive scientists usually assume the existence of such [i.e. empirical necessary] truths with natural faith. If this assumption could be *disproved,* there would, indeed, be no reason why they should continue their efforts. But I have argued that the common attempts [embodied in the alternative theories examined before] to disprove it rest on a misconception;

> and this is all that is required, at least until someone produces an objection which is more difficult to meet. For we want to make true conjectures about the boundaries of possibility, and induction is the only systematic way of trying to do what we want to do.[31]

Kneale concludes by saying :

> A traveller in the desert who is dying of thirst will struggle towards the place where he thinks he sees an oasis. If presently he is satisfied that what he saw was only a mirage, he may as well lie down and die. But, for a man who understands his situation, even the thought that he may reach water by going in that direction is enough to justify further effort.[32]

These words of Kneale carry conviction indeed.

More light on his theory of natural necessity may be thrown through consideration of the Kantian view as to natural necessity. Kant's view is considered, and then Kneale's view is compared with it, in the next section.

9.4 Consideration of Another Source of Inspiration for Kneale - The Kantian Theory of Natural Necessity

9.4.1 Kneale's reference to Kant

Kneale writes at one place in his *Probability and Induction*:

> When we look for an explanation we want to discover not merely a theory which co-ordinates some, or even all, of the empirical generalizations hitherto established by primary induction, but, if possible, *the* theory under which all possible generalizations can be subsumed. *As Kant maintained, our thought is guided by the ideal of a single, all-inclusive system of natural necessity.* Why we should have a craving to

> discover this I cannot say, but the fact seems to be beyond doubt.[33] [Italics not in the text]

In the above passage Kneale explicitly refers to Kant's theory of natural necessity. Kneale here takes Kant to have connected the necessitarian status of natural laws with scientific systematization[34]. Although he has given here no textual reference to any passages in Kant's work, such passages can be adduced in plenty, and will be adduced soon from Kant's third *Critique*. Meantime, it is worth pointing out that, as the above observation about Kant made by Kneale is not frequently noted, Kant's influence on Kneale's theory of natural necessity is usually overlooked.

Note.[35] The reason why, among Kant's writings, it is his third *Critique* which is here selected for special consideration is that only there all the relevant points bearing on his theory of natural necessity are stated - and stated clearly.

But even in his first *Critique* - *Critique of Pure Reason* -, Kant has not failed to give a kind of indication of his commitment to natural necessitarianism.

Thus at B 198 / A 159 of the first *Critique* he observes: 'Even natural laws, viewed as principles of the empirical employment of understanding, carry with them an expression of necessity, ...'[36]

Kant hastens to add in the paragraph that follows that 'necessity according to concepts' is not found in any 'empirical proposition, however general its application'.[37]

There is no contradiction between Kant's observation that natural laws carry with them an expression of necessity and his second observation implying that this necessity is not necessity according to concepts. His point comes to this:

The necessity of natural laws is not conceptually comprehensible; it is opaque to our (human) intellect. Unlike the necessity of the categorial principles of pure understanding, which is a transparent necessity, the necessity of the empirical laws of nature is an opaque one, which is why it is that man's intellect cannot comprehend it.

The point will become clearer when the third *Critique* comes to be studied. It will be clear then that, although human understanding, for lack of insight into natural necessity, is not in a position to admit it, there is yet something - namely, reflective judgment - which has to admit it, because necessity goes with the law-character of certain empirical rules which are regarded as *laws*, namely, empirical natural laws, and unless certain empirical rules are regarded as laws, scientific systematization in accordance with them cannot be carried out.

Incidentally, it may be well to recall one question which was previously raised: what is the *source* of the idea of natural necessity? To this - it may be said - the Kantian answer is: reflective judgment in the sense of the third *Critique* is the source of the idea of natural necessity.

9.4.2 Kant's theory of natural necessity

In his third *Critique* – *Critique of Judgment* ('Judgement')[38]- Kant observes in the Introduction, section IV, about empirical natural laws:

> These laws, being empirical, may be contingent as far as the light of *our* understanding goes, but still, if they are to be called laws, (as the concept of nature requires,) they must be regarded as necessary[39] [Italics in the text]

Again in section V:

> ...the objects of empirical cognition are determined, or, ... are determinable, in divers ways ... ; and each of these modes must ... have its rule, which is a law, and, consequently, imports necessity: although owing to the constitution and

> limitation of our faculties of cognition we may entirely fail to see this necessity.[40]

Still again in section V:

> ... Understanding ...needs a certain order of nature in its particular rules which are only capable of being brought to its knowledge empirically, and which, so far as it is concerned, are contingent. These rules ... must be regarded ... as laws, i.e. as necessary - for otherwise they would not form an order of nature - though it [i.e. understanding] be unable to cognize or ever to get an insight into their necessity.[41]

A careful examination of these three passages serves to bring in full relief three important points:

First, the empirical laws of nature, so far as the light of our (i.e. human) understanding goes, are contingent; for it cannot cognize, or get an insight into, their necessity.

Secondly, the empirical rules, if they are to be called laws, have to be regarded as necessary, because - as the second of the passages above indicates - to be a law is to import necessity. Thus the necessitarian character of empirical laws goes with their lawlikeness.

Thirdly, as the third of the above-quoted passages says, the empirical rules have to be regarded 'as laws, i.e. as necessary' because otherwise they would not form an *order of nature*. This means that there cannot be an intelligible *order of nature*, and so a satisfactory scheme of scientific explanation of natural phenomena, unless the empirical rules are endowed with a necessitarian, lawlike, character. This point needs to be clarified. When the clarification is given, it will be seen that, with Kant, natural necessitarianism is connected with scientific systematization.

Systematization of natural phenomena in accordance with empirical laws, (which, as laws, have to be regarded as necessary) is, for Kant, the work, not of understanding, but of reflective judgment ['judgement'] in the sense of the third *Critique*. For the sake of providing textual evidence, some brief passages need to be quoted again from the 'Critique of Judgment':

> The reflective judgement which is compelled to ascend from the particular in nature to the universal, stands . . . in need of a principle. This principle it cannot borrow from experience, because what it has to do is to establish just the unity of all empirical principles under higher, though likewise empirical, principles, and then the possibility of the systematic subordination of higher and lower. Such a transcendental principle ...the reflective judgement can only give as a law from and to itself....[42]
>
> ...the principle of judgement, in respect of the form of the things of nature under empirical laws generally, is the *finality of nature in its multiplicity*....[43]
>
> The finality of nature is ... a particular *a priori* concept, which has its origin solely in the reflective judgement. For we cannot ascribe to the products of nature anything like a reference of nature in them to ends, but we can only make use of this concept to reflect upon them in respect of the nexus of phenomena in nature - a nexus given according to empirical laws.[44]

If the whole Introduction to Kant's third *Critique* is gone through carefully, his view will be clearer without the help of any commentary. He has indeed a number of considerations in explanation of his view. However, the following clarification presented by G. Buchdahl by reference particularly to one of Kant's arguments in the fourth section of the First Introduction may be of some use:

> An infinity of uniformities is always possible; it is our 'need' alone to 'think experience as a system' that limits this infinity, by demanding that 'nature' should be 'characterized as experience qua empirical system', by for instance putting

> particular laws under more general ones... [Thus] the necessitarianism of empirical laws, their lawlikeness, is a function of the unifying procedure of... [reflective] judgment ....[45]

It is also worth mention that the principle on which, according to Kant, reflective judgment proceeds is characterized by Robert E. Butts as 'systematic finalty'[46]. As he explains it: ' "systematic finality" is ... intimately connected with concepts of system, e.g. simplicity, lawlikeness, parsimony, and the like.'[47]

In the above exposition of Kant's theory of natural necessity the relevant major points have all been covered and sufficiently substantiated by textual citations so as to leave no scope for suspicion on any point. There are some Kant-interpreters (e.g. A. F. Apett)[48] who think that Kant has laid the basis for a correct theory of induction in the Transcendental Analytic of the first *Critique*. Buchdahl has shown[49] that this is a wrong interpretation. In the above exposition, which depends considerably on Buchdahl's Kant-interpretation, it has been suggested that Kant has laid the firm basis for a correct theory of induction, rather, in his third *Critique* by highlighting, in this *Critique*, the necessitarian status of empirical natural laws and clearly connecting natural necessitarianism with the methodological procedure of scientific systematization.

9.4.3 Kneale's theory of natural necessity compared with that of Kant

A comparison of Kneale's theory of natural necessity with that of Kant can now be made.

First, Kneale, like Kant, admits that we (i.e. our, human, intellect) cannot cognize, or get an insight into, the necessity of empirical natural laws.

Secondly, Kneale, like Kant, thinks that certain empirical generalizations have nevertheless to be accorded a lawlike, necessitarian, status if a firm basis of a correct theory of induction has to be laid.

These two points of agreement together serve to strengthen what has already been said previously, namely, that Kneale's theory of natural necessity is a theory of opaque necessity[50] - a necessity not transparent to our, human, intellect, but still worthy of acknowledgement and emphasis for our urgent scientific needs.

Thirdly, the scientific needs in question are the needs for scientific systematization and explanation of natural phenomena in accordance with empirical natural laws ascending from the lower to the higher, and thence to the still higher, and so forth. On this point, Kneale only shares the view of Kant (as the quotation from the former's work at the outset of this section, i.e. 9.4 indicates).

But, whereas Kant has developed his theory subjectivistically, Kneale has rather developed his theory along the realist line. This suggests that Locke's influence on Kneale surpasses Kant's influence on him.

Note[51]. That Kant's theory of natural necessity has been developed *subjectivistically* is evidenced by the fact that, with him, natural necessitarianism connects with the methodological procedure of scientific systematization as guided by an *a priori* principle which reflective judgment 'can only give as a law from and to itself'. (See one of the passages quoted before in 9.4.2.) Kant puts this point more clearly in a later passage in the third *Critique* by saying: 'Thus judgement . . . is equipped with an *a priori* principle for the possibility [i.e explanation] of nature, but in a subjective aspect. By means of this it prescribes a law, not to nature (...), but to itself (...), to guide its reflection upon nature.[52]

9.5 A Brief Statement of a Recent Form of Natural Necessitarianism

A theory of natural necessity developed along a different line has been published lately (in 2006). The object of this section is not to explain, but only to state briefly, this theory, because explanation of it (which demands explaining a number of issues) does not belong to the assignment in this work.

Alexander Bird in his paper entitled 'Laws and Essences'[53] espouses a view called 'Dispositional Essentialism'[54] according to which[55]

> (DE) Some properties are essentially dispositional and these properties include the properties that figure in the fundamental laws of nature.
>
> This view is opposed to Categorialism which is a widespread view to the effect:
>
> (C) All properties are categorical.
>
> To the categorialists-
>
> (CL) The laws are metaphysically contingent relations among categorical properties.[56]

Bird has sought to show that dispositional essentialism (DE), which he promotes, leads rather to partial necessitarianism about laws, which is to the effect:

> (PNL) At least some of the laws of nature are metaphysically necessary.[57]

The question arises whether it is possible to go beyond partial necessitarianism to full necessitarianism about the laws of nature, such as this:

> (FNL) All the laws of nature are metaphysically necessary.[58]

Bird concedes that it is possible to accept (PNL) without accepting (FNL). But he says that this would give a mixed view of laws, according to which some of the laws of nature are necessary, while others are contingent. This would be, he concedes, 'an untidy metaphysic, with two classes of laws'. Theorists have generally sought a unified account of laws. Accordingly, Bird says: 'if we accept:

> (U) Whatever it is, the true account of fundamental laws is a unified account then a commitment to (PNL) becomes a commitment to (FNL).'[59]

Bird goes on to develop this theory, distinguishing in the process between a strict law and a *ceteris paribus* law, and seeking to show that his dispositional essentialism gives a natural account of both strict laws and *ceteris paribus* laws.[60] In the end, however, he comes to express a worry, hoping nevertheless that something better may emerge out of future discoveries in physics.

As already said before, the objective in this section is not to explain, but only to state briefly, Alexander Bird's theory of natural necessity. The purpose of this brief statement is to indicate that a theory of natural necessity as such has not yet become outmoded. It is still being developed, although along a different line.

With regard to Kneale's theory of natural necessity (and connected doctrines), C. D. Broad observed in 1950:

> ...It is a very happy circumstance that doctrines which are at the moment unfashionable should be put forward by a man like Mr Kneale, who is fully aware of the strength and the weakness of the current orthodoxy... .[61]

Kneale's necessity theory of natural laws - to consider this one particularly - might have seemed 'unfashinable' at that time - i.e. during the heyday of the regularity theory. That, however, cannot be said about it at this time. A revival of interest in natural necessitarianism has taken place. It is, indeed, true that such a theory is being developed along a different line. This is nothing unexpected: some, from time to time, work on an old topic in a new way, while others try to investigate how much an old theory is still working. As regards Kneale's theory of natural necessity, it has to be said that there is yet some need for further research on it. There are indeed some serious difficulties in it. Kneale himself has admitted it. He says in the Preface to his *Probability and Induction*:

> ...I am acutely conscious of the difficulties of my views and the insufficiency of my arguments, and yet I cannot see any other way of describing matters which seems at all plausible.[62]

The last sentence in this observation is immensely significant. For one thing, it has considerable merit, because it has been seen that some other ways of describing the relevant matters (such as the ways of the regularists, regionalists, prescriptionalists, and instrumentalists) have not proved more convincing. For another thing, it is a source of inspiration to some who are eager to pursue further research on the subject along his line.

A concluding note is added hereinafter.

Notes

1 In his CRITICAL NOTICE of Kneale's 'Probability and Induction', in *Mind*, IX, 1950, pp. 94 - 115. See the last para. of this CRITICAL NOTICE.

2 For the expression 'objective necessity', see, e.g. W. and Martha Kneale, *The Development of Logic*, Oxford, 1962, (reprinted 1964), p. 651.

3 See (i) W. Kneale, 'Truths of Logic', *Proceedings of the Aristotelian Society*, vol. 46, 1946, pp. 207 - 34;

(ii) W. Kneale, 'Are All Necessary Truths True by Convention?' *PAS*, sup. vol. XXI, 1947, pp. 118 - 33;

(iii) W. Kneale, *Probability and Induction*, First edition 1949, reprinted 1966, § 9; and also pp. 257 f .

(iv) W. and Martha Kneale, *The Development of Logic*, pp. 628 ff.

4 In 1.5 above.

5 Kneale, 'Truths of Logic', *PAS*, vol. 46, 1946, p. 223.

6 'Marks' if the words are written, and 'sounds' if they are uttered.

7 See p. 226 in 'Truths of Logic'.

8 *Ibid.*, p. 227.

9 *Ibidem.*

10 'Carnapian', because Kneale develops his criticism in reference to Carnap's *Logical Syntax of Language*, pp 302 ff.; see *Probability and Induction*, p. 34 n.

11 See first para. of p. 34 of his book under reference.

12 In what Chisholm calls sentence *T*, where he was supposed to write 'Being red excludes being blue', he writes 'Being blue excludes being red'. His point is, however, sufficiently clear.

13 R. M. Chisholm, *Theory of Knowledge*, 2nd ed., Prentice-Hall of India Private Limited, New Delhi, 1987, p. 54.

14 In *The Development of Logic* also (p. 639) Kneale says that in the objective (i.e. extra-linguistic) world 'there is a range of distinct hues which can be divided as we divide it by use of our colour words. Anyone who accepts conventionalism ignores this... .' There is an objective incompatibility of characters which a necessary statement of the sort under consideration expresses, and modern conventionalists who find necessity, and so impossibility and even incompatibility, in language alone ignore this.

15 *The Development of Logic*, p. 638.

16 *Ibid.*, pp. 634 - 35.

17 *Ibid.*, p. 638.

18 Cited from Strawson's *Introduction to Logical Theories* [London, 1952], p. 12, in *The Development of Logic*, pp. 638-9.

The omission-sign, [...], after the sentence 'They are already drawn', is not inserted in their citation from Strawson's book under reference by Kneale and Kneale. It is inserted by us from Strawson's *Introduction to Logical Theory*, Methuen, London, University Paperback edition 1963 (reprinted 1971), p. 12.

19 *Ibid.*, p. 639, second para.

20 Kneale and Kneale here give no reference. But it is well known that Chisholm (e.g.) would count the proposition cited here as an example among those which are known *a priori* and still are not analytic. Cf. Chisholm, *op. cit.*, p. 60.

21 *The Development of Logic*, p. 637.

22 *Ibidem.*

23 The reference here is to Ayer's *Language, Truth and Logic*, 1936, p. 103. In Ayer's *Language, Truth and Logic*, Victor Gollancz Ltd., London, 1967, his definitions in question occur on p. 78.

24 Kneale and Kneale, *loc. cit.*

25 *Ibid.*, pp 637 - 638.

26 Kripke, *Naming and Necessity*, Oxford, 1980, p. 38.

27 See above, 1.5.

28 Chisholm, *op. cit.*, p. 47.

29 *Ibidem.*

30 Kneale, *Probability and Induction*, p. 258.

31 *Ibid.*, pp. 258 - 259.

32 *Ibid.*, p. 259: last three sentences of the last para.

33 *Ibid.*, p. 253.

34 Cf. also Gerd Buchdahl, 'The Conception of Lawlikeness in Kant's Philosophy of Science', in Lewis White Buek, (ed.) *Proceedings of the Third International Kant Congress,* March 30 - April 4, 1970, D. Reidel Publishing Company, Dodrecht: Holland, 1972, p. 157.

35 This note is inserted in order to set the record straight.

36 See N. Kemp Smith's translation (Macmillan, London, First ed. 1929, 2nd impression with corrections 1933, reprinted 1968), p. 195.

The words which Kemp Smith has translated as

'carry with them an expression of necessity'

have been translated by J. M. D. Meiklejohn (Colonial Press, New York,1900, p. 112) as

'possess also a characteristic of necessity'

and have been translated by F. Max Müller (Anchor Books, Doubleday & Company, Inc., New York,, 1966, p. 133) as 'carry with them a character of necessity'.

Meiklejohn's and Max Müller's translations of the relevant portion here appeared to be more straightforward.

Kant's original German words (see *Kritik der reinen Vernunft,* B 198, in Band 1, 1922, of Immanuel Kant: *Samtlitche Werke*, hg. v. O. Buek, P. Gedan, W. Kinkel, J. H. v. Kirchmann, K. Vorlander, F. M. Schiele, Th. Valentiner; Felix Meiner, Leipzig) are

'führen zugleich einen Ausdruck der Nothwendigkeit'.

37 Kemp Smith's trans., p. 195, second para.

38 The spelling 'Judgement' is James Creed Meredith's. The spelling followed by us with many others is 'judgment'. This is not to say that the latter spelling is better. (We are aware that, according to Fowler, the former is the better spelling.) Anyway, the spelling 'Judgement' is adopted in this work in those quotations where that spelling occurs.

39 Kant, *The Critique of Judgement*, translated by James Creed Meredith, Clarendon Press, Oxford, 1928 (reprinted 1978; 1980 impression printed by Morrison & Gibbs Ltd., London), p. 18.

40 *Ibid.*, 183, Meredith's trans., p. 22.

41 *Ibid.*, 184, Meredith's trans., p. 24.

42 *Ibid.*, 180, Meredith's trans., pp. 18 -19.

43 *Ibid.*, 180, Meredith's trans., p. 19.

44 *Ibid.*, 181, Meredith's trans., p. 20.

45 See p. 157 in Buchdahl's paper in Beck, *op. cit.*

46 Robert E. Butts, 'On Buchdahl's and Palter's Papers', *ibid.,* p. 190.

47 *Ibid.*, p. 199.

48 See Buchdahl's paper, *ibid.*, p. 151.

49 In his paper under reference.

50 For Kneale's use of the phrase 'opaque to the intellect', see his *Probability and Induction*, p. 97, end of the second para.

51 This note is inserted in order to provide a clarification that is needed.

52 *Critique of Judgement*, 185 - 6, Meredith's trans., p. 25.

53 Alexander Bird, 'Laws and Essences', in Alice Drewery, ed. *Metaphysics in Science*, Blackwell Publishing, Melden, MA, USA, 2006, chap 5.

[54] *Ibid.*, p. 64.

[55] *Ibid.*, p. 63.

[56] *Ibid.*, p. 64, see also p. 63.

[57] *Ibid.*, p. 65.

[58] *Ibid.*, p. 68.

[59] *Ibidem.*

[60] *Ibid.*, p. 69.

[61] *Mind*, vol. LIX, 1950, p. 94.

[62] Kneale, *Probability and Induction*, p. v.

CONCLUDING NOTE

Kneale's theory as to the logical character of natural laws, which is known as his theory of natural necessity, has been explained, and its main sources have been explored. Some of the principal objections to the theory have been examined by Kneale, and it has been seen that his criticisms are sound. The main alternatives to the theory have been considered by him seriously, and no one of these alternatives has been found to be any more satisfactory than his theory. There are some strong positive recommendations in favour of his theory in its turn. Thus it has been mentioned in the Introductory Chapter that the theory is in keeping with the actual practice of natural scientists in their conjectures of law, and it has been pointed out in the Final Estimate that the theory provides a straightforward explanation of the belief that ampliative induction is a *rational* policy. It seems, therefore, that there are good grounds for supposing that the theory has a title to acceptance, in the sense that withholding it is not more reasonable than accepting it.

The fact that the theory has been defended by Kneale at great length against its powerful critics like Karl Popper and the fact that it has been found susceptible of defence against other critics not attended to by him amply prove that it is *eminently defensible.* And the fact that so acute a philosopher as Karl Popper - to refer to him again - has been led ultimately to revise his own definition of physical or natural necessity as a result of Kneale's criticisms is the best proof that the latter's theory under reference is *fairly intelligible.*

So it appears that there are good reasons for believing that the primary objective of the present work, as set out in the Preface, has been achieved. This is not to deny, however, that still some further research on the subject is necessary.

APPENDIX I

HUME'S CRITIQUE OF CAUSAL NECESSITY: SOME SOPHISTICATED VERSIONS

I
Foreword

In the History of Western Philosophy, Hume, an eighteenth century philosopher, remains contemporary even today with his epistemological and metaphysical ideas drawing a vast literature upon it. Hume is a staunch empiricist reacting strongly against his rationalist predecessors, who founded their philosophy on what they consider as self-evident principles, deducing their epistemological and ontological theories from them. Hume is influenced by Locke's rejection of innate ideas and maintains, like Locke, that all our ideas must originate from experience. Hume follows Newton's experimental methods in investigating the powers and workings of human mind. Just as Newton discovered the general laws of physical objects such as the laws of motion and the law of gravitation by examining the behaviour of physical objects, Hume relies on introspective study of the human mind to discover the general principles related to human mind in order to develop a science of human mind.

Three important notions found in Hume's epistemology are : 'perception', 'impression' and 'idea'. By 'perception' Hume means any conscious state of the mind and perception is subdivided into two, viz., impression and idea. Impression again may be of two types - sense experiences such as visual, tactual, olfactory, gustatory, auditory and kinesthetic, and introspective feelings such as anger, desire, joy etc. He refers to the former in his *Enquiry* as 'outward impression' and in his *Treatise* as 'impression of the sensation'. The latter is called by him in his *Enquiry* as 'inward sensation' and in his *Treatise* as 'sensation of reflection'. By an idea Hume means any conscious state other than impression. The distinction between impressions and ideas, according to Hume, lies in points of vivacity and force. While the impressions are more lively or vivid and forceful, the ideas are comparatively dull and faint. Hume, however, is cautious enough to add that a person in a disordered state of mind may have ideas as lively and vivid as impressions. There is another tacit point of difference between impression and idea, as pointed out by Jonathan Bennett[1], in terms of objectivity. Impressions of sensation are those obtained in the actual perception of things. Scholars find difficulty in these two incompatible criteria of distinction between impression and idea, but let us grant that Hume has made his point and proceed further to find how Hume utilizes his empiricist criterion to explain the idea of causal connection.

Before the discussion on Hume's theory of causal connection, reference to what is known in present day as Hume's 'Fork' seems essential. The Fork is fundamental to Hume's empiricism and the twentieth century version of it. In section iv of his *Enquiry* Hume presents the Fork thus: 'All objects of human reason or enquiry may naturally be divided into two kinds, to wit, 'Relations of Ideas and Matters of Fact'. The former are absolutely certain and discoverable by mere thought, independent of experience. The latter are based on experience and are never certain, for there is no logical contradiction involved in its denial. In other words, propositions about relations of ideas are intuitively or demonstratively certain and they do not assert the existence of any non-abstract entities. Propositions concerning matters of fact, on the other hand, are neither intuitively nor demonstratively certain and they do assert the existence of non-abstract entities.

There is one type of proposition which Hume considers as concerning matters of fact even though do not assert the existence of any non-abstract entity. They may be called the bridging propositions. They are the propositions, which taken together with a proposition reporting the sense-experience at a particular time or through a series of time-sequence, imply the existence of some non-abstract entity not observed at the same time or the time-sequence. For example, the causal maxim 'every event has a cause'. Though the proposition does not assert the existence of any non-abstract entity, taken along with the proposition reporting some observed event, it implies the existence of its cause though the cause may remain unobserved. Another important bridging proposition is the proposition asserting the law of uniformity of nature. In fact, all laws of nature are regarded by Hume as bridging propositions, which imply the existence of a non-abstract entities.

As has been stated earlier, Hume maintains that propositions concerning matters of fact including the bridging propositions are neither self evident nor demonstrable. Hume's reasons for maintaining this has been brought out in a candid manner by George Dicker in his book entitled *Hume's Epistemology and Metaphysics*. The reason for the propositions concerning matters of fact are not self-evident, is this:

If a proposition states a matter of fact then it asserts or implies the existence of some non-abstract entity.

If a proposition asserts or implies the existence of some non-abstract entity then it is not self-evident.

∴ If a proposition states a matter of fact then it is not self-evident.[2]

The first premise of the above argument is true by Hume's definition. Hume's reason for maintaining the second premise as true is that any proposition is self-evident if its truth may be ascertained just by examining it but the truth of propositions asserting or implying the existence of some non-abstract entity cannot be known in this way.

Now, the reason why a proposition concerning matters of fact is not demonstrable may be stated. A proposition is demonstrable, according to Hume, if there is a set of self-evident propositions such that the set, taken along with the contradictory of the proposition, is self-contradictory. The propositions concerning matters of fact are not demonstrable for there is no set available, comprising of self-evident propositions, such that the set, taken along with the negation of the statement concerning matters of fact, leads to self-contradiction.

In Part I of section IV of his *Enquiry* Hume states that all reasoning concerning matters of fact seem to be based on causal connection. Using this relation alone one may go beyond his perception or memory. But what is the exact nature of this relation, according to Hume ? The next section is devoted to the discussion of the nature of causal relation.

II

Hume's Theory of Causal Connection

The rationalist predecessors of Hume believed that the cause possesses a power to produce the effect. There is a necessary connection between the cause and the effect such that if the cause occurs the effect is bound to occur. Inference about the future is justified only on the ground of this necessity of causal connection.

Hume is guided by his empirical principle in his analysis of causal connection. The meaning of any idea, for him, is understood only if we can trace some impression corresponding to it. He says:

> ...When we entertain, therefore, any suspicion that a philosophical term is employed without any meaning or idea (as is but too frequent), we need but enquire, *from what impression is that supposed idea derived*? And if it be impossible to assign any, this will serve to confirm our suspicion.[3]

The proper application of this dictum, Hume hopes, would enable us to achieve clarity and precision in cases of philosophical reasoning. If there be any obscurity or ambiguity in any complex idea, then we have to define, that is, enumerate, the simple ideas that compose the idea. But, even after the definition is 'pushed up' to the simplest ideas, if some confusion or vagueness still remains, then Hume's suggestion is to produce the impression or the original sensation of which the idea is a copy.

Hume launches his search for the impression of necessary connection in his *Enquiry* 'in all the sources, from which it may possibly be derived'[3a]. Obviously, one may begin the search with cases of causal situation involving material objects like Hume's favourite example with billiard balls. Hume finds that when one billiard ball strikes another, all one can see is that the cue ball strikes the object ball and the second ball rolls away, perhaps one can also hear a clicking noise when the former strikes the latter and nothing more. We do not see the first ball exercising any power to roll the second ball. Upon this Hume remarks:

> ...When we look about us toward external objects, and consider the operation of causes, we are never able, in a single instance, to discover any power or necessary connexion; any quality, which binds the effect to the cause, and renders the one an infallible consequence of the other. We only find that the one does actually, in fact, follow the other.[3b]

Hume next turns towards mental phenomena in search for the impression of necessary connection. Hume examines the situations involving our will and the voluntary action performed upon it and also between our will and deliberate thinking. He then argues that in none of them a necessary connection is detected in introspection. If we were aware of a necessary connection between our will and its effect in voluntary action, then we would understand how the mind interacts with the body, but since we do not understand the secret connection between mind and body, it has to be admitted that there is no experience of necessary connection between our will and the resulting voluntary action. Certainly if a force is detected in such cases then we would know as to why we can move some parts of body at our will but not some other parts. For, the force may be regarded as present in the former cases, but not in the latter. However, the fact is that one does not know as to why certain parts of the body may be moved at will but not others. Further, the limbs are moved not because of the will alone, there are other neurological factors and brain events. But the brain events are not known, neither a connection between the brain event and the neurological and muscular events are apprehended. Similarly, when we deliberately involve ourselves to think in a certain manner after we will to do so, we do not understand the mechanism through which the will acts to produce the thought. Mental causation, according to Hume, is more mysterious.

Thus all one can find in experience is an *exceptionless* regularity of a relation. The unfruitful search for the impression of necessary connection leads him to conclude that the ideas of cause and effect (and similarly all the ideas involved in our thought about necessary connection) are separable in the sense that the idea of the one does not include that of the other. Thus, Hume says in his *Treatise* :

> ...as all distinct ideas are separable from each other, and as the ideas of cause and effect are evidently distinct, 'twill be easy for us to conceive any object to be non-existent this moment, and existent the next, without conjoining to it the distinct idea of a cause or productive principle. The separation, therefore, of the idea of a cause from that of a beginning of existence is plainly possible for the imagination; and consequently the actual separation of these objects is so

> far possible that it implies no contradiction nor absurdity; and is therefore incapable of being refuted by any reasoning from mere ideas, without which 'tis impossible to demonstrate the necessity of a cause.[4]

When Hume denies the necessary connection between cause and effect, or between any two features connected by a law of nature, he has obviously logical necessity as his model of necessity. Had there been a necessary connection, Hume thinks, it would have been known *a priori*. But can we know the necessity of causal connection by conceptual analysis, that is, by the mere examination of the idea of cause ? Certainly not. In perception of the cause for the first time, we do not see its necessary connection with the effect. Even if the cause and the effect are both present before the senses for the first time, that is, even if we are witnessing their conjunction for the first time, we do not know any necessary connection holding between them at that moment. Hume says:

> ...The mind can never possibly find the effect in the supposed cause, by the most accurate scrutiny and examination. For the effect is totally different from the cause, and consequently can never be discovered in it. Motion in the second billiard-ball is a quite distinct event from motion in the first: nor is there anything in the one to suggest the smallest hint of the other.[5]

What, then, is the source of this idea of necessity ? There is no impression of necessary connection in the perception of the objective world or introspection of mental states. All that we note in our experience is the constant conjunction of two types of event. Because of the regular co-presence of the two relate in our experience and no experience of any exception to the regularity, the mind is 'determined by custom' to consider its usual attendant whenever any one is experienced, and it is this determination which enables us to talk of necessity. This expectation of one event on perception of another is the impression of reflection from which one obtains the idea of causal necessity. This necessity, then, is mind-dependent. We project our mental expectation outward into the physical world and think that there is a necessary connection between the two events or objects. A passage from the *Treatise* is worth quoting here:

> ...Upon the whole, necessity is something, that exists in the mind, not in objects; nor is it possible for us ever to form the most distant idea of it, considered as a quality in bodies. Either we have no idea of necessity, or necessity is nothing but the determination of the thought to pass from causes to effects and from effects to causes, according to their experienced union.[6]

Hume's reason for denial of necessary connections in nature may be analyzed into two points. These are:

1. The things or states of affairs involved in the so-called necessary relation are separate, for the connection is not known to be necessary, when the connection is perceived for the first time. Upon experiencing any one of the kind for the first time, it is not possible to infer or predict the other. This *impossibility of prediction* of one from the other suffices to prove that they are separate, and if they are separate then there is no necessary connection between them.

2. It is possible to imagine the things bound by a law of nature as separate. That is, it is always possible to conceive one in separation from the other. This means that a change in the course of nature described by a law is conceivable. Though bread, for example, has always nourished in the past, we may very well think of a piece of bread which does not possess this property. *Conceivability of the opposite* of a law suffices to prove the absence of necessity of natural laws.

Some present day thinkers, like Evan Fales, contend that actually Hume 'provides two distinct criteria for assaying the existence of necessities in nature'[7]. Taking logical necessity as the paradigm of necessity, a statement may be taken to convey a necessary connection, for Hume, if (i) its opposite is inconceivable, and (ii) it states a connection between two things or states of affairs such that it is possible to infer each of the connected ones from the experience of the other. The failure of natural law to comply with these two conditions, namely, the 'inconceivability of the opposite' and the 'possibility of prediction' leads Hume to conclude that laws are not expressive of necessary connections existing in nature. Fales, however, remarks that in Hume's argument the two criteria are deemed as 'interchangeable'[8] and that Hume himself has been found to conflate the two.

To summarize, the essence of causal connection, according to Humean analysis, lies not in necessary connection but in the regular succession or constant conjunction of two phenomena. All laws are not anything more than regularity. This view, in the history of philosophy, is known as the 'regularity theory'.

III

An Examination of Hume's View

The regularity theory attracted great many philosophers of different ages. The doctrine, its supporters claim, has removed the problematic notion of necessity - a notion, which cannot be defined after logical necessity, from the notion of causal and other laws. But the theory has invited some strong objections against it. Some of the criticisms of Hume's regularity theory are taken up.

3.1 The problems involved in Hume's search for the impression of necessary connection

It is a fundamental principle for Hume that every simple idea is preceded by a corresponding impression. Since Hume goes in search of an impression of necessary connection, obviously for Hume, the idea of necessary connection is a simple one. Hume argues that there is no objective necessary connection, as the idea of necessary connection cannot be traced to any impression of sensation or reflection. How far is this argument acceptable ? First of all, how did Hume come to know the truth of his fundamental principle ? The principle, according to Hume himself, has exceptions. If a person is presented with a spectrum of all the different shades of blue except one - the one which he has never experienced. Hume is convinced that the person will have an idea of the missing shade. Obviously then, Hume allows the possibility of having an idea without the corresponding impression. It is needless to find out whether someone in fact gets the idea of the missing shade in this manner. What is important is that Hume himself is aware of a counter-example to his general maxim. The maxim then is not a necessary truth. And if it is so, then the search for the impression of necessary connection and, subsequently, the rejection of an objective necessity on the ground that no such impression may be found seem not inevitable.

Again, Hume never doubts that we possess an idea of necessary connection, but he considers it impossible to trace it to any impression received from the objective world. In this connection, Stout contends:

> If we never get an impression of the necessary connection between cause and effect in any particular instance of causality, it would seem that Hume's main methodological principle must be abandoned.[9]

Hume intends to show that our belief in objective necessity is false. However, Stout points out that in order to have a false belief about necessity we are, nevertheless, to have an idea of necessity and in absence of the idea we cannot even have a false belief about it. In Stout's words again :

The trouble stems from Hume's tendency to conflate the question of what our idea of necessity is an idea of, or what is our idea of necessity, and the quite different question of how that idea ever gets into the mind, or why we ever ascribe necessity to certain things we find in the world.[10]

3.2 Hume's search for an impression of necessary connection seems unnecessary

There are eminent philosophers who regard causal power as perceptible. We all have experience of the waves eating away the shore; the planes are seen hitting the twin towers of the World Trade Centre at New York and the buildings crumble down. Examples of experiences like these may be multiplied. The direct perception of causal power stands as the warrant of the existence or objectivity of causal relation. Hume's endeavour to find out a rational justification for the authenticity of what is given in perception seems unnecessary. Normally what is given in perception is accepted as true and no reason is required to prove the existence of the objects known in perception, unless there are counter-examples pointing to the opposite direction. We have direct experience of causal power and scientific experiments corroborate its validity. There is no need for further justification.

Of course, the perception of causal powers, as pointed out rightly by Harre and Madden, is not similar to the perception of colour, for 'a (A) potent entity does not wear its causal powers like a ripe apple wears its redness'. The perception of causal efficacy of a thing, to them, is similar to perception of the motion of a thing. There can be no doubt about the perception of the motion of a thing. We can clearly distinguish the states of motion of a thing from the states it stayed static. Yet, the thing seems to acquire no change in essence as it starts moving. They say:

> A moving thing is not perceptually distinct from a motionless thing. The perception of its motion is a genuine perception.

> Its motion is not inferred from its successive occupations of different relative positions. An iron ball depressing a cushion is qualitatively no more than an iron ball, yet we see it pushing upon and reshaping the cushion.[11]

Besides, if necessity is a determination of the mind, then can we take the idea of necessity to be an idea of this 'determination'? To maintain this is to move away from the standard linguistic usage of causality. If necessity is a determination of the mind, then all our talks about a necessary relation between two phenomena become statements about us and not of the external world. Hume perhaps could see this absurdity and he intends to avoid the subjectivist and psychological view. For this purpose, Hume introduced his "associationistic explanation" in terms of custom or habit and its "projection" upon the things and events. However, upon examination, this associationistic account turns to be inadequate. Hume never cares to show as to how habit generates the idea of necessity. Nor does he clearly spell out the way in which the habit or expectation is projected upon the external objects and events of the natural world. Further, as Harre and Madden puts succinctly:

> ...We have no more the impression of 'habit' than we have one of 'causal power'. Cause, repetition and habit are all in the same boat, so to speak, because they all seem to presuppose non-Humean elements... his (Hume's) explanation is made in terms of the notion of repetition which ... presupposes a more adequate analysis of memory than he gives and one which seems difficult to formulate in his own framework.[12]

3.3 The cause and the effect are not two distinct phenomena

Hume argues that the idea of the cause and that of the effect are distinct ideas. There is no necessary connection between them for the negation of the causal maxim is not self-contradictory. Does he here offer distinctness of two ideas as a proof of the absence of necessary connection between them ? It seems that he is not arguing but merely stating his views. What is the test of distinctness of two ideas, according to Hume ? It may be said that it consists in the possibility of conceiving one without the other. And possibility of conceiving means absence of self-contradiction. Stout's comments deserve our notice. He says:

> ...a statement is contradictory if it is the negation of a principle of logic either directly or when any terms in the statements are replaced by other terms which stand for the same idea. But then the notion of sameness or distinctness of ideas is being used in the test of contradictoriness whereas contradictoriness was originally invoked to explain the sameness or distinctness of ideas. Hume has no non-circular argument on this point at all.[13]

Hume succeeds in showing that constant conjunction cannot be a reason to prove necessary connection with *deductive* certainty. But the fact that there is no deductively sufficient reason for a conclusion does not make the conclusion unjustified. To say that there is no deductive reason is not to say that there is no reason at all. If Hume claims that no argument is valid where the conclusion does not follow deductively from the premises, then he is accepting an unnecessarily strict and narrow criterion of validity for arguments. This criterion would make most of the scientific inferences invalid and it is not compulsory to accept it.

Hume regards the cause and effect as isolated independent things or events because they may be identified and consequently described independently of each other. However, it may be pointed out that the description in which they are identified independently does not refer to their causal potency. Considered as cause and effect they are not independent of each other. Rather 'they are related through the generative mechanisms upon which they operate and through which they are produced'[14]. Hume's argument against causal necessity and his explanation of our feeling of necessity as due to habit, formed because of repetition, hinge upon his atomistic epistemic presupposition. If objects are taken as independent and isolated, we can never claim to see their causal connection. If our impressions indeed furnish us with atomic isolated ideas, then it is but natural that there would be no impression of a connection. However, this very assumption is wrong, according to many philosophers.

Harre and Madden think that Hume is right in saying that statements about matters of fact are not logically necessary. That a change in nature is logically conceivable proves this obvious fact. However, from that it does not follow that there can be no necessary connection between matters of facts.

3.4 Inductive scepticism

Inductive inference is central to our normal life and scientific procedure. If laws of nature are believed to assert nothing more than regularity, then inductive scepticism becomes inevitable. A non-Humean philosopher's reaction to inductive scepticism would be very strong for it seems to 'question part of the bed-rock of our beliefs'[15]. And any philosophical theory that puts the rationality of our inferences from the observed to the unobserved into question goes counter to the most basic belief of our life and calls for its rejection. The regularity theory may be abandoned just on that account.

Inductive inference, according to Hume, is an invalid inference for in induction we pass from the observed to the unobserved cases. Hume is right in maintaining that we cannot offer any deductive justification of our inductive procedure because a law, being a regularity, means 'all observed cases' + 'all unobserved cases'. Understandably, the deductive rules of logic do not permit us to infer a law from all the observed cases; that would certainly be going beyond the premises. Nevertheless, it is a truth that induction is rational. Armstrong's justification is:

> The sort of observational evidence which we have makes it rational to postulate *laws* which underly, and are in some sense distinct from, the observational evidence. The inference to the laws is a case of inference to the best explanation. If the inferred laws exist, then, of course, they entail conditional predictions about the unobserved (if it is an F then it will be a G').[16]

Of course, the best explanation is no proof of the truth of the explanation. The laws with natural necessity justify our inductive practice, but the regularists have no justification for the inductive practice. A law, for a regularist, is a conjunction of observed manifestation of regularity with unobserved similar manifestation. This account of law fails to explain the observed regularity, e.g., that Fs are Gs, and also fails to show why a law implies regularity in unobserved cases. The theory that laws are *more* than mere regularities is in a better position to explain observed regularity. It allows us to infer the continuation of observed regularity in unobserved cases. Upon this view, inductive justification takes the following pattern:

Observed regularity → law → unobserved regularity

(Observations of togetherness of F and G lead us to postulate the law that 'All Fs are Gs'. This is a case of inference to the best explanation - an inference that is non-deductive but reasonable enough. The law asserts an objective necessary connection between Fs and Gs and this necessity justifies our inference that the unobserved Fs are Gs.)

The regularists' inference, on the other hand, is reduced to:

Observed regularity → law (observed regularity + unobserved regularity) → unobserved regularity

This is equivalent to:

Observed instances → unobserved instances.

Armstrong argues that the rationality of inductive inference is a necessary truth. If the truth that inductive inference is rational is believed to be contingent, then a question would arise immediately: what leads us to believe in this contingent truth ? Accepting some inductive justification for this contingent truth is to be involved in a vicious regress of justification. Thus that inductive inference is rational must be a truth and a necessary truth.

Again, if events are momentary phases, then persistence or continuity of physical objects becomes inexplicable. Hume tries to explain the experiences of continuity in terms of resemblance. But, Harre and Madden observe that the idea of a substance with its causal potency can provide the material basis for the continuity of things. This continuity is essential in order to speak of change in nature for every change implies some continuous elements. Without an idea of substance, Hume is left only with accidental persistence of patterns. The Necessitarian doctrine is in a better position for there is an ontological tie to bind things or properties together. To put in the language of Harre and Madden:

> Physical systems do not necessarily exist, but if there are any systems of natural kinds at all in a universe (and how else can we speak of a universe ?) then something will necessarily follow in that universe[17]

They explicate little later:

> If this stuff is as a matter of fact hydrogen, and if hydrogen is as a matter of fact an aggregate of atoms, each of the same structure, and if that structure accounts for both the valency and for the spectrum of that element, then if it has this set of chemical properties it is *not possible that* it does *not* have this spectrum and vice versa.[18]

A Humean, however, remains unperturbed by these difficulties.

Simon Blackburn calls this demand for some persistence in nature a demand for some 'secret spring or principle' in virtue of which the world retains its order; 'the desire for a Straight-jacket on the possible course of nature: something whose existence at one time guarantees constancies at any later time'. This demand for the Straight-jacket is specially made to dispel 'the inductive vertigo'. But, in Hume's work Blackburn finds a distinction made between the Straight-jacket and a 'causal nexus' - a nexus between two events over and above regular succession. The connection in a Straight-jacket has to be efficacious through changes of time; otherwise, it would itself be 'a case of coincidence or fluke, another contingency crying out for explanation and engendering inductive vertigo'[19]. The nexus, however, can change in principle - the power that works at one point of time may cease to be effective at some other time and there is no contradiction in supposing the change. The nexus does not provide a Straight-jacket but is equally efficacious in dispelling the inductive vertigo. Hume's intention, Blackburn observes, was to reject the apprehension of a Straight-jacket in cases of causal connection. His positive theory is sketched by Blackburn as below:

> ...The mind's perceptions, which form the material with which it must work, come to us only as a regular succession of events. However, upon acquaintance with a regular succession the mind changes, but *not* by forming an impression or idea of anything not given in one instance alone. It changes *functionally*: it becomes organized so that the impression of the antecedent event gives rise to the idea of the subsequent event. No new aspect of the world is revealed by this change: it is strictly *nonrepresentative*,.[20]

Blackburn feels that Hume disallows a representative idea of thick connection in causality. But, that does not take away anything significant from 'a Bare Humean':

> ...she goes through the functional change which Hume describes, and conducts her expectations and actions accordingly. She can be an enthusiastic natural scientist, finding concealed features and concealed patterns in nature to aid prediction. . . . she will be a virtuoso at the salient features that are usable day by day to control her world. What else does she need ? Are we sure she is missing anything at all - isn't she a bit like you and me ?[21]

Molnar points out that the Humean theory of laws 'fails to reveal what it is about laws that enables them to limit possibilities'. Humeans take the laws as *de facto* generalizations. It leaves unexplained 'how something's being just so can make its not being so impossible'[22]. If the mind is functionally changed to expect and act in a certain way by the repetition of constant conjunction of two phenomena, this expectation becomes nothing more than a 'lucky guess'. A pragmatist may not want anything more than this, but some philosophers may still remain unsatisfied !

3.5 Conceivability of the contradiction of laws does not disprove the necessity of laws

We may utilize Kneale's reply to Hume in his *Probability and Induction* to make this point. Kneale states in following words (the passage is often cited in philosophical writings):

> In any sense of the word 'conceive' which is relevant to the argument, an ability to conceive the contradictory of a supposed law of nature does not disprove the suggestion that the supposed law is a principle of necessitation. This can be seen from consideration of a mathematical analogy. In 1742 Goldbach, an otherwise unknown correspondent of the Swiss mathematician Euler, suggested that every even number greater than two is the sum of two primes. This conjecture has been confirmed for all the even numbers for

> which it has been tested, but during the past two centuries no one has succeeded in demonstrating its truth. The attitude of the mathematicians towards it can, therefore, be expressed by the statement 'Goldbach's conjecture looks like a theorem, but it may conceivably be false'.[23]

Kneale admits that there is an important distinction between Goldbach's conjecture and the case of natural laws; for, unlike a mathematical proposition, a natural law is not ever in principle demonstrable. He points out that this difference only strengthens his argument. 'If the conceivability of the contradictory is not to be taken as a disproof of necessity in mathematics, where proof is attainable by *a priori* reasoning, why should it be supposed to furnish such a disproof in natural science ?'[24]

Kneale's argument has been explained not exactly in the same manner by different writers. Goldbach's conjecture, falling short of demonstrative proof, is not known to be true or false. But if subsequent demonstration proves Goldbach's conjecture to be necessarily true, what then ? If it is necessarily true, then its contradictory is necessarily false, and therefore surely *inconceivable* according to Hume's principles. For Hume, in the case of a mathematical proposition, its negation is inconceivable in the sense of involving a contradiction. But if it is inconceivable, how can it still be *conceivable* (as it is required to be, if Kneale is to be right) ? Here one may utilize a point made by Karl Popper in the course of his criticism of Kneale's argument. One may say that the contradictory of Goldbach's conjecture, if the conjecture is necessarily true, can still be *conceived* in the sense in which we, in an indirect proof, start by *conceiving* a proposition to be true and end by concluding that this proposition is nevertheless inconceivable. Popper says: 'Indeed, an indirect proof may well be put thus: "*Conceive* that *a* is true. Then we should have to admit that *b* is true. But we know that *b* is absurd. Thus it is *inconceivable* that *a* is true." '[25]

Here when it is said to be *inconceivable* that *a* is true, 'inconceivable' means the same as 'leading to a contradiction'. When, however, the indirect proof starts by *conceiving* that *a* is true, *conceive* does not mean what does not lead to a contradiction. The word is used in a different sense. This sense is, as Popper points out, 'a little vague and ambiguous'. But it would be misleading to say that it is *not conceivable* that *a* is true, 'considering that we did start by conceiving, precisely, the truth of '*a*'[26]. It will have been clear by now that the contradictory of Goldbach's conjecture, supposing that it is proved to be necessarily true, is after all *conceivable* (in some sense), even though, it is inconceivable in the sense of leading to a contradiction.

But if one utilizes Popper's point in the above way, Kneale's argument cannot be expected to give general satisfaction. This is indeed the view of Popper, who says:

> ...Thus 'inconceivable' in logic and mathematics is simply another word for 'leading to an obvious contradiction'. *Logically* possible or 'conceivable' is everything that does not lead to an obvious contradiction, and logically impossible or 'inconceivable' is everything that does. When Kneale says that the contradictory of a theorem may be 'conceivable', he uses the word in another sense.[27]

The implication of Popper's observation is that Kneale's argument 'operates with a sense of 'conceivable' different from the one intended'[28] and is therefore not satisfactory.

Ayer, who is also critical of Kneale's argument, does not, however, contend that Kneale, in saying that we can conceive the contradictory of Goldbach's conjecture, operates with a sense of 'conceivable' which is different from the intended sense. Ayer argues that in so far as Goldbach's conjecture has not been *demonstrated* as either true or false, both the conjecture and its contradictory are conceivable. As he puts it:

> ... It may happen, in doing logic or pure mathematics, that one formulates a statement which one is unable to prove or disprove. Surely in that case both the alternatives of its truth and falsehood are conceivable.[29]

Accordingly Ayer concludes that 'Kneale makes his case'[30].

3.5.1 Ambiguity of the phrase 'a change in nature'

Hume's argument against natural necessity relies on the assertion that a change in the course of nature is conceivable, for it is not self-contradictory. But, what does Hume mean by a 'change in nature'? The phrase is ambiguous according to Harre and Madden. Either it means that a particular object of a certain kind retains its essential nature while its ability to produce its usual effect changes, or, it is interpreted to suggest that the particular looses some or all the characters it previously had and retains 'at worst only a dubious numerical identity derived from temporal continuity of the occupation of a place or continuous sequence of places'[31]. A 'change of nature' in any of the above senses has its own difficulties.

The first sense of "change in nature", stated above, is logically inconsistent, according to Harre and Madden. The essential nature of a thing is identified in natural science by reference to its causal potency. To imagine a situation where a thing retains its essential nature is to imagine a situation where it is capable of producing its usual effect. Therefore, to say that a thing retains its essential nature and does not produce its usual effect is to say that a thing is both capable and not capable of producing its usual effect. This is sheer self-contradiction.

If the particular is found without its usual attendant, i.e., if a thing behaves differently in identical circumstances, then we explain it as a case where the essential nature of the thing has undergone a change. This is a case of explicable change where a substance in course of time looses some of its causal power and yet maintains a continuity and identity in respect of some other properties. A particular medicine, e.g., a capsule, may retain its numerical identity and yet loose its causal efficacy after the date of expiry. Such an account of change in nature is acceptable for there is a material basis for the change - 'an unproblematic material basis for the identity of the substance through change'. However, 'such cases cannot be offered in support of the Humean contention'. Thus 'change in nature' in the second sense is irrelevant for Hume's purpose. It is irrelevant to say that there is no necessary connection between the nature of a thing and the effect it brings about for the essential nature of a thing might change. What is needed for the Humeans is an inexplicable change in which a fountain pen becomes a pig, a flower vase becomes a woman. And Harre and Madden think that such inexplicable changes are only to be 'sought in the fertile imagination of Humeans'[32]. These changes can be viewed as change of one thing into another or they may be held as cases in which one thing is suddenly replaced by another thing. In the former case, we are induced to find a rationale behind the change while the second prevents the possibility of any explanation of the change. There are attempts in science to explain the sudden change in nature rationally by inventing 'a quasi-substance to be the bearer of continuity through change'[33]. But a thing cannot retain its essence and possess an altogether different nature or causal potency. 'An electron and a positron *cannot* turn into a pig, but then neither can a pen, and we all know that'[34].

Hume contends that there is no logical contradiction involved in conceiving a violation of a natural law. We may easily conceive that the sun will not rise tomorrow or an apple instead of falling downward would fly upward in the air. But, a critic of Hume finds these counter-examples to natural laws 'intolerable', 'rendering as they do, all common-sense and scientific explanations and predictions empty'[35].

3.5.2 Further point in Kneale's reply to Hume

Kneale points out that when Hume maintains that we can *conceive* the contradictory of a supposed law of nature, what he can be taken to mean is that we can *imagine* its contradictory. To conceive or think of a *matter of fact* is, for him, to imagine it. An idea, he says, is an image. An image is a copy of an impression. An impression in Hume's terminology is what is called in modern terminology a sensum. It follows that, according to him, we can imagine (that is, have an image of) a sensum or sensa only. When we imagine, e.g. lightning, we really imagine a bright visual impression which is a sensum. When we imagine thunder, we really imagine a loud auditory impression which again is a sensum. When, therefore, we imagine the contradictory of the law, for example, that lightning causes thunder, we really imagine that a bright visual sensum is not sometimes followed by a loud auditory sensum. But the difficulty is that a natural law is not a statement about sensa. It is a statement about perceptual objects. Indeed, when we speak of lightning, we are speaking about a public event which can be perceived by other people or photographed. When we speak of thunder, we are indeed speaking about a public event which again can be perceived by other people or recorded in a machine. A natural law being in this way a statement, not about sensa, but about perceptual objects, Hume's objection ultimately proves to be irrelevant.

IV

Sophisticated Versions of the Regularity Theory

Kneale's criticism of the regularity theory of natural laws has brought to light the problem of explicating the true character of natural laws from the pure regularity point of view. A satisfactory answer to Kneale's objection is not found at least in Hume's own work. The main point of Kneale's objection is that a law of nature has a counterfactual import and is on that account logically stronger than an accidental generalization. It is by this counterfactual import that a law of nature can be distinguished from a universal statement of facts.

The regularists also have felt the need to distinguish a law from a non-law, though the naive version of the regularity theory, as considered before, fails to offer a satisfactory criterion for this purpose. There are also other difficulties for the theory. Armstrong has shown that there are laws which do not satisfy the Humean stipulations. Again, there are many universal statements which the Humeans themselves would refuse to call laws, even though they satisfy all the Humean stipulations for a law. Various attempts have been made, on behalf of the regularists, to bring improvements upon Hume's theory to avoid these difficulties. In this way certain sophisticated versions of the regularity theory have arisen.

The attempts to improve upon the regularity theory have been broadly classified by Armstrong under two heads: (i) those versions which introduce 'an external criterion' to distinguish laws from non-laws, and (ii) the versions which give 'an internal criterion' - a characteristic belonging to the very nature of laws demarcating laws from non-laws. Suchting construes the rationale that might have dwelled in the regularists' minds to have led them to choose any of these two alternative modes of sophistication. He observes that since, for the regularists, a law-statement cannot be anything more than a mere contingent universal statement about matters of facts, the only way in which a law can be distinguished from other universal statements is by an appeal to 'certain specific relations that they bear to other items'[36]. The other item in the relation may be either the persons entertaining the statements as laws, or, some other statements. As the improvement attempted in terms of the former appeals to certain epistemic matters, viz. the attitude towards the uniformities, the nature of evidence supporting the laws, etc., this version of sophistication upon the regularity theory is called by Armstrong the 'epistemic version'. Suchting calls it the 'pragmatic version'[37], because the attitude towards a law is reflected in the special way in which a law-statement is used in guiding human action. This is the kind of explanation offered by Goodman, Ayer, and Strawson, besides Braithwaite and Ramsey. The latter alternative has again taken two forms: (i) the resiliency version offered by Brian Skyrm, and (ii) the systematic version adopted by Ramsey, Lewis, and others. The systematic version seeks to distinguish a law-statement from a universal statement of fact by means of some logical relation which obtains between a law-statement and some other statements. On this interpretation, the laws are, as Suchting puts it, 'objects of certain characteristic human attitudes, expressed . . . in the uses made of them and not others, in guiding human action. But these attitudes are taken not to constitute, but rather to be a consequence of, their being law-statements'.[38]

The above classification of the different attempts to improve upon the regularity theory is not intended to suggest that one version is an exclusive alternative to the other. The different versions are often found to go hand in hand. Suchting has mentioned Walters who has combined two versions. Mention may also be made of Braithwaite. In an article published in *Mind* (vol. 36, 1928) he has sought to explain the distinction between a law and a non-law in terms of belief. However, after twenty-four years in his *Scientific Explanations* he has justified people's belief in laws by reference to the relation a law-statement bears to the total system of believed or accepted statements. This explanation, he claims, is far superior in subtlety to his earlier solution, and this combines the epistemic version with the systematic one.

4.1 The Epistemic Version of Sophistication

Beauchamp and Rosenberg maintain that there is circularity in the sort of objection that Kneale has urged against the regularity theory of natural laws from the point of view of the counterfactual import of laws. Laws, according to Kneale, are distinguished from statements of accidental generalizations in that they support counterfactuals, but the notion of counterfactuals in its turn depends on an implicit understanding of the concept of laws. Hence, they contend, 'the supposed death knell of the regularity theory ultimately goes unexplained by Hume's opponents'. On the other hand, 'the Humean avoids a circular explanation of lawlike generalizations and counterfactuals by analysing *both* in terms of epistemically warranted attitudes'[39]. They further write: 'Lawlikeness and counterfactual support alike can be treated as a function of the degree of confidence generated by and vested in the supporting evidence.'[40]

The origin of this interpretation of law may also be traced in Hume. Hume regards the notion of a necessary connection as the most important component of our idea of causal connection. He recommends that this idea of necessary connection be understood as being due to habit, that is, a psychological fact 'about human beings and other animals, viz. propensities to associate in a reflex-like manner certain impressions with certain ideas'[41]. It would be more interesting, however, to see how this Humean way of explaining the idea of necessary connection in *psychological* terms has been developed further by Hume's followers in later years.

Thus Braithwaite suggests that the distinction between a law of nature and the other kind of universal statements may be explained on the ground of people's 'rational corpus of knowledge and reasonable belief'[42]. A law of nature, for him, is a subset of true statements. The honorific title of 'law of nature' is reserved only for those true statements which one has some special reason to believe. As he puts it:

> ... This account of natural law makes the application of the notion dependent upon the way in which the hypothesis is regarded by a particular person at a particular time as having

> been established: 'lawlike' may be thought of as a honorific epithet which is employed as a mark of origin.[43]

He specifies the conditions in which a statement is believed to be a law of nature. A law is accepted or believed on nondemonstrative grounds, that is, on grounds other than the complete enumeration of its instances. A statement is a law if it is supported by direct observation of some of its instances and is also indirectly supported by instances of other hypotheses which are subsumed with the first statement under a higher-level hypothesis. The statement 'All men are mortal' would not be called a law if the only evidence available in its support were the instances of men. There must be other reasons for believing in the law than the evidence of its instances alone. If the above statement is deduced from a higher-level hypothesis, namely, 'All animals are mortal', then the evidence supporting other general propositions, like 'All horses are mortal', 'All cats are mortal', etc., which are placed along with the general statement 'All men are mortal' on the same level and subsumed under the higher-level hypothesis 'All animals are mortal', would constitute its indirect evidence. Thus the statement 'All men are mortal' is accepted as true upon direct observation of the mortality of some of its instances and also on such other pieces of evidence that horses have died, cats have died, etc., and is for this reason regarded as a law of nature.

Braithwaite admits that this explanation has a paradoxical consequence. Upon it, a statement like 'All men are mortal' would be regarded as a natural law because 'it occurs in an established scientific deductive system at a lower level than a hypothesis (e.g. 'All animals are mortal') which has other lower-level hypotheses under it which are directly confirmed by experience....'[44] Paradoxically, the higher-level hypothesis, 'All animals are mortal', would not be considered a law because the only evidence supporting it is the evidence of its own instances. Braithwaite thinks that the paradox corresponds to the way a law of nature is generally put to use. A law is usually understood to provide an explanation of the instances coming under it. If the sole reason for believing a general statement is the 'direct knowledge of the truth of its instances', it is 'a poor sort of explanation of these instances'. On the other hand, if the general statement, besides its direct evidence, is also supported by indirect evidence, it has a greater explanatory power. The law, in that case, provides the grounds for believing the truth of its instances 'independently of any direct knowledge of such truth'[45]. Thus Braithwaite goes on to define lawhood in the following manner:

> The condition for an established hypothesis *h* being *lawlike* (i.e. being, if true, a natural law) will then be that the hypothesis either occurs in an established scientific deductive system as a higher-level hypothesis containing theoretical concepts or that it occurs in an established scientific deductive system as a deduction from higher-level hypotheses which are supported by empirical evidence which is not direct evidence for *h* itself.[46]

The formulation of lawlikeness, in so far as it is a formulation in terms of deducibility from higher-level hypotheses, has two obvious advantages. It provides an account that puts due emphasis upon the explanatory character of a law of nature. Secondly, though a law is distinguished from a non-law by means of the reasonable belief on the part of individual subjects, it does not reduce lawfulness to a purely subjective notion varying from person to person. As the 'rational corpora of many people with the same scientific education and culture agree in the scientific deductive systems at a given time'[47], there would be a general agreement that some statements, if true, are statements of laws of nature and that some others are accidental generalizations, though 'each of the people will mean something different by his statement'[48].

Braithwaite also includes hypotheses containing theoretical concepts in the class of laws; for these hypotheses, though not deduced from higher-level hypotheses, are not established by the process of induction by complete enumeration. The hypotheses containing theoretical terms are obtainable by the hypothetico-deductive method - the method of formulating the hypothesis and then deducing testable consequences from it. Both forms of hypothesis mentioned by Braithwaite have an explanatory role - they explain their instances, besides covering them. A true statement, then, is regarded as a statement of law after considering the 'way in which it could enter into an established scientific deductive system'[49].

P. F. Strawson begins his exposition of law-statements with the observation that if a statement is a law then it must be true omnispatially and omnitemporally. Any person uttering a law-statement anywhere at any point of time is uttering a true statement. Thus an ideal law-statement contains no such words the reference of which 'depends in any way upon the situation in which they are uttered'[50].

Strawson distinguishes a law-statement from a mere general statement which is not a law. Contingent general statements, according to him, are of two types: (i) restricted generalizations, that is, generalizations about a closed class, and (ii) unrestricted generalizations, that is, generalizations about an open class. To take, e.g., the statement 'All cats like fish': many of us would be inclined to regard this statement as expressive of unrestricted generality. Strawson, however, points out that the statement is not about an open class. He observes:

> ...But it would be possible to say: 'It *used to be true* that all cats like fish; but now X has bred a new strain of cats which detest fish.' When the pre-X talkers uttered the sentence, they made a true statement; but when the post-X talkers uttered it, they made a false one. So the class referred to was not ideally open.[51]

A law-statement, on the other hand, is a statement about an open class, and is, therefore, 'independent of contextual conditions'[52].

To regard statements as expressions of laws 'is both to emphasize the unrestrictedness of their application and to say something about the nature of evidence by which they are supported'[53]. The evidence for the truth of a law-statement, or, the evidence for the acceptance of a law, should in no way indicate that the law is about a class of which the members are 'limited in a very definite temporal sense'. The assertion of the law 'All S is P' should not depend on the evidence 'that there will be no more members, and that there never were more than the limited number of which observations have been recorded' of S. Finally, Strawson adds that the 'evidence which is both permissible and adequate to establish a law will . . . be adequate to establish also the related unfulfilled conditionals'[54].

Strawson admits that some contingently true generalizations of the form '(x) (Sx k Px)' are not laws. But from this it does not follow that no law-statements are contingent, that is, that no law can be of the form '(x)(Sx kPx)'. Strawson takes up the objection raised by Kneale. Kneale maintains that laws are not mere unrestricted generalizations, but are stronger than these. The counterfactual import of laws remains unexplained in the regularity account. An accidental generalization, 'All S is P', standing on the evidence that (i) there is a limited number of members of S and (ii) that there would not be any more added to this number, will not permit us to say that had there been another S then it would have been P. Thus the evidence that there is no S that is non-P does not suffice to make the statement, 'All S is P' a statement of law. Strawson seeks to explain the counterfactual import of laws within the regularity scheme. He maintains:

An *essential* part of the evidence for the conclusion that

> there (omnitemporally) is no *s* which is not *p* in our imagined case consists of evidence that the class of members of the species is limited in a very temporal sense; i.e. evidence that there will be no more members, and there never were more than the limited number of which observations have been recorded. All we need to add to our characterization of natural laws is the requirement that such evidence as this shall not be an essential part of our grounds for accepting them. Evidence which is both permissible and adequate to establish a law will then be adequate to establish also the related unfulfilled conditionals.[55]

To use law-statements, for Strawson, 'is both to emphasize the unrestrictedness of their application and to say something about the nature of evidence by which they are supported'[56].

The exposition of the epistemic version remains incomplete without a brief reference to Ayer. Ayer has sought to explain the distinction between a statement of law and a generalization of fact not in terms of the fact that makes the statement true or false, but in terms of the attitude people have in proposing the law. He maintains that the factual content of every form of general proposition is the same. But a law, as distinguished from an accidental generalization, has a counterfactual import. The scope of a law is not restricted to the actual; it extends equally to the possible. Understandably, then, the law is not different from a mere generalization in terms of what actually happens. The difference is only a difference in attitude. Ayer proposes 'to explain the distinction between generalization of law and generalization of fact, and thereby to give some account of what a law of nature is, by the indirect method of analysing the distinction between treating a generalization as a statement of law and treating it as a statement of fact'[57].

Ayer does not claim to provide a definition of natural law. He is well aware that there cannot be a one-one correspondence between every proposition that expresses a law of nature and a particular attitude that people actually have towards it. There may be natural laws that remain unknown to the human intellect. Such laws then may exist, but the laws being unknown, people do not have any attitude towards them. However, Ayer claims that the notion of unknown laws is not inconsistent with his theory that seeks to explain the distinction between a law and an accidental generalization in terms of people's attitude. Ayer does not explain this point. In the next section, the reason Ayer possibly has in mind will be examined. This exposition of Ayer's view may be concluded by noting what, according to him, are the specialities of the attitude towards a law. He writes:

> ...for someone to treat a statement of the form 'if anything has F it has Y' as expressing a law of nature, it is sufficient (1) that subject to willingness to explain away exceptions 'he believes that in a non-trivial sense everything which in fact has F has Y', (2) that his belief that something which 'has F has Y' is not liable to be weakened by the discovery that the object in question also has some other property X, provided (a) that X does not logically entail not-Y, (b) that X is not a manifestation of not-Y, (3) that the discovery that something had X would not in itself seriously weaken his belief that it had F, (4) that he does not regard the statement 'if anything has F and not-X it has Y' as a more exact statement of the generalization that he was intending to express.[58]

4.2 Some Difficulties of the Epistemic Version

The prima facie difficulty of the epistemic version is the explanation of unknown laws. Ayer has admitted the possibility of unknown laws, and Suchting believes that other thinkers, as mentioned before, 'implicitly' accept them. The problem is: If the epistemic version does not rule out the possibility of unknown laws, can it explain lawlikeness in terms of people's attitude ?

It is generally believed that the laws of nature are independent of human minds. They obtain irrespective of the existence of human beings and their knowledge. It is quite possible that some of the laws remain unknown to human minds. Thus Suchting maintains that 'it is unnecessary for the obtaining of laws that any law-statement ever be known or believed by any human being'[59]. But the recognition that there may be law-statements towards which people have no attitude undermines the very theory of laws that makes an essential reference to people's attitude. In the epistemic version, what would be the status of the unknown law-statements towards which people do not possess the special attitude which they have for other, that is, known, laws ? The epistemic version faces this problem here: A statement, S, which was not a law previously when the law was unknown and accordingly there was no attitude towards it, becomes a law when it is known and people develop an attitude towards it. This has led Ayer to make a modest claim that the explanation of the distinction between a law and a mere generalization in terms of people's attitude may at most be taken as an explanation in terms of the sufficient condition and not a necessary condition of lawlikeness. Though Ayer has not spelled out his position about unknown laws within the framework of his epistemic version, Suchting conjures up the possible reason which Ayer could have provided. The reason may be stated in the following words:

> ... to say that there is an unknown law expressible by sentence S is to say that what would normally be asserted by S is true, though nobody in fact asserts S, and that there are certain situations which would be the subject-matter of evidence-statement E relevant to S, such that if someone were to be in possession of E, and also consider S, then that person would have an attitude to S satisfying conditions on laws.'[60]

Thus the only way the epistemic version can tackle the problem of unknown laws is by an introduction of the subjunctive mood as to what people would have believed under unfulfilled conditions. Under the explanation provided by the epistemic version, a law is a statement of uniformity, if either we actually possess a certain attitude, A, towards it, or, if certain other (epistemic) conditions had been fulfilled, we would have the attitude, A, towards it.

Armstrong points out that the introduction of the language of counterfactuals would not really help the epistemic version. The counterfactuals of the epistemic theorists 'apparently demand the existence of certain laws about epistemic attitudes'[61]. Only some laws like 'Whenever there is a law, L, people have an attitude, A, towards it under circumstance, C, can justify their counterfactuals. But these laws themselves are regularities, and people must have a certain attitude to them. Thus the use of counterfactuals by the epistemic theorists makes their theory open to the charge of circularity.

Armstrong observes that even though it is not clear whether the attempt to sophisticate the regularity theory by the introduction of an epistemic condition can survive the charge of circularity, the following objection can be brought against it in any case:

> ...It is clearly possible that there should be a universe governed by laws, and one in which there were some Humean uniformities which we would not wish to account laws, but in which there were no minds. ... But in this universe there would be no Humean regularities involving epistemic attitudes, and hence, according to the Epistemic theorist, no laws.[62]

How in the knowerless world do we distinguish between a law and a non-law ? One might answer that in a knowerless world the distinction is not of any great significance. Nevertheless, one cannot deny that there is a difference, and if there is a difference at all, then what is the differentiating criterion ? In the epistemic version, the concept of unknown laws is explained in terms of subjunctive conditionals about human behaviour, and this in turn is explained in terms of laws about human behaviour. Consequently, in a knowerless world where there is no human being, there cannot be any unknown law. Again, as Suchting points out, in such a world, there would be no known laws either, for there are no human beings to possess any attitude towards them. Therefore, in a knowerless world there would be total lawlessness.

Besides, it is not clear why certain regularities are objects of the epistemic attitudes appropriate for laws, but not others. If this difference of attitude is not arbitrary, there must be a 'real or supposed difference in the objective nature of the uniformities in question'[63]. But recognition of an objective difference undermines the epistemic version itself. If there are objective differences, they should be enough to differentiate a universal statement of law from a universal statement of fact. Armstrong writes:

> This last objection shows that an attempt to modify the Epistemic view by talking only about the regularities which it would be *rational* to treat in certain epistemic ways, must appeal to differences in the regularities which make rational the difference in epistemic attitude. The modification therefore passes over into one of the Objectivist or internal solutions although in a concealed manner.[64]

Molnar argues that necessity and possibility are not epistemic concepts: what is necessary or possible does not depend on the knowledge of any one scientist or all the scientists of all times or the manner in which scientific knowledge is acquired or the evidence supporting scientific knowledge. The concepts of 'necessity' and 'possibility' and the distinction between a law and an accidental generalization are metaphysical issues. A law sets a limit to possibility, and the world is restricted by laws irrespective of our knowledge of the laws. How do we distinguish, for example, between the falsity and the impossibility of the statement: 'Nothing is a river of Cocacola' ? It has to be determined by reference to metaphysics, and not by epistemology.

We find that the epistemic theory does not succeed in explaining the difference between a law-statement and a statement of fact. Earlier a fusion of the epistemic and the systematic version has been observed in Braithwaite. Ayer's version of the theory has been found to be incomplete.

Attention may be drawn to another difficulty of the epistemic version. If the laws, following the epistemic version, are statements to which we have a special attitude, then, Suchting says 'the members of law-statements depend on *de facto* modes of functioning of human organisms'. Here arises a problem. The behaviour-pattern of people is not logically a fixed phenomenon; it may change owing to many factors. It is also possible to think about a world that has everything identical with our present world except the way people form their beliefs there and use those beliefs in regulating their lives. Again, there may be two different behaviour-patterns in the same world. But the epistemic view seems to disallow this. If the status of a law ultimately depends on people's attitude or the inductive policy people decide to adopt, then Suchting surmises, 'membership of the class of law-statements would be, logically, a matter of convention'[65]. If, instead of maintaining that a statement may be used for predictive purposes because it is a law, it is maintained, as Goodman does, that a statement is a law because of its predictive use, then 'there are as many possible sets of law-statements as there are possible predictive practices'[66]. This is, however, hardly acceptable as a satisfactory account of natural laws.

In defence of the epistemic theory, it may be urged that the criticism to the effect that if lawhood is explained in terms of people's attitude then there would be different laws for people with different habits or attitudes is not really damaging. If people's habit changes in the world, then the new world is not identical with the previous world, even though other physical elements remain the same. Likewise two worlds having identical elements except people's behaviour-patterns are not the same. And if the worlds are not the same, the laws in them need not be the same. Suchting replies that this is contrary to the commonly accepted theory of laws. A statement is a law of nature not in any special individual world inhabited by a special group of people. Once a statement is accepted as a law of nature, its status would remain unchanged even after a different set of people with different behaviour-patterns enter into the universe. The status of a law is independent of the existence of any individual. And if a theory is found to be inconsistent with the ordinary understanding, the inconsistency may be regarded as an objection to the theory.

Notes

1 Bennett J., *Locke, Berkeley, Hume: Central Themes*, Oxford University Press, Oxford, 1971, pp. 224-225.

2 Dicker G., *Hume's Epistemology and Metaphysics: An Introduction*, Routledge, London, 1998, p. 57.

3 David Hume, *Enquiries Concerning Human Understanding and the Principles of Morals*, ed. P. H. Nidditch, 3rd edn, Clarendon Press, London, 1975, Sec. II, p. 22.

3a Hume, D., *Enquiries Concerning Human Understanding and Concerning the Principles of Morals*, ed. Selby Bigge and P.H. Nidditch, Oxford University Press, Oxford, 1975, p. 63.

3b *Ibid.*, p. 63.

4 David Hume, *Treatise of Human Nature*, L. A. Selby-Bigge ed. Oxford, 1888, p. 80.

5 *Enquiries*, p. 29.

6 *Treatise*, pp. 165-166.

7 E. Fales, *Causation and Universals*, Routledge, London, 1990, p. 22.

8 *Ibidem.*

9 B. Stout, *Hume*, Routledge and Kegan Paul, London, 1977, p. 45.

10 *Ibid.*, p. 84.

11 *Ibid.*, p. 51.

12 *Ibid.*, p. 64.

13 Stout, 1977, p. 48.

14 Harre and Madden, *Causal Powers: A Theory of Natural Necessity*, Basil Blackwell, Oxford, 1975, p. 130

15 D. M. Armstrong, *What is a Law of Nature ?*, Cambridge University Press, 1983, p. 53.

16 *Ibid*, pp. 52-53

17 Harre and Madden, *op. cit.*, p. 80.

18 *Ibid.*, p. 131.

19 S. Blackburn, 'Hume and Thick Connexions', *Philosophy and Phenomenological Research*, Vol. 50, 1990, p. 241.

20 *Ibid.*, p. 247.

21 *Ibid.*, p. 250.

22 Molnar, 'Kneale's Argument Revisited', *The Philosophical Review.* Vol. LXXVIII, 1969, p. 88.

23 *Ibid.*, pp. 79-80.

24 *Ibid.*, p. 80.

25 K. R. Popper, *The Logic of Scientific Discovery,* Hutchinson, London, 1959, p. 429.

26 *Ibidem.*

27 *Ibidem.*

28 *Ibidem.*

29 A. J. Ayer, 'What is a Law of Nature?' in *Revue Internationale de Philosophie*, no. 36, 1956, reprinted in Ayer, *The Concept of a Person*, Macmillan, London,1964; here taken from B. A. Brody, ed. *Readings in Philosophical Analysis*, Prentice Hall, New Jersey, 1970 , p. 42.

30 *Ibidem.*

31 Harre and Madden, *op. cit.*, p. 143.

32 *Ibid.*, p. 106.

33 *Ibid.*, p. 108.

34 *Ibid.*, p. 109.

35 *Ibid.*, p. 70.

36 W. A. Suchting, 'Regularity and Law', *Boston Studies in Philosophy of Science,*
vol.14, D. Reidel Publishing Co., Dordrecht: 1974, p. 75.

37 *Ibidem.*

38 *Ibidem.*

39 T. L. Beauchamp and A. Rosenberg, *Hume's Theory of Causal Connection*, Oxford University Press, Oxford, 1981, p. 157.

40 *Ibid.*, p. 151.

41 R. B. Braithwaite, *Scientific Explanations*, Cambridge University Press, 1953, p. 302.

42 *Ibid.*, p. 301.

43 *Ibid.*, p. 302.

44 *Ibidem.*

45 *Ibid.*, pp. 302-303.

46 *Ibid.*, pp. 301-302.

47 *Ibid.*, pp. 304-305.

48 *Ibid.*, p. 305.

49 *Ibid.*, p. 303.

50 P. F. Strawson, *Introduction to Logical Theory*, Methuen & Co. Ltd., 1971, p. 198.

51 *Ibidem.*

52 *Ibid.*, p. 215.

53 *Ibid.*, p. 200.

54 *Ibid.*, pp. 199-200 .

[55] *Ibid.*, pp. 199-200.

[56] *Ibid.*, p. 200.

[57] A. J. Ayer, 'What is a Law of Nature?', *Revue Internationale de Philosophie,*

No. 36, 1956, reprinted in B. A. Brody, ed. *Readings in the Philosophy of Science*, Prentice Hall, Englewood Cliffs, 1970, p. 51.

[58] *Ibid.*, p. 53.

[59] Suchting, *op. cit.*, p. 78.

[60] *Ibidem.*

[61] Armstrong, *op. cit.*, p. 62.

[62] *Ibid*, p. 63.

[63] *Ibidem.*

[64] *Ibidem.*

[65] *Ibidem.*

[66] *Ibid.*, p. 81.

APPENDIX II

WHITEHEAD'S METAPHYSICS AND HIS REGIONALISM CONCERNING NATURAL LAWS

1. Foreword

Laws of science are considered to have a universal scope. Contrary to this view, Whitehead suggests that a scientific or natural law is a restricted generalization even though every instance coming under it is not enumerated individually. According to Whitehead, a thing of a particular kind may follow different behaviour-patterns and the same thing may possess different properties at different times and places, although the other prevailing conditions remain the same. This view, in philosophy of science, is called regionalism. Incidentally, Armstrong refers to two different interpretations of regionalism: (1) Regionalism may be interpreted to mean that there are different laws obtaining at different cosmic epochs. Though none of these laws are reducible to any other, all of them may be subsumed under a higher second-order law, when 'this second-order law determines that, for any time t, if the laws at time t are L, then, given a time g(t) which is a certain function of t, the laws at g(t) will be a certain function, f, of L'[1]; or, (2) Regionalism may be interpreted to assert that there are different laws in different cosmic epochs and that there are no higher-order laws to subsume the laws of different cosmic epochs. The law of each epoch is different from that of another epoch. The second version, according to Beauchamp, matches perfectly with a 'process and time-oriented philosophy such as Whitehead's.[2] ...Whitehead, with his introduction of novelty in different natural epochs, has rejected the idea of a single law of uniformity of nature running through different cosmic epochs. Laws, according to Whitehead, are mere contingencies holding in one epoch but failing in some other. An understanding of Whitehead's metaphysics seems essential to properly understand his theory of laws.

2. The Metaphysical Background of Whitehead's Theory of Laws

Whitehead's metaphysical view, which is described as process philosophy, first appeared in his *The Concept of Nature* (1920) and it was expanded in his *Science and the Modern World* (1925), *Process and Reality* (1929), and *Adventures of Ideas* (1933). Whitehead created a comprehensive metaphysical system, which is sometimes called by him speculative philosophy. He defines it as 'the endeavour to frame a coherent, logical, necessary system of general ideas in terms of which every element of our experience can be interpreted'. By the notion of interpretation he means that 'everything of which we are conscious, ... , shall have the character of a particular instance of the general scheme.[3].

Whitehead's process philosophy has developed, in part at least, as his reaction to the rapid change in landscape in contemporary physics witnessing a challenge to Newtonian theory by Einstein's theory of relativity and also by the quantum theory. He finds that science is concerned with the 'description and measurement' of real objects and that the objects are 'abstracted forcibly from the totality of things' for this purpose. Science accordingly does not represent reality in its true form - 'it is more like a blueprint'. On the other hand, '. . . the task of seeing wholes can belong only to philosophy'[4]. Whitehead speculates that reality, rather than being independent of experience, may itself bend to experience.

Whitehead rejects the Newtonian idea of nature as absolute, and 'attacks the time-honoured dichotomies of sense-experience and thought...'[5]. He rejects the 'bifurcation of nature' into perceived qualities known through sense-experience and the theoretical entities of scientific theories constructed out of the sense-data. His philosophy of science seeks to analyse 'the ontological status of scientific and mathematical concepts in terms of their derivation from the elements and relations of nature as disclosed in sense-experience'[6].

In his *Science and the Modern World* and also in his *Process and Reality*, Whitehead adopts a point of view called by him the 'organic point of view'. He recommends for every science 'a new aspect which is neither purely physical nor purely biological'. He finds that the words of our common language often cannot express his unique ideas. He has gone on to enrich language by developing some special coinages which stretch the applicability of language to his novel ideas. An understanding of his coinages is difficult even to a trained philosopher. Next some concepts important in Whitehead's philosophy are explained.

2.1 Whitehead's Notion of Actual Entities

Whitehead rejects the dualism between the mind and matter and the long tradition of philosophy to classify things of the real world into substance and attributes. The world, according to Whitehead, is made of infinite number of actual entities. Such entities are not anything permanent; they are representatives of momentary experience. The actual entities, for Whitehead, are all in a process. They arise and pass away. Following A. N. Johnson[7], the following features of a Whiteheadian subject or actual entity may be identified: (a) The actual entity is a component unit; (b) The content of the experience of the actual entity is mainly, though not entirely, affective; (c) The actual entity has its environment acting on its nature; (d) The actual entity becomes what it is as a result of its subjective reactions to the data provided by its environment; (e) The actual entity is autonomous - it selects data from its environment in accordance with a conceived ideal.

2.2 Whitehead's Theory of Prehension

The process by which an actual entity reacts to its environment is called 'prehension', and there are different types of prehension.

A prehension is conceptual if the actual entity prehends a general idea or ideal. Such prehensions constitute the mental pole of an actual entity. If the actual entity reacts to another concrete actual entity, then the prehension, according to Whitehead, is physical. Physical prehensions constitute the physical pole of an actual entity. Thus an actual entity is analyzable into component prehensions, conceptual and physical.

In every prehension there are three factors involved: (i) the subject, i.e. the actual entity in which a prehension takes place; (ii) the datum, i.e. the content or material of prehension; and (iii) the subjective form or attitude taken by the actual entity toward the prehended datum. Sometimes Whitehead also uses the term 'subjective form' to mean the entire inner life of an actual entity. Through the data prehended, an actual entity gives rise to another actual entity and the process of emergence of a new actual entity through grasping of data into its life is called by Whitehead concrescence.

Prehensions, again, can be positive or negative. When the data of prehension are included in the internal constitution of the new actual entity, the prehension is positive. In this type of prehension, the process of concrescence absorbs the data of prehension into the inner life of the new entity so much so that the data no longer remain external facts to which the entity reacts but become part of its private life. Positive prehension is sometimes described by Whitehead as 'feeling'. A negative prehension is one in which certain data are recognized as available, yet they are rejected as unsuitable. Negative prehension involves elimination where the data are inactive and does not culminate in any feeling. Even though the data are rejected in a negative prehension, this kind of prehension has a significant contribution in the making of the inner life of a newly arising actual entity.

2.3 Whitehead's Notion of Eternal Object

The process of development of an actual entity is guided by an ideal or abstract pattern, called by Whitehead an 'eternal object', i.e. 'any entity whose conceptual recognition does not involve a necessary reference to any definite actual entity of the temporal world'[8]. An eternal entity is often described in philosophy as a universal. An eternal entity, according to Whitehead, may be simple or complex. Whiteness, hardness, army etc. are simple eternal entities. A definite finite relationship involving a particular group of eternal objects is a complex eternal object, which, in philosophy, is often described as abstract essence.

Each eternal object is unique and different from all other eternal objects. They all possess an individual essence. They also possess a relational essence. The eternal objects are involved in a general system of mutual relation. The relation of one eternal object to others is internal, while the relation that an eternal object possesses to an actual entity is said to be external. Though an eternal object is not necessarily related to any actual concrete entity, it is not totally isolated from the world of actuality, firstly, because of its presence in God's primordial nature. Secondly, and there is a continuous striving toward its realization in some actual entities. The eternal entities are infinite and fixed in number; they cannot be created or destroyed. For Whitehead, actual entities and eternal objects are the only fundamental types of entities, while all other types of entities stand for the type of relation between these two fundamental types.

2.4 Whitehead's Rejection of Subject-Object Dualism

While explaining the relation between a prehending and a prehended entity Whitehead rejects the water-tight distinction between the subject and object. In physical prehension of an actual entity B by another actual entity A, the data for prehension into A are available only after the internal essence of B has 'evaporated, worn out and satisfied'. The relationship between the two entities, is, to put in the words of Whitehead, 'appropriation of the dead by the living'. Thus the actual entities 'perpetually perish' subjectively to become immortal objectively. In other words, the subject confronts the object and appreciates certain aspect of the object into its internal constitution. The relation between the subject and object involves two factors: i) the causal potency of the past impressing itself into the prehending entity's phenomenological field, and ii) the way in which the subject decides to ingress the object. The process of prehension, in this way, leads to transform the objectively given into subjective immediacy and process of concrescence. Thus the process of becoming proceeds from objectivity to subjectivity. The subject becomes what it is by arising from the object and it perishes to become a datum, available for future prehension. To quote Whitehead: 'Actuality in perishing acquires objectivity, while it loses subjective immediacy'[9]. The subject, so to say never exists independent of its previous objective environment. An actual entity is at once the subject of experience and the superject of its experiences. The superject is the objective aspect of the subjective form. It is, for Whitehead the data of objects that conditions the process of concrescence 'exercising its function of objective immortality'[10]. The superject has a transcendent function as an object. It is itself the projection of the subject that aims at satisfaction. It is essentially the subjectified object in the process of becoming objectively immortal.

2.5 Further elaboration of Whitehead's Metaphysics

A primary organism, according to Whitehead, is 'identified as the emergence of some particular pattern grasped in the unity of a real event', and 'each event involves the pattern of aspects of other events which it grasps into its own unity (its own prehension)'[11].

However, the process of physical prehension does not mean the total transfer of data from the old to the new entity. The transfer of data or content from entity B to entity A entails some elimination and loss because, when A arises, B is already dead and its contents are not available in immediacy. Besides certain data are eliminated according to the free will of the emergent actual entity A and the data prehended are arranged in the new subjective experience of A.

The actual entities of nature are not independent bits of existence; they are interrelated societies[12]. A group of actual entities forms a society 'when they all manifest a common eternal object'[13]. A society, which arises from the immanence of one actual entity in others by prehension, is different from a nexus in which the entities are related with each other in the most general sense.

Obviously then Whitehead's process metaphysics is not opposed to permanence. The actual entities are transitory, but the societies 'endure, at least for a time'[14]. Societies have antecedents and consequents. When there is a continuous succession of actual entities, there is a common element present in the series because the preceding entity is objectified in the immediately succeeding actual entity. This series of actual entities is called by Whitehead a personal society. A complex society, involving various series of personal societies, is called by Whitehead a corpuscular society. And the universe is made up of societies of societies of societies. The actual entities in the world exist in mutual cooperation in the sense that all past actual entities are the available data for the use of all present actual entities and all present actual entities furnish data for the use of all future actual entities.

Whitehead has jettisoned the idea of a simple location dominant in classical physics where matter is believed to exist in one particular point in the universe at a certain time without any relation to other forms of matter existing in different places and times. A particle of matter, for Whitehead, has no existence in isolation; 'it is essentially related to every other item of nature by the spatio-temporality of nature, and...has no meaning apart from this spatio-temporality'[15]

Events stand in a general relation to each other. This general relation is called by him 'extension', which 'is a part and whole relation and is hence transitive'[16]. Extension gives continuity to events. Every event extends over others. The relation of extension makes the events actual matters of facts by means of properties which arise in spatial relations. Further, events are involved in the process of 'becoming of nature' by means of the properties issuing in temporal relations. Nature is thus viewed by Whitehead as 'an interrelated structure of events'. Each event here possesses volume and duration and stands in the 'part and whole relation of extension which is more general than the specific notions of space and time'[17].

Whitehead rejects also the Newtonian concept of space and time. Things are generally believed to exist in space and time when the latter are said to be independent of things. For Whitehead, there can be no space and time apart from the actual entities. The actual entities are spatial and temporal, but space and time do not house the actual entities - they are internal relations. The nature of the actual object is determined by its spatio-temporal relations. In a different spatio-temporal relation, there is a different actual entity.

Another uniqueness of Whitehead's theory lies in his conception of time as a continuous process, a succession of different quantum of times. It does not flow; rather it moves by taking jumps. The universe is a series of successive cosmic epochs. In each cosmic epoch, a set of laws emanates, or rises to predominance. The set has a stage of endurance, and it gradually fades away as the society undergoes change.

Whitehead maintains a holistic attitude in understanding and interpreting the world. The entities of the universe possess an internal relation amongst them, and the changes in the entities bring about certain changes in their interrelations. Whitehead observes:

> ... an individual entity, whose own life-history is a part within the life-history of some larger, deeper, more complete pattern,

> is liable to have aspects of that larger pattern dominating its own being, and to experience modifications of that larger pattern reflected in itself as modifications of its own being. This is the theory of organic mechanism.

According to this theory, the evolution of laws of nature is concurrent with the evolution of enduring pattern. For the general state of the universe, as it now is, partly determines the very essences of the entities whose modes of functioning these laws express. The general principle is that in a new environment there is an evolution of the old entities into new forms.[18]

Beauchamp offers a schema as a 'simplification and reconstruction of Whitehead's view that it is logically possible, and not known to be empirically impossible, that relevantly similar and fully described causal items may produce dissimilar effects in different cosmic epochs'[19]. The schema is stated below:

1. 'All ag things are b & - p' is true in Cosmic Epoch 1.
2. 'All ag things are b & p' is true in Cosmic Epoch 2.
3. 'All ag things are p & - b' is true in Cosmic Epoch 3.

For Beauchamp, 1, 2, and 3, as they are stated above, cannot be true omnitemporally, since each falsifies the others. Nevertheless, there is no logical reason prohibiting their joint possibility; for such a reason would make the law of uniformity of nature logically necessary. It would also beg the question by denying the plausibility of the doctrine that different laws evolve in different cosmic epochs.

3. Whitehead's Theory of Natural Laws

By now it is clear that upon the Whiteheadian metaphysics some causal or natural laws arise in a definite society prevailing in a particular cosmic epoch. The society undergoes a change with the change in interrelations among actual entities. And in a different society there is a different set of laws. The laws of nature are understood not as laws running across different cosmic epochs.

Recurrences or uniformities are to be expected within a single cosmic epoch.

Whitehead, at the same time, recognizes the importance of the concept of natural laws. He admits that an accurate expression of the notion of law which 'has entered into the explicit consciousness of various epochs under every variety of specialization, arising from its coalescence with other components in the popular cosmology'[20] is an extremely difficult matter. He says:

> ...Let us grant that we cannot hope to be able to discern the laws of nature to be necessary. But we can hope to see that it is necessary that there should be an order in nature. The concept of order of nature is bound up with the concept of nature as the locus of organisms in process of development.[21]

That the laws are required for our understanding of the world is also insisted on by Whitehead in a different work:

The relations of sense-objects to their situations are complex in the extreme, requiring reference to percipient events and transmitting events. Apart from some discovery of laws of nature regulating the associations of sense-objects, it is impossible by unintelligent unsorted perception to form any concept of the character of an event from the sense-objects which might be situated there for percipients suffering from any normal or abnormal perceptions.[22]

A paragraph from his *Adventure of Ideas* expresses the same view:

> The notion of law, that is to say, of some measure of regularity or of persistence or of recurrence, is an essential element in the urge towards technology, methodology, scholarship and speculation. Apart from a certain smoothness in the nature of things, there can be no knowledge, no useful method, no intelligent purpose. Lacking an element of Law,

> there remains a mere welter of details, with no foothold for comparison with any other such welter, in the past, in the future, or circumambient in the present.[23]

Whitehead accepts the doctrine of immanence of laws. According to this view, the order of nature expresses the character of real things of the natural world. To know the essential character of these things is also to know the relations obtaining amongst them. If there are certain common elements found in the essences of these real things, then that accounts for the identities found in their mutual relations. Whitehead writes: 'some partial identity of pattern in the various characters of natural things issues in some partial identity of pattern in the mutual relations of those things. These identities of pattern in the mutual relations are the Laws of Nature'[24]. This view presupposes the essential interdependence of things. This doctrine is recognized by Whitehead as a rationalistic doctrine leaving an open possibility for understanding nature.

Whitehead also points out the following features of this theory:

1. Sciences provide us with explanations and not mere descriptions of observed facts.

2. In science, exact conformation to the laws is never expected. If all the things of the world had exactly the same essence everywhere, then the laws of nature would have to be considered to be strictly universal. In actuality, though the majority of the things of a particular kind are found to have the same character, the character is, nevertheless, absent in a few. In these cases, 'the mutual relations of these things will exhibit lapses when the law fails to obtain illustration'[25]. Understood in this sense, the laws of nature may be understood to have a statistical character.

3. Again, the laws are not viewed as permanent or fixed. The laws of nature evolve concurrently with the changes of natural things which constitute the environment. There could be no eternal law.

4. The theory recommends a 'limited trust' in the processes of induction. If the world is conceived as an environment in which we do only partly know the nature of a large number of objects, then we may claim to have some knowledge of the laws of nature governing the environment. Without the doctrine of immanent law and the supposed theory of the nature of the world, 'we should then acknowledge blank ignorance, and not make pretences about probability'[26].

5. The doctrine of immanent law becomes untenable without a plausible metaphysical doctrine, according to which the characters of the relevant natural objects are the outcome of their interconnections and 'their interconnections are the outcome of their characters' [27]. In other words, the doctrine is based on the doctrine of Internal Relations.

Whitehead, in his *Adventure of Ideas*, discusses three other theories of natural laws. They are considered below along with Whitehead's criticisms of them.

3.1 Whitehead's examination of the doctrine of imposition

Understandably this doctrine of imposition is based upon the doctrine of external relations between things in the natural world. Each of the existent beings may be understood in isolation from others. These ultimate beings are conceived to exist with 'private qualification', and they share no characteristic in common. Nevertheless, there is a necessity imposed on these entities for which they enter into relationships with one another. And 'these imposed behavior patterns are the laws of nature'[28]. These laws are not to be discovered by inspection of the nature of the ultimate existents of the world, nor can the nature of the things be inferred from the laws.

Deism lies at the root of this theory. Imposition implies an imposer, and the imposer, according to some such thinkers as Newton, is the transcendent imposer, i.e. God. Further, if the laws of nature are imposed by God, then they are to be exactly obeyed by all the entities of nature without exception. This is how the doctrine successfully explains the universality of laws and endorses a belief in the efficacy of laws in spheres lying beyond the range of meticulous observation. However, this theory is unacceptable to Whitehead. First, it is not compatible with his metaphysics of internal relation. Secondly, the things in nature are not exactly identical in their minute details. Nature is full of surprises, and there is no fixed law obtaining at all spaces and times. Whitehead remarks: 'the physicists in their recent researches have disclosed a novel illustration of capriciousness'[29].

3.2 Whitehead's examination of the positivist theory

Whitehead mentions another theory, described by him as the positivist theory. Upon this theory, the laws of nature are 'observed persistence of pattern in the observed succession of natural things ....Thus a law says something about the things observed and nothing more'[30]. No doubt, the theory puts the right emphasis upon a fundamental truth of scientific methodology. A great scientist like Newton insists that he is neither 'speculating nor explaining', he is rather 'enunciating a formula which expresses observed correlations of observed facts'[31]. Positivism has greatly influenced the Humean sort of atomism. The laws are believed to be the 'formulation of observed entities'[32]. Since Hume deals with subjective experience, he maintains that we have only a psychological expectation that the regularities or recurrences observed in the past would also recur in the future. Whitehead observes that Hume has no answer to the question whether there would be actual recurrences in the future, and, if so, why they occur at all. He has developed no metaphysics to support this expectation; he only tells that human life cannot be carried out without the 'metaphysical persuasion that the past does in fact condition the future'[33]. Now, Whitehead observes that nature is full of surprises; it does not always satisfy our anticipations.

Again, science is not satisfied with a general description of facts. It provides an 'explanatory description' that justifies the extension of laws beyond the observed actual instances. The positivists cannot appeal to statistics to justify an inductive leap from the observed to the unobserved. Whitehead's remarks in this context are noteworthy. He says:

> ... statistics tell you nothing about the future unless you make the assumption of the permanence of statistical form . . . There is no valid inference from mere possibility to matter of fact, or, in other words, from mere mathematics to concrete nature.[34]

Whitehead further points out that the theory is unable to explain the existence of alternative theories on the same subject. Moreover, if laws are only descriptions of what has been observed, 'we can describe what has happened, but with that description all possibility of knowledge ends'[35]. The main problem of this view is the restriction imposed by the theory upon our scope of knowledge. Upon this, we may know only the facts of observation which are 'rough, inaccurate and sporadic' and 'we must not ascribe, we must not expect, one step beyond our direct knowledge'[36]. The theory is unable to justify the strong urge of the scientists to go beyond the mere descriptions of facts and offer an *explanation* of the observed facts with some speculations about the future. The bridge that has been built at present between science and metaphysics with the doctrines of metaphysics modified to provide an explanation of actual events points towards the inadequacy of positivism.

3.3 Whitehead's examination of the doctrine of conventional interpretation

Whitehead mentions another doctrine which explains laws as conventions. To put it in the words of Whitehead: it 'certainly expresses the procedure by which free speculation passes into an interpretation of Nature. But Nature has subsequently been interpreted in terms of mathematical laws. The conclusion seems to be, that Nature is patient of interpretations which happen to interest us'[37].

Whitehead, however, thinks it erroneous to interpret natural laws in terms of mathematics and treat the laws as arbitrary conventions. Undoubtedly, convention plays an important role in the discovery or formulation of a natural law. The statements of laws are developed by human beings of a particular age. And the formulations of laws, to some extent, are dependent on abstract sciences which the scientists have chosen to develop. Nevertheless, the scientific 'convention should not be twisted to mean that any fact of nature can be interpreted as illustrating any laws that we like to assign'[38].

4. The Attractiveness of Regionalism

Beauchamp observes that Whitehead's view is indeed quite acceptable to all, unless one treats it as a 'conceptual truth' that the laws of nature express unrestricted uniformity without any exception. To Beauchamp, the theory of Whitehead's opponents does not possess an intuitive certainty. At least, Whitehead's view coaxes us to examine it critically. Whitehead believes that the laws neither express any omnitemporal and omnispatial truth, nor have any universal reference. As Beauchamp puts it:

> ...the most one can say about laws is that (A) no known data indicate that the examined instances of contemporary laws constitute the complete class of instances, and that (B) we have reasonable grounds for holding laws to be unrestrictedly universal within a certain spatio-temporal scope (whereas we can, by experimentation, know that accidental universals are close or subject to exceptions). The evidence

> for the knowledge claim in (A) coincides with the reasonable grounds of (B).[39]

J. P. Day points out that the question whether there are truly universal laws, is by no means so easy to settle...[40].

Regionalism is certainly a convincing doctrine in social sciences. In the study of human nature and economics, certain laws are accepted as true only within a certain age and domain. We all know that the laws determining the economy of a developing country are different from the economic laws of a developed country[41]

Day thinks that universalists are mistaken in taking scientific law-statements literally. As said earlier, though the law-statements are expressed in the timeless present, there is always some tacit qualification restricting the 'scope' of such generalizations. One wonders whether there exists at all an empirical law or a true universal proposition which is unconditionally true.

Again, since laws are established by inductive generalizations upon instances of a certain spatio-temporal zone, there is hardly any guarantee that the general propositions, so obtained, would be true at all places for all times. Certainly, it would be more rational to suggest that a law holds only under certain conditions ideal for the efficacy of the law. This ideal condition need not always be a single phenomenon; rather it may be a set of several conditions. Surely, our knowledge being limited, we are never absolutely certain of these special conditions to be able to incorporate them into our statements of laws. The law about the boiling point of water, or the law concerning the melting point of a metal, say gold, is true against a definite background. A change in the background often baffles the predictions based on the laws.

Whitehead's view is surely a reasonable one, if, in maintaining a regionalist attitude, he intends to endorse the importance of the conditions under which the law holds. Understood in this sense, the scientific laws may be viewed as 'conjectures about uniformities in limited regions of space-time'[42].

Toulmin, in his discussion of the nature of natural laws, examines Whitehead's theory. He holds that there is definitely a merit in Whitehead's contention. For 'a few hundred years' experiments on this Earth could hardly justify us in advancing generalizations of a completely unrestricted kind'[43]. A statement of a law of nature, in practice, is regarded as true within a certain region of space and time, and its trustworthiness is adjudged in reference to the size of this region. In fact, the strength of the truth of a law-statement is proportionate to the restrictions imposed upon it. Thus the greater is the scope of the law-statement the lower is the probability of the generalization. The validity of a law-statement and the magnitude of its field vary inversely.

5. An Examination of Whitehead's Regionalism

As has been said earlier, if regionalism is interpreted to mean the doctrine that a statement of a law of nature is true only in a set of ideal conditions and that the truth-value of such a statement gets affected when the basic conditions vary, then certainly the theory has an appeal. Both Whitehead and Kneale refer to a common fact. It is a common fact that the scientists observe great caution and special care while applying the laws to remote cases. This caution has been construed by Whitehead to prove his regionalism. For Kneale, on the other hand, the general practice adopted by the scientists of applying laws to remote cases stands rather as evidence of the universality of laws. He observes:

> Indeed, the considerations which make the scientist cautious in such a case cannot be stated without an assumption that precisely formulated laws of nature have unrestricted universality.[44]

A scientific law is established after observation of some instances at a particular time and space. It is quite legitimate to doubt whether or not the recurrent feature of the observed instances is present in all unobserved cases as well. There is every possibility that the feature noticed uniformly in the observed cases is not invariably present in every sample of the class. Kneale writes:

> ... If we have found all *a* things in our experience to be *b*, we may assert that all *a* things without restriction are *b* and yet presently feel some hesitation in using this proposition as a premiss for inferences about remote instances of *a*-ness because we reflect that all the instances we have observed may be subject to some local or temporary condition (e.g. of temperature or atmospheric pressure) not mentioned in our statement of the supposed law.[45]

However, the recognition of local conditions does not compel us to embrace regionalism. One may still support universalism by taking law-statements as elliptical statements. They may be formulated in full by incorporating a reference to the ideal conditions. Such conditions are not generally mentioned in a statement of law because they are either obvious or overlooked. If they are overlooked, every care is taken by the scientists of the next genre to consider them and state them specifically in the formulation of the law-statement. In this manner, the law-statements become refined or reformulated in course of time. Thus, instead of saying 'All *a* things are *b*', we should rather say: 'All *a* things, in the presence of the condition g, are *b*', i.e. 'All *ag* things are *b*'. However, once this is accepted as a law, every time everywhere there is an *a* in *g*, it is bound to be coupled with *b*. Thus the universality claim may be still retained. It is found that Kneale and Whitehead have alternative explanations of a common scientific practice.

Kneale's position may be elaborated further. He seems to hold that when, in the history of science, an earlier law, e.g. 'All α

things are β' is refined to 'All $\alpha\gamma$ things are β', the refinement is not to be understood as the rejection of the earlier law. Nor is the introduction of the qualification of 'γ' construed to impose a restriction on the law 'All α things are β'. In fact β-ness is considered a regular feature of α which normally has the qualification of 'γ'. The law 'All $\alpha\gamma$ things are β' is an improved version of the earlier law, 'All α things are β'. And if the refined version of the law-statement is not a rejection of the earlier law, then the universality claim, implicit in the law, is also not given up.

Kneale seems to hold further that it is the feature of universality, which distinguishes a local generalization from a law. A law is true and is a universal statement. Thus the statement 'All crows are black' is not a law, since it is not true. The crows of the snowy region and the crows of Australia are white. But if we add a qualification to the above statement and say instead that 'All crows of Calcutta are black' - even though it is true, will it be considered to be a law ? No one, perhaps, is ready to ascribe the title of 'law' to such generalizations that are true within a limited region. Laws are more than mere statements of facts. They provide rational justification for future prediction. And such predictions are possible because the laws are regarded as universally true.

Gary Gutting's interpretation of Whitehead also demands our attention. Gutting observes that Whitehead introduces his theory of internal relations to solve the riddle of induction. Gutting quotes the following passage from Whitehead's *Process and Reality*:

> Another way of stating this explanation of the validity of induction is, that in every forecast there is a presupposition of a certain type of actual entities, and that the question then asked is, under what circumstances will these entities find themselves ? The reason that an answer can be given is that the presupposed type of entities requires a presupposed

> type of data for the primary phases of these actual entities; and that a presupposed type of data requires a presupposed type of social environment. Hence when we have presupposed a type of actual occasions, we have already some information as to the laws of nature in operation throughout the environment.[46]

Gutting clarifies Whitehead's position thus:

> What any given actual entity is depends, to a large extent, on what the actual entities in its past were . . . . Since on this view an actual entity is, to a great extent, itself a projection of the past, it would seem that we are justified in projecting its future behaviour on the basis of the known behaviour of past actual entities.[47]

In his paper entitled 'Metaphysics and Induction', Gutting argues that the problem of induction is an epistemological problem which cannot be solved by any metaphysical theory. To infer that the future would be like the past, e.g. that in future bread will nourish as it did in the past, one has to be convinced that the future example is a regular piece of bread, like B_1 and B_2, sharing the common essential property of producing nourishment (N). But how can we be sure that the future and the past instances do not differ in any important respect ? Gutting apprehends that there may be objects like 'y', that is, a loaf of bread 'laced with arsenic' or 'a clever synthetic product which simulates all external properties of bread but has no nutritional value'[48]. We must be sure that what we take as bread in our inference is really a piece of bread and not the kind of an object like 'y'. The problem of the scientist is not whether there is uniformity in nature; '... the problem is rather, *which* of these laws apply to y'[49]. Gutting finds that the doctrine of internal relations is neither necessary nor sufficient to solve the problem of induction. Further, internal relations between entities, even if they exist, must be known by some non-inductive method. They cannot furnish the ground of validity for inductive reasoning without being circular. To infer that the future bread would be like the past bread in producing nourishment is already to *know* the law of nature that bread nourishes. As Gutting says:

> ...according to the Whiteheadian doctrine of internal relations, to be a loaf of bread means to have incorporated a certain kind of structure from things in one's past... . But this, in turn, means that to be a loaf of bread is to be a part of a certain kind of environment- i. e., to have certain types of entities in one's immediate past. Consequently, as soon as we talk about 'a loaf of bread', we are necessarily talking about a certain kind of physical environment. But part of being 'a certain kind of physical environment' is being governed by certain kinds of physical laws (). As a result, when we talk about today's loaf of bread, we are necessarily discussing something that obeys the same laws of nature as did yesterday's loaf of bread. Since nutrition follows the eating of bread in virtue of laws of nature, we can justifiably conclude that today's bread, like yesterday's, will produce nutrition.[50]

Gutting refers to two special assumptions Whitehead had to make to justify inductive inference. They are about the relation of actual entities or occasions to their environments:

> Each actual occasion objectifies the other actual occasions in its environment. This environment can be limited to the relevant portion of the cosmic epoch. *It is a finite region of the extensive continuum, so far as adequate importance is concerned in respect to individual differences among actual occasions.* Also, in respect to the importance of individual differences, we may assume that *there is a lower limit to the*

extension of each relevant occasion within this region. (PR 313, italics added)[51]

Whitehead thus makes use of Keynes' principle of limited variety to justify inductive procedure. Of course, he reformulates this principle in terms of his doctrine of internal relation, but he has not worked out any necessary connection between the two. Keynes' principle is not a necessary outcome of the doctrine of internal relation. It may be utilized even by a Humean to justify his inductive inferences. Whitehead seeks to justify our inference about the future and for this purpose he introduces his metaphysical doctrine that any real entity is historically determined by its past, and that its future is to a great extent determined by its present state. Is this not a kind of general regularity ? If so, then this is a return of the principle of Uniformity of Nature in a new garb.

Notes

1 *Ibid.*, p. 25.

2 T. L. Beauchamp, 'Cosmic Epochs and the Scope of Scientific Laws', *Process Studies*, vol. 2, 1972, p. 298.

3 *Process and Reality*, p. 3.

4 J. Martin, *New Shapes of Reality*, George Allen and Unwin, London, 1968, p. 17.

5 *Ibid.*, p. 144.

6 J. Bradley, *Routledge Encyclopedia of Philosophy*, vol. 9, Routledge and Kegan Paul, London, 1998, p. 715.

7 A. H. Johnson, *Whitehead's Theory of Reality*, Dover Publications Inc., New York, 1962, p. 17.

8 Quoted from Johnson, *op. cit.*, 1962, p. 19.

9 *Process and Reality*, p. 29.

10 *Ibid*, p.45.

11 *Ibid.*, p. 61.

12 Whitehead speaks of 'society' in *Process and Reality* and *Adventure*

of Ideas; but, in *Science and the Modern World*, he uses the term 'organism'.

13 Johnson, *op. cit.*, p. 51.

14 *Ibid*, p. 19.

15 A. N. Whitehead, *The Interpretation of Science*, The library of Liberal Arts, The Bobbs-Merrill Co. Inc., New York, 1961, p. 140.

16 Mays, *op. cit.*, p. 52.

17 *Ibid.*, p. 53.

18 A. N. Whitehead, *Science and the Modern World*, Cambridge, 1927, p. 134.

19 *Ibid.*, p. 299.

20 A. N. Whitehead, *Adventure of Ideas*, Penguin Books, London, 1933, p. 130.

21 Whitehead, *Science and the Modern World*, p. 92.

22 A. N. Whitehead, *An Enquiry Concerning the Principles of Natural Knowledge*, Cambridge University Press, Cambridge, 1955, p. 186.

23 Whitehead, *Adventure of Ideas*, p. 130.

24 *Ibid.*, p. 133.

25 *Ibid.*, p. 134.

26 *Ibidem.*

27 *Ibid.*, pp. 134 -135.

28 *Ibid.*, p. 135.

29 *Ibid.*, p. 137.

30 *Ibid.*, pp. 137-138.

31 *Ibid.*, p. 139.

32 *Ibid.*, p. 149.

33 *Ibid.*, p. 150.

34 *Ibidem.*

35 *Ibid.*, p.147.

36 *Ibid.*, p.148.

37 *Ibid.*, pp. 161-162.

38 *Ibid.*, p.165.

39 Beauchamp, *op. cit.*, p. 299.

40 *Ibidem.*

41 Day on pp. 187 - 188 refers to the British classical school of economics, followed by Smith and others, where the economic laws are prevalent universally and to the German historical school for which different laws are true of different countries at different point of history. Mill tries to arrive at a compromise by distinguishing between Pure and Applied Economics. Universalism is true in the former and Regionalism is true in the latter. Mill tries to develop a new science called 'Political Ethnology' to determine what important features are to be taken into consideration when the laws of economics are applied to a particular country.

42 *Ibid.*, p. 73.

43 S. Toulmin, *The Philosophy of Science*, pp. 98-99.

44 *Ibidem.*

45 *Ibidem.*

46 A. N. Whitehead, *Process and Reality,* Social Sciences Book Store, New York, 1941, p. 311.

47 G. Gutting, 'Metaphysics and Induction', *Process Studies,* vol. 1, 1971, p. 174.

48 *Ibid.*, p. 176.

49 *Ibidem.*

50 *Ibid.*, p. 175.

51 *Ibid.*, p. 176.

APPENDIX III

SOME PROBLEMS CONCERNING THE LOGICAL CHARACTER OF NATURAL LAWS

The aim of natural science is to discover the laws of Nature. These laws not only describe the natural phenomena, they also explain, predict and control them. Determining the logical form of a natural law statement is a difficult problem. Years of research on this topic could not yield a satisfactory solution. The aim of this paper is not to offer any solution to this thorny problem, but to draw attention to some of the problems involved in the suggestions coming from different important schools of philosophy. Such deliberations are not totally uncalled for. A satisfactory theory on the exact logical form of natural laws can emerge by mitigating, if not, eliminating, the defects of the earlier formulations.

The first part of the paper refers to the age-old controversy between regularists and the necessitarians regarding the logical character of natural laws. It focuses on certain objections raised by the necessitarians. These objections seem to be strong enough to show the inadequacy of the regularity theory to elicit the true character of natural laws. The second part dwells upon a particular version of the necessitarian doctrine formulated by Dretske, Armstrong and Tooley. An attempt is made to determine the cogency of this formulation. Finally, the ontological theory of laws proposed by Chris Swoyer and Milton Fisk shall be taken up to show its relative merit.

I

To remain confined to the controversy between the necessitarians and the regularists is to give an incomplete picture for these are not the only theories available on this matter. There are the logical positivists who consider that the sentences expressing laws of nature are not propositions at all. A law cannot be true or false. A law, for them, is rather a rule of inference. Ryle, for example, describes a law of nature as 'inference-ticket'[1]. The law viz., all men are mortals permits us to undertake the inference-path from 'x is a man' to 'x is mortal'. The doctrine of logical positivism is based on their peculiar theory of meaning which has no merit of its own to render its acceptance compulsory. Further, it is legitimate to question the justification of such rules. Is not this rule of inference based on the objective fact that men in this world are mortals? A rule of inference, which is not based on objective facts, is only a matter of linguistic convention. But if that be so, then all scientific laws become arbitrary. No natural scientist is ready to accept that the laws are arbitrary fabrications. If the natural laws are arbitrary, then how can they be used as the ground of successful prediction about natural events?

Whitehead considers that the statements of natural laws are restricted in generality. They are true in a particular cosmic epoch, a certain domain of space and time. As an evolutionary philosopher, Whitehead thought it pertinent to believe that the world undergoes change, and with the change in the nature of the world, there are changes in the laws that hold in it. Thus, what holds good in one cosmic epoch may not be true in another. Whitehead has only limited faith in inductive inference. Any inference about the future must be restricted within the boundary of one cosmic epoch. Many philosophers, like Kneale, find this theory a 'peculiar'[2] one. This paper omits Whitehead's theory for its counter-intuitive nature.

A law in language is expressed in the form of a categorical statement of unrestricted generality. A universal statement is usually expressed in logic to have the form $(x)(Fx \supset Gx)$. Of course, there are many other laws, like the functional and probabilistic laws which are not expressed in the form of categorical statements.

For the sake of simplicity, our discussion shall refer only to the categorical form of law-expression. Whatever is said of the above form may be said with little modification in connection with other forms of law as well.

The regularists regard a natural law as a universal truth concerning the matters of fact. They maintain that a law may be truly represented in the form of a material conditional. The necessitarians, on the other hand, maintain that a law of nature is concerned with necessary connexion between natural phenomena. A material conditional is inadequate to represent a law of nature. A material implication may be true when its antecedent is false. But a law statement is not true just because it talks about an empty class. Some further restriction must be brought upon a material implication to capture the true character of natural laws. Can we add the stipulation that the subject of a law statement must be a non-empty term? That, however, would be an illegitimate demand, for there are uninstantiated laws like the Newton's law.

Again, every universal truth is not a law. There is a distinction between a law of nature and a 'historical accident on a cosmic scale'[3], e.g. all tom-cats are blue-eyed. The necessitarians and the regularists both have to accept the following equation:

Law = universal truth + x (where x stands for different values to signify the special status or function of x).

The necessitarians are better equipped to explain the differentia. Since a law statement, according to them, states a necessary connexion, the law covers the observed and the unobserved, the actual and the counterfactual. Thus if all F are G is a statement of an accidental truth of generality, they talk about things that are. It cannot talk about counterfactual situations. On the other hand, a law has a counterfactual import. If it is a law of nature that all F are G, then Fs are Gs necessarily, then there is a justification of the counterfactual assertion that if this x, which is not in fact F, were F, then it would have been G.

The regularists attempt to explain the counterfactual import of laws and the distinction between laws and accidentally true statements in different manners. Since a law statement is not anything more than a mere contingent universal statement about matter of facts, the regularists can distinguish law statement from other universal statements by an appeal to 'certain specific relations that they bear to other items'[4]. The other item in this relation may be either external to the uniformity or something inherent in the uniformity itself. The first alternative refers to certain epistemic matters, viz., people's attitude towards the laws, the nature of evidence supporting a law etc. in order to distinguish between a law and an accidental generality. This theory, suggested by Ayer, Goodman, Strawson and others, may be called the epistemic version of regularity view. The latter alternative has taken two forms: i) the resiliency version offered by Brian Skyrm and ii) the systematic version adopted by Ramsey, Lewis and others.

According to the epistemic version what distinguishes a law from a non-law is the special attitude which people have towards laws. The prima facie difficulty of this version is the explanation of unknown laws. If the epistemic version does not rule out the possibility of unknown laws, then how can it explain lawlikeness in terms of people's attitude? What, according to the epistemic version, would be the status of an unknown law towards which people do not possess the special attitude which they have for the known laws? On this account the same statement, S, which did not stand for a law at one time (when the law is unknown and accordingly there is no attitude towards it) becomes a law statement as soon as it is known and people develop an attitude towards it. This has led Ayer to make a modest claim that the explanation of the distinction between a law and a mere generalization in terms of people's attitude may be at most be taken as the sufficient condition and not a necessary condition of lawlikeness. The epistemic version can tackle the problem of unknown laws by introducing a counterfactual conditional about what people would have believed under unfulfilled conditions. A law statement may be understood as a statement of uniformity, if either people actually possess a certain attitude towards it, or, would have the attitude towards it, provided certain other (epistemic) conditions had been fulfilled. Again, let us imagine a totally uninhabited world which is governed by natural laws. How, in the knowerless world, do we distinguish between a law and a non-law? One might answer that the distinction is not of any great significance in a knowerless world. Yet there is a difference and if, at all, there is a difference, then what is the differentiating criterion. Prof. Suchting[5] points out that, if the epistemic version is accepted, in a knowerless world, then there can be no known or unknown laws for there is no one to possess any attitude towards them. Therefore, there would be total lawlessness in a knowerless world. Molnar rightly argues that necessity and possibility are not epistemic concepts. Whether a statement represents a necessity or a contingent truth does not depend upon the knowledge of any one scientist or all the scientists, or, the manner in which the scientific knowledge is acquired, or, the evidence supporting the scientific hypotheses. The concepts of 'necessity' and 'possibility' and consequently, the distinction between a law and an accidental generalization are metaphysical issues. A law sets a limit to possibility and the world is governed by the laws irrespective of our knowledge of the laws. The discussion above shows that the epistemic account has not explained the difference between a law-statement and a statement of fact satisfactorily.

Let us now turn to the Resiliency version of regularity theory. Brian Skyrm wishes to replace the modal notion in the expression of natural laws with the concept of resiliency. High resiliency, for Skyrm, 'can be thought of as a statistical notion of necessity'[6]. If all Fs are Gs, then there is a certain probability for an F to be a G, and this probability is invariant under varying circumstances. In other words, if Fs are Gs regularly, then there is a certain limiting frequency of Gs among Fs and this limiting frequency is maintained through the variation of circumstances accompanying Fs. The concept of resiliency, Skyrm thinks, provides an insight into the nature of universal laws. A universal law statement may be understood to assert that everything falling within the scope of its quantifier has the *propensity of one* for not being a counter-example. For example, if it is a law that 'All ravens are black', it means 'Every raven has a propensity of one to be black'. Negatively speaking, the law has the propensity of one to deny the existence of any counter-example, i.e. the existence of a non-black raven. Thus, the above law means that everything has a propensity of one to be either black, or not a raven, or both.

It would be of interest to examine the tenability of the resiliency interpretation of laws. Prof Armstrong observed a resiliency account in general introduces a 'considerable arbitrary and convenient element'[7] in the explanation of probabilistic laws. When a law is assigned a precise probability, a, to F for being G, 'this conceals the fact that there will regularly be an element of decision that the facts are to be so described.'[8] This, however, is not true of Skyrm, who is honest enough to live with 'imprecision' and relativity'[9]. Skyrm admits that absolute resiliency is impossible to achieve, for no such thing exists. The only kind of physical randomness one may claim is 'randomness relative to a given set of physical properties'[10].Skyrm's notion of resiliency which holds the key to an understanding the notion of laws and other related concepts and helps in the objective test of laws is, at most, a 'potentially resiliency'.

Now, how far the notion of resiliency can explain the distinction between a law statement and a general statement stating the truth of facts? According to Skyrm, a general statement 'All F are G' is a law statement, if Fs are Gs resiliently. This resiliency is not an absolute resiliency to claim that all the *actual* Fs are Gs in 'every nomically possible circumstance'[11]. A law is relatively resilient. The relative resiliency claims that all actual Fs in a wide range of suitable circumstances are Gs. That is *actual* Fs, which are also Hs or Js or Ks...., are Gs. The factors, H, J, K.... are taken to cover a wide range of suitable circumstances in which Fs are Gs.

Now, if H, J, K accompany actual Fs when they are Gs, then is there any role played by these factors to make an F, G? If actual Fs are always accompanied by Hs or Js or Ks nature has provided no room for an objective test of the law. Further, how wide is the range of suitable circumstances? One way of putting the law to test is to produce a situation (provided it is nomically possible) that would falsify the law. For example, whether 'all Fs are Gs" is a law or not may be decided by trying to produce (if nomically possible) a situation where there are Fs that are non-Gs. But this criterion is not decisive. There may be laws which cannot be put to test because no resources, natural or artificially created by men, are available to produce an appropriate situation conducive to carry out such a test. Armstrong makes use of Tooley's example of Smith's garden to explain his point. It has been found that all the fruits in Smith's garden has been successful. Oranges brought into the garden became elephants, bananas turned to apples, while pears, resisted by an insurmountable force, failed to cross the boundary and all the cherry-plants in the garden either bear apple or stand fruitless. The generalization about fruits in Smith's garden has high resiliency because it holds in a wide range of circumstances that would have falsified the generalization, provided the generalization is falsifiable at all. But how can we have confirmation of laws under every variety of circumstances?

Besides, only the actual variations of circumstances are available to us. The resiliency of a law is the resiliency over the actual instances only and this resiliency may be constant. Why that may be said to be constant in the possible and the counterfactual cases as well? Again the counterfactual supported by a probabilistic law must inherit the probabilistic character from the law. Now a counterfactual implied by a law is of the form 'if a were F then a would be G' and not of the probabilistic form 'if a were F then probably it would be G'. In the latter case the counterfactual is simply not asserted. Thus the resilient version has its own problems.

Upon the Systematic version, a law statement is distinguished from a universal statement of fact by means of a logical relation which obtains between a law-statement and some other statements. R.B. Braithwaite proposes to distinguish law statements from other universal statements on the ground of people's 'rational corpus of knowledge and reasonable belief'[12]. Similar suggestions are made by J.S. Mill, C.G. Hempel, and P. Oppenheim and B. Berofsky. The F. P. Ramsey and David Lewis provided the best model to distinguish between a law of nature and an accidental generalization within the Humean tradition.

Ramsey points out that a universal statement of law cannot be distinguished from a universal of fact by syntactical considerations alone. It is not enough to say that a law is a statement where the subject term does not mention any 'particular portion of space-time'. We can easily construct an example of a statement where the subject term does not refer to any particular portion of space-time; yet, people may hesitate to regard the statement as a law. Again, there may be statements having reference to a particular point of space and time and yet, they may be recognized as laws, for example, Kepler's law. The laws hold a place of importance in our epistemic system and they determine, in a significant manner, the character of the world to which they belong. For Ramsey, the laws are 'consequences of those propositions which we should take as axioms if we knew everything and organized it as simply as possible in a deductive system'[13]. Simplicity and strength or information content are the two guiding principles to form a system with true propositions. In fact, many such systems may be formed with true statements. The best system is one which strikes a balance between the two guiding principles. Endorsing the same view, Lewis says that 'a contingent generalization is a law of nature if and only if it appears as a theorem in a in each of the true deductive system'[14].

The Primary problem of the systematic version is that it leaves ample scope for the insurgence of subjective element in the theory. A system, according to this version, must satisfy the demand for simplicity and strength. However, the theory is clueless as to what that universally accepted standard is. Lewis's account further requires a balance between simplicity and strength. But, Armstrong asks: 'May there not be irresoluble conflicts about the exact point of balance?'[15] Different people might attempt to balance the two principles in different manners. Again if people have different standards of simplicity and strength, then a conflict becomes inevitable. For example, a rationalist might emphasize on simplicity, while an empiricist would prefer strength and as a result of this difference between points of emphasis a conflict emerges. If the system that we in fact possess is not strong or simple enough, then we might fail to include certain laws.

A systematic theorist must distinguish between a law and a pseudo law. Laws are parts of a deductive system of uniformities. How a new object which is imagined to have a property which in fact it does not possess could fit in such system? Where is the guarantee that such an object would fit in the system of *de facto* generalities? Lewis believes that the laws imply the counterfactuals because the deductive system is considered as important. That is why we seem to retain the law in cases of any new object. This reduces counterfactual import of laws to a matter of habit or preference.

We may now turn to another objection brought against the regularity theory by Kneale. George Molnar develops the objection in the following manner. He begins with the Humean definition of a law of nature as

D_1: p is a statement of a law of nature iff

1. p is universally quantified.
2. p is true omnitemporally and omnispatially.
3. p is contingent.
4. p contains only non-local empirical predicates, logical connectives and quantifiers.

Now, a state of affair is regarded as empirically possible if it does not contradict a law of nature. A state of affair is an unrealized possibility, if it is possible but it does not occur. Thus, we come to two more definitions:

D_2: If p is a statement asserting the existence of a state of affair, then what it says is possible, provided p expresses a state of affair which is not inconsistent with any law of nature.

D_3: p states an unrealized possibility (a state of affair which is conceived as 'neither actual nor impossible') iff

1. p states a possible state of affair.
2. p is false.

With the help of these three definitions and other rules of inference, Molnar constructs a formal proof which has ten steps[16] to prove that no 'contingent unrestricted existential proposition containing only empirical predicate' can be both false and 'consistent with every law of nature'.

1. "Something is F" is false. (Assumption)
2. "Nothing is F". (1 Equivalence)
3. "Nothing is F" is a law of nature. (2 D_1)
4. "Something is F" is inconsistent with "Nothing is F". (Tautology)
5. "Something is F" is inconsistent with a law of nature. (3, 4)
6. "Something is F" is not a statement of possibility. (5 D_2)
7. "Something is F" is false, then "Something is F" is not a statement of possibility. (1 - 6 Conditional Proof)

8. It is not that in both case "Something is F" is false and that "Something is F" is a statement of possibility. (7 Equivalence)
9. "Something is F" is not a statement of unrealized possibility. (8 D_3)
10. For any x, if x is an unrestricted empirical existential proposition, then x is not a statement of unrealized possibility. (9 UG)

The above argument shows that there can be no unrealized possibility. But this is counterintuitive. There are statements, like 'there is a golden mountain', which is empirically false, though the fact it describes is both logically and empirically possible. Some empiricists, like Popper, seek to defend empiricism at the cost of maintaining that unrealized possibility is instantiated sometime somewhere. Molnar proceeds to show that the problem can be evaded only by rejecting the conjunction of the definitions D_1, D_2 and D_3. To him, the best option seems to be to reject the third clause of D_1. The laws express an objective necessary connexion.

It may be noted that law statements are expressed in the form of categorical propositions are synthetic necessary statements. The subject concept is neither wholly nor partly identical with the predicate concept. The connexion between the subject and predicate is established inductively. According to the necessitarians, the relation involved in a law is an objective relation that holds between phenomena. Thus the truth of a law statement does not follow from logic alone; there is something more than logic. What is then the difference between logical possibility and empirical possibility?

Let us consider two characters F and G. Then, in respect of an individual a, there are the following possibilities in terms of possession of F, G and their negations:

1. The possibility that a has both F and G.
2. The possibility that a has both F but not G.

3. The possibility that a does not possess F but possesses G.
4. The possibility that a has neither F nor G.

Now, all the above are logical possibilities since there is no logical contradiction involved in F. G. Yet, if it is a law that all F are G then it is really impossible for an individual *a* to be F but not G. Thus the law allows 1, 3, and 4 and prohibits 2. The set of permissible logical possibilities has only one option where an individual possesses F and as per 1 then it also possesses G. This connexion is not accidental; it is grounded on the nature of the physical objects.The real possibility is then only a subset of the set of logical possibility.

The Humeans reduce all kinds of necessity to psychological expectation arising from the regularity of connexion. However, for the necessitarians, if that be so, then all inductive inferences become worthless. There is no guarantee that our expectations shall be fulfilled by nature. If experience at all provides a support for our interference about the yet-to-be experienced, then there must be an objective basis of such inference. Our inference to the future is guided by the past experience and this proceeds by projecting the features of the observed instances on to the unobserved. Such projections are justified only if there is a chance that when the observed individuals have the feature of being G if they are F, any arbitrarily selected unobserved individual is also G if it is F. However, such chances do not exist if all the features of the experienced cases are contingent. Only the real necessity of a feature can make it likely that an unobserved individual would also be a similar feature. The projected features must be those which possess things of a certain kind by law. The ontology of objectively based real necessity, Milton Fisk points out, is a rich one - there are entities with strings of properties and actions and all the entities have fixed natures.

The necessitarians often adopt a univocal meaning of necessity. The logical truths are known to be necessary and their contradictories are self-contradictory. The scientific laws are inductively established and their negations are not self-contradictory. The truth of these law statements is depended on ontological connexions. Considering the limitations of human intellect, such connexions may remain 'opaque to the intellect'[17]. Yet, their epistemic status does not imply that of the two kinds of necessity. The meaning of necessity is same everywhere. Necessity restricts alternatives. The regularists presuppose a difference between the two and then 'cudgel their brains'[18] to find out a special meaning of physical necessity and remark at the meaning of physical necessity is totally unexplained and unfathomable. A necessitarian, like Kneale, on the other hand, points out that necessity everywhere sets a limit to possibility. That is to be construed as the general meaning of necessity. The source of restriction in logic comes from the nature of ratiocination; in the natural world it comes from the structure of the world. To conceive of a distinction between the logical and physical necessity is to confuse the epistemological with the ontological issues.

This account successfully explains the counterfactual import of laws. If it is a law that all F are G, then surely the counterfactual that if this x, which is not in fact F were F, then it would have been G is true. But an accidental truth has no such import. From an accidental generalization like all coins in my purse are rupee-coins, it cannot be inferred that if this 25p coin, which is not in my purse, were there, then it would have been a rupee-coin. If the laws are mere records of actual regularity, how such regularity can be stretched to the counterfactual cases? But, if Fs are Gs because of a necessary connexion in their inherent natures, then any individual (actually or possibly) possessing the nature of F must also possess the nature of G. The theory that a law, like all F are G, boils down to the fact that there is something in the nature of F that is responsible for its being G. This theory is described in current literature as the property theory of laws. The next part of the essay deals with the theory of law suggested by Dreske, Armstrong and Tooley.

II

Dreske points out that if a natural law is something more than a mere universal truth then the form of natural law is not $(x)(Fx \supset Gx)$. The predicate position in a universal proposition $(x)(Fx \supset Gx)$ is transparent. If F and K co-extensive, i.e. $(x)\ (Kx = Fx)$, then by co-extensive predicate substitution we may conclude that $(x)\ (Kx \supset Gx)$. The truth-value of a general proposition remains unchanged after such a substitution. The predicate or the descriptive term of a law statement occurs in an opaque position. The expression's status as a law might be affected by substitutions of terms. Only when $(x)\ (Kx = Fx)$ is a law, the statement obtained by substitution of F by K in the statement 'all F are G' remains a law statement. Dreske offers a plausible explanation of the opacity of the predicate in a law statement. Taking this suggestion from Frege, Dreske observes that when it is said that it is a law that all F are G, it is the law operator (it is a law...) that converts the transparent position of F and G to opacity. Within this operator, the terms F and G do not stand for their usual referents. All F are G is not a statement about the extensions of the predicates F and G; it is a singular statement describing universal properties F-ness and G-ness. Universal is one and exists in many, though it is ontologically different from the many in which it resides. The form of a law then is

$$\text{F-ness} \rightarrow \text{G-ness}.$$

This is viewed as the extensional relation between intensions. The relation between F-ness and G-ness imposes a restriction on the particulars which fall within the scope. The '$\rightarrow$' here does not stand for material implication. Because F-ness, in its essence, is related to G-ness the instantiation of one property yields or generates the other. Since there is no reference to the extension of the predicate expressions involved in the law, the extension of one may be hypothetically stretched to match the antecedent of the counterfactual conditional and the consequent may be obtained using the connexions involved in the law.

Armstrong in essence suggested the same theory of laws. If it is a law that all F are G, then there must be a higher level connexion between the universals F-ness and G-ness. The form of law, according to him is

$$N\ (F,G)$$

And it is also true that N(F,G) implies the Humean regularity however, a Humean regularity does not imply a law. Thus

1. $N(F,G) \supset (x)\ (Fx \supset Gx)$
2. $(x)\ (Fx \supset Gx) \neq N(F,G)$

The law stands for a stronger connection than mere regularity. Where there is a law there is regularity, but every kind of regularity is not a law. For example, that all moas die before the age of fifty is an observed regularity. In fact some virus killed all the moas at New Zealand and all of them were below 50 years when they died. But, there is nothing in the nature of moas to confine their life to 50 years.

Tooley held a similar view. For him, if it a law that all F are G, then the ordered pair < P, Q > must be nomically related. Such relation subsists only between universals and nothing else. The universals according to Tooley, are the truth makers of laws. Universals are believed to have properties and they stand in relation to other universals. This relation among universal 'logically necessitates some corresponding generalization about particulars, and when this is the case, the generalization in question expresses a law'[19]

This theory is not above criticism. Is this ontological ascent from particulars to universals absolutely necessary to retain the model character of laws? If laws are relations amongst universals, then surely the universals exist. Many consider the notion of universal ambiguous, besides being ontologically extravagant. Further, what is the nature of the relations between universals? According to Dreske, Armstrong and Tooley it is a contingent relation and the snag of their theory lies here. If a first order relation is made necessary by a second order relation and the second order relation is believed to be contingent, then it is only the Humean picture of the higher order. If the relation between the universals is contingent then there would be different relations between the two in different possible worlds. That would make the fact that a certain law holds in a certain possible world a matter of cosmic co-incidence. That relinquishes the very theory of necessity of natural laws. Thus a contingent relation at the second order cannot bestow necessity on the first order relation.

III

We turn now to another version of the property theory coming from Chris Swoyer and earlier by Milton Fisk. According to this version, a law of nature expresses objective connexions between properties. A property may be a quality like colour etc, a vector, a propensity, temperature or disposition. To Swoyer, the laws of nature may be regarded to involve properties because the discovery of properties in science goes hand in hand with discovery of laws. The basic tenet of the property theory that if it is a law that all F are G, then there is something about the things being F which causes its being G. Obviously this connexion is not regularity. The laws are objective facts signifying a nomic implication between properties such that whenever an individual possess the first, it is bound to possess the second. Nomic implication cannot be obtained by putting a modal operator before a Humean regularity statement. Chris Swoyer begins with the formulation of law as:

Ifg (where I stands for the nomic connexion between f

and g; g and f are variables for abstract singular terms resulting from nominalization transformation of F, G which are predicate variables)

I can successfully represent the objectivity of natural laws, for a statement of law involves properties, whereas a statement of mere regularity refers to individual facts. Ifg cannot be understood as $\Box$ $(\forall x)$ $(x\alpha f \supset x\alpha g)$ for then the law must be regarded as true if f necessarily fails to exist. Some further restrictions must be made so that Ifg may represent the true character of laws. Let us replace Ifg by the following :

N : $\Diamond$ (Exists g and Exists f) & $\Box$ $(\forall x)$ $(x\alpha f \supset x\alpha g)$

The above account reveals that in all worlds where F exists, it is accompanied by G. The connexion is grounded on the properties themselves. So the law holds not because $(\forall x)$ $(x\alpha f \supset x\alpha g)$ is true in all possible worlds, but because the very natures of F and G make it impossible for there be any world in which it is false. Thus Ifg holds even in worlds where F and G do not occur because of the natures of property in the actual world.

But what if F and G do not occur in the actual world? Clearly there are laws, like the Newton's law which talk about the possible world. We may infer about the counterfactual or the possible on the evidence of the actual world. But can the merely possible determine the claim of truth for the actual world? The question can be answered if the laws about the impossible are considered as derivable from the laws concerning the actual entities. But what if the laws are not so derivable? Swoyer finds that his position then would be no 'worse shaped' than his opponents.

Fisk maintains that a law of nature 'involves three things, two properties and a relation. The two properties are necessarily connected as properties of things of that kind, but not as properties of things of a different kind.'[20]. Fisk further proceeds to show that a thing is said to belong to a natural kind on the basis of certain stable behaviour-pattern or uniform association of attributes. A property is a trans-world identity. In that case, a thing belonging to a certain natural kind is not a contingent matter. Let us take a grain of salt that necessarily dissolves in water. To imagine that in some possible world this salt is a diamond is to embrace a contradiction. It is tantamount to admit that in a possible world an object, which is a grain of salt, dissolves in water and at the same time it, being a diamond there, does not dissolve in water. Hence if an object is a grain of salt in actual world, it is of that kind in all worlds. Thus

$(x)\ (Nx \rightarrow \Box\ Nx)$ (where N is a natural kind term)

A law of nature then is said to have the form

1. "$((x)\ (Nx \rightarrow \Box\ (Fx \rightarrow Gx))$" (where N is natural kind term F and G are predicate variables.)

Here we are dealing with a modal operator within the scope of the quantifier. We are speaking about the necessity of something of the natural kind 'N', falling within the range of the quantifier, to possess a certain nature. This necessity is a real or *de re* necessity which is different from propositional or *de dicto* necessity.

But classification of natural objects into their kinds and discovery of relation is not an easy task. And the necessity of connexion between the properties remains unknown for many reasons which can be developed here. Considering the limitations of our intellectual faculty and techniques, scientists' endeavour to discover the properties and laws about natural objects remain everlasting process.

NOTES

1 Ryle

2 W.C.Kneale

3 W.C. Kneale, *Induction and Probability*, Clarendon Press, 1949, p. 72

4 W.A. Suchting, "Regularity and Law", *Boston Studies in Philosophy of Science*, vol. XIV, D.Reidel Publishing Co., Dordrecht, 1974, p.75

5 *Ibid*

6 B. Skyrm, *Casual Necessity*, Yale University Press, New Haven, 1980, p.12

7 Armstrong, 1983, p.36

8 Armstrong, 1983, p.36

9 *Ibid*

10 Skyrm, *ibid*, p.15

11 Armstrong, *ibid*, p.36

12 *Ibid*, p.301

13 Ramsey, 1978, p.138

14 Lewis, Counterfactual, p.73

15 Armstrong, *ibid*, p.67

16 G.Molnar, Kneale's Argument revised, The Philosophical Review, vol. LXXVIII, 1969, pp 80-81

17 Kneale......

18 Kneale......

19 M. Tooley, The Nature of Laws, Canadian Journal of Philosophy, vol. 7, 1977, p.672

20 Fisk, 1970, p.388

BIBLIOGRAPHY

Aaron, R. I., *John Locke*, 2nd ed., Clarendon Press, Oxford, 1955.

Achinstein, P., 'From Success to Truth', *Analysis*, vol. 21, 1960-61, pp. 6 - 9.

Achinstein, P., *Law and Explanation*, Clarendon Press, Oxford, 1971.

Alexander, H. G., 'General Statements as Rules of Inference?' in H. Feigl, M. Scriven and D. Maxwell, eds. *Minnesotta Studies in the Philosophy of Science*, University of Minnesotta Press, Minneapolis, 1958, pp. 309 - 329.

Armstrong, D. M., *What is a Law of Nature?* Cambridge University Press, 1983.

Ammerman, R. R., ed. *Classics of Analytic Philosophy*, McGraw-Hill Publishing Ltd. India, Bombay - New Delhi, 1965,

Ayer, A. J., 'What is a Law of Nature?' *Revue Internationale de Philosophie*, No. 36, 1956, reprinted in B. A. Brody, ed. *Readings in the Philosophy of Science*, Prentice Hall, Englewood Cliffs, 1970, pp. 39 - 54.

Ayer, A. J., 'The Elimination of Metaphysics', *Language, Truth and Logic*, Victor Gollancz Ltd, London, 1964, pp. 33-45.

Baker, G. P. and Hacker, P. M. S., *Wittgenstein: Rules, Grammar and Necessity-An Analytic Commentary on the Philosophical Investigations*, vol. 2, Basil Blackwell, Oxford, 1985.

Beauchamp, T. L., 'Cosmic Epochs and the Scope of Scientific Laws', *Process Studies*, vol. 2, 1972, pp. 296 - 300.

Beauchamp, T. L. and Rosenberg, A., *Hume and the Problem of Causation*, Oxford University Press, Oxford, 1981.

Beck, L. W., ed. *Proceedings of the Third International Kant Congress,* March 30–April 4, 1970, D. Reidel Publishing Company, Dodrecht: Holland, 1972.

Bennett, J., 'Substance, Reality, and Primary Qualities', *American Philosophical Quarterly,* vol. 2, 1965, reprinted in Martin and Armstrong, eds. *Locke and Berkeley: A Collection of Critical Essays* (see below), pp. 86 - 124.

Biglow, B., Ellis, B. and Caroline Lierse, 'The World as One of a Kind: Natural Necessity and Laws of Nature', *The British Journal of Philosophy,* vol. 43, 1992, pp. 371 - 388.

Bigelow, J. and Pargetter, R., 'From Extroverted Realism to Correspondence: A Modest Proposal', *Philosophical and Phenomenological Research,* vol. L, no. 3, 1990, pp. 435 - 609.

Bird, A., 'Laws and Essences', in Alice Drewery, ed. *Metaphysics in Science,* Blackwell Publishing, Melden, MA, USA, 2006, chap 5.

Black, M., 'Necessary Statements and Rules', *Philosophical Review,* 1958, reprinted in H. Feigl, W. Sellars, and P. Lehrer, eds. *New Readings in Philosophical Analysis,* Appleton Century Crofts, New York, 1972.

Broad, C. D., Critical Notice of Kneale's 'Probability and Induction', *Mind,* vol. LIX, 1950, pp. 94 -115.

Bradley, J., *Routledge Encyclopedia of Philosophy,* vol. 9, Routledge and Kegan Paul, London, 1998.

Buchdahl, G., *Metaphysics and Philosophy of Science,* Basil Blackwell, Oxford, 1969.

Buchdahl, G., 'The Conception of Lawlikeness in Kant's Philosophy of Science', in Beck, ed. *Proceedings of the Third International Kant Congress,* March 30–April 4, 1970 (see above).

Butts, R. E., 'On Buchdahl's and Palter's Papers', in Beck, ed. *Proceedings of the Third International Kant Congress*, March 30 - April 4, 1970 (see above).

Braithwaite, R. B., *Scientific Explanations*, Cambridge University Press, Cambridge, 1953.

Campbell, N. R., *Relativity*, Cambridge University Press, Cambridge, 1923.

Carnap, R., 'Testability and Meaning', *Philosophy of Science*, vols. III and IV, 1936 - 1937, reprinted in Ammerman, ed. *Classics of Analytic Philosophy*, (see above), pp. 214 - 230.

Cartwright, Nancy, *How the Laws of Physics Lie*, Clarendon Press, Oxford, 1983.

Carroll, J. W., *Laws of Nature*, Cambridge University Press, Cambridge, 1994.

Chisholm, R., 'The Problem of Empiricism', *Journal of Philosophy*, vol. 45, 1948, pp. 512 - 517.

Chisholm, R. M., 'Law Statements and Counterfactual Inference', *Analysis*, vol. 15, 1955, pp. 97 - 105, reprinted in E. Sosa, ed. *Causation and Conditionals*, Oxford University Press, London, 1975, pp. 147 - 155.

Chisholm, R. M., *Theory of Knowledge*, 2nd ed., Prentice-Hall of India Private Limited, New Delhi, 1987.

Cohen, J., 'The Problem of Natural Laws', in D. H. Mellor, ed. *Prospects for Pragmatism*, Cambridge University Press, Cambridge, 1980, pp. 211 - 228.

Day, J. P., *Inductive Probability*, Routledge and Kegan Paul, London, 1961.

Dewey, J., *The Quest for Certainty: A Study of the Relation of Knowledge and Action*, George Allen & Unwin, London, 1930.

Dewey, J., *Logic: The Theory of Inquiry*, Henry Wolt and Company, New York, 1938.

Earman, J.,'The Universality of Laws', *Philosophy of Science*, vol. 45, 1978, pp. 173 - 181.

Fisk, M., 'Are There Necessary Connections in Nature?'*Philosophy of Science*, vol. 37, 1970, pp. 385 - 404.

Fraassen, B. van, *The Scientific Image*, Clarendon Press, Oxford, 1980.

Goodman, N., *Fact, Fiction and Forecast*, Bobbs-Merrill, Indianapolis, New York, 1973.

Gillies, D., *Philosophy of Science in the Twentieth Century: Four Central Themes*, Blackwell Publishers Ltd, Oxford, 1993.

Gutting, G.: 'Metaphysics and Induction', *Process Studies*, vol. 1, 1971, pp. 171 - 178.

Hacker, P. M. S., *Wittgenstein's Place in Twentieth-Century Analytic Philosophy*, Blackwell Publishers Ltd, Oxford, 1996.

Hempel, C., 'Problems and Changes in the Empiricist Criterion of Meaning', in Ammerman, ed. *Classics of Analytic Philosophy* (see above), pp. 214 - 230.

Hempel, C., *Aspects of Scientific Explanation and Other Essays in the Philosophy of Science*, The Free Press, New York, 1965.

Hiz, H., 'On the Inferential Sense of Contrary-to-Fact Conditional', *Journal of Philosophy*, vol. 48, 1951, pp. 586 - 587.

Hooker, M., 'Descartes's Denial of Mind-Body Identity', in M. Hooker, ed. *Descartes: Critical and Interpretative Essays*, The John Hopkins University Press, Baltimore, 1978.

Jackson, R., 'Locke's Distinction between Primary and Secondary Qualities', *Mind*, vol. 38, 1929, reprinted in Martin and Armstrong, eds. *Locke and Berkeley: A Collection of Critical Essays* (see below).

Johnson, A. H., *Whitehead's Theory of Reality*, Dover Publications Inc., New York, 1962.

Kant, I., *Kritik der reinen Vernunft* [1781 and 1787], hg. v. Th. Valentiner, DER PHILOSOPHISCHEN BIBLIOTHEK BAND 37, Felix Meiner, Leipzig, 1922.

Kant, I., *Critique of Pure Reason*, trans. :

(i) J. M. D. Meiklejohn, Colonial Press, New York,1900;

(ii) N. Kemp Smith, Macmillan, London, First edition 1929, 2nd impression with corrections 1933, reprinted 1968;

(iii) F. Max Müller, Anchor Books, Doubleday & Company, Inc., New York, 1966.

Kant, I., *The Critique of Judgement* [1790], trans. James Creed Meredith, Clarendon, Oxford, 1928, reprinted 1978, 1980 impression printed by Morrison & Gibbs Ltd, London.

Kneale, W., 'Truths of Logic', *Proceedings of the Aristotelian Society*, vol. 46, 1946, pp. 207 - 34.

Kneale, W., 'Are All Necessary Truths True by Convention?' *PAS*, sup. vol. XXI, 1947, pp. 118 - 33.

Kneale, W., *Probability and Induction*, Oxford, First edition 1949, reprinted 1966.

Kneale, W., 'Natural Laws and Contrary-to-Fact Conditionals', *Analysis*, vol. 10, 1950, pp. 121-125, reprinted in Margaret Macdonald, ed. *Philosophy and Analysis*, Basil Blackwell, Oxford, 1954.

Kneale, W. 'Universality and Necessity', *The British Journal for the Philosophy of Science*, vol. 46, 1961, pp. 89 - 102.

Kneale, W. and Kneale, Martha, *The Development of Logic*, Clarendon Press, Oxford, 1962, reprinted 1964.

Kripke, S. A., *Naming and Necessity*, Basil Blackwell, Oxford, 1980.

Lewis, C., *Counterfactuals*, Basil Blackwell, Oxford, 1973.

Locke, J., *Essay Concerning Human Understanding*, ed. P. H. Nidditch, Clarendon Press, Oxford, 1975.

Locke, J., Draft A of the *Essay*, in R. I. Aaron and J. Gibbs, eds. *An Early Draft of Locke's Essay*, Oxford University Press, Oxford, 1936.

Loon, J. F. G. van, 'Rules and Commands', *Mind*, vol. 62, 1952, pp. 514 - 521.

Mackie, J. L., 'Counterfactuals and Causal Laws', in R. J. Butler, ed., *Analytic Philosophy*, Series-I, Oxford, 1966, pp. 66-80.

Mackie, J. L., *Truth, Probability and Paradox*, Clarendon Press, Oxford, 1973.

Mackie, J. L., *The Cement of the Universe*, Clarendon Press, Oxford, 1974.

MacKinnon, E. 'Epistemological Problems in the Philosophy of Science', *The Review of Metaphysics*, vols 22 and 23, 1968, pp. 113-135, and 329-358.

Martin, C. B. and Armstrong, D. M., ed. *Locke and Berkeley : A Collection of Critical Essays*, Modern Studies in Philosophy, Macmillan, London, n.d.

Martin, J., *New Shapes of Reality*, George Allen and Unwin, London, 1968.

Mays, W., *Whitehead's Philosophy of Science and Metaphysics*, Martinus Nijhoff, The Hague, Netherlands, 1977.

Mellor, D. H., ed. *Philosophical Papers: F. P. Ramsay*, Cambridge University Press, Cambridge, 1990.

Mill, J. S., *A System of Logic*, Longman, London, 1970.

Molnar, G., 'Kneale's Argument Revisited', *The Philosophical Review*, vol. LXXVIII, 1969, pp. 79 - 89.

Moore, G. E., 'Wittgenstein's Lectures in 1930 - 1933', *Mind*, vol. LXIII, 1955, reprinted in Ammerman, ed. *Classics of Analytic Philosophy* (see above), pp. 214 - 230.

Morgenbesser, S., 'The Realist-Instrumentalist Controversy', in S. Morgenbesser, S. Patrick, and M. G. White, eds. *Philosophy, Science and Method*, St. Martin Press, New York, 1969, pp. 200 - 218.

Mulder, H. and Velde-Schlick, Berbara F. B. van de, eds. *Moritz Schlick : Philosophical Papers*, vol. II (1925 - 1936), trans. Peter Heath, Wilfred Sellars, Herbert Feige and May Brodbeck, D. Reidel Publishing Company, Dodrecht: Holland, 1979.

Musgrave A., 'Wittgensteinian Instrumentalism', *Theoria*, vol. 47, 1981, pp. 66 - 105.

Nagel, E., *The Structure of Science: Problems in the Logic of Scientific Explanations*, Indian edition, Macmillan India Limited, New Delhi, 1984.

Nerlich, G. and Suchting, W. A., 'Popper's Revised Definition of Natural Necessity', *The British Journal for the Philosophy of Science*, vol. 18, 1967, pp. 63 - 65.

Passmore, J., *A Hundred Years of Philosophy*, Penguin Books Ltd, England, 1980.

Pap, A., *Semantics and Necessary Truth*, Yale University Press, New Haven, 1958.

Popper, K. R., 'A Note on Natural Laws and so-called "Contrary-to-Fact Conditionals" ', *Mind*, vol. 58, N. S., 1949, pp. 62 -66.

Popper, K. R., *The Logic of Scientific Discovery*, Hutchinson and Co. Ltd, London, 1959.

Popper, K. R., *Conjectures and Refutations: The Growth of Scientific Knowledge*, Routledge & Kegan Paul, London, 1963.

Popper, K. R., 'A Revised Definition of Natural Necessity', *The British Journal for the Philosophy of Science*, vol. 19, 1968, pp. 316 - 321.

Ramsey, F. P., 'Universals of Law and of Fact' (1928), in D. H. Mellor, ed. *Philosophical Papers: F. P. Ramsey* (see above), pp 140 -144.

Ramsey, F. P., 'General Propositions and Causality' (1929), in D. H. Mellor, ed. *Philosophical Papers: F. P. Ramsey* (see above), pp. 145 -163.

Rescher, N., 'Belief-Contravening Suppositions', *Philosophical Review*, vol. LXX, 1961, pp. 176 - 196.

Stope-Roe, H. V., 'Recipes and Induction: Ryle v. Achinstein', *Analysis*, vol. 21, 1960 - 1961, pp. 115 - 120.

Ryle, G., 'John Locke on the Human Understanding', in J. L. Stock, ed. *Tercentenary Addresses on John Locke*, Oxford University Press, Oxford, 1933, reprinted in Martin and Armstrong, eds. *Locke and Berkeley: A Collection of Critical Essays* (see above), pp. 14 - 39.

Ryle, G., '"If", "So" and "Because"', in Max Black, ed. *Philosophical Analysis*, Cornell University Press, Ithaca, 1950, reprinted in *G. Ryle: Collected Papers*, vol. 2, *Collected Essays (1929 - 1968)*, Hutchinson of London, 1971, pp. 234 - 249.

Ryle, G., 'Predicting and Inferring', *Proceedings on the Colston Research Society*, vol. 9, University of Bristol, 1957, reprinted in *G. Ryle: Collected Papers*, vol. 2, *Collected Essays (1929 - 1968)* (see above), pp. 373 - 380.

Ryle, G., 'Comment on Mr. Achinstein's Paper', *Analysis*, vol. 21, 1960 - 61, pp. 9 - 11.

Ryle, G. *The Concept of Mind*, Penguin Books Ltd., England, 1976.

Schlick, M., 'Causality in Contemporary Physics' ('Die Kausaliät in der Gegenwä rtigen Physik', *Die Naturwissenschaften*, 19, 1931, trans. Peter Heath), in Mulder and Velde-Schlick, eds. *Moritz Schlick: Philosophical Papers*, vol. 2 (see above), pp. 176 - 237.

Schlick, M., 'Causality in Everyday Life and in Recent Science', in *University of California Publication in Philosophy*, Berkeley, vol. 15, 1932, pp. 99 - 125, reprinted in Mulder and Velde-Schlick, eds. *Moritz Schlick: Philosophical Papers*, vol. 2 (see above), pp. 238 - 258.

Schlick, M., 'Meaning and Verification', *Philosophical Review*, vol. 45, 1936, reprinted in H. Feigl and W. Sellars, eds. *Readings in Philosophical Analysis*, Appleton Century Crofts, New York, 1949.

Schlick, M., *Philosophy of Nature*, Philosophical Library, New York, 1949.

Shapere, D., 'Natural Science and the Future of Metaphysics', *Boston Studies in the Philosophy of Science*, vol. 14, D. Reidel Publishing Company, Dodrecht: Holland, 1974, pp. 161 - 171.

Skyrm, B., *Causal Necessity*, Yale University Press, New Haven, 1980.

Sosa, E., ed. *Causation and Conditionals*, Oxford University Press, London, 1975.

Strawson, G., *Secret Connexion: Causation, Realism and David Hume*, Clarendon Press, Oxford, 1989.

Strawson, P. F., *Introduction to Logical Theory*, Methuen & Co. Ltd, London,1971.

Stopes-Roe, H. V., 'Recipes and Induction: Ryle v. Achinstein', *Analysis*, vol. 21, 1960 - 1961, pp. 115 - 120.

Suchting, W. A., 'Regularity and Law', *Boston Studies in the Philosophy of Science*, vol. 14, D. Reidel Publishing Company, Dordrecht: Holland, 1974, pp. 73 - 90.

Suchting, W. A., 'Popper's Revised Definition of Natural Necessity', *The British Journal for the Philosophy of Science*, vol. 20, 1969, p. 340 - 352.

Swartz, N. and Bradley, R., *Possible Worlds: An Introduction to Logic and Its Philosophy*, Indianapolis, Hackett, 1979.

Swartz, N., *The Concept of Physical Laws,* Cambridge University Press, Cambridge, 1985.

Tooley, M., 'The Nature of Laws', *Canadian Journal of Philosophy,* vol. 7, 1977, pp. 667 - 697.

Toulmin, S., *The Philosophy of Science: An Introduction,* Hutchinson University Press, London, 1955.

Whitehead, A. N., *Science and the Modern World,* Cambridge University Press, Cambridge, 1927.

Whitehead, A. N., *Adventure of Ideas,* Penguin Books, London, 1933.

Whitehead, A. N., *Process and Reality,* Social Sciences Book Store, New York, 1941.

Whitehead, A. N., *An Enquiry Concerning the Principles of Knowledge,* Cambridge University Press, Cambridge, 1955.

Whitehead, A. N., *The Interpretation of Science,* The Library of Liberal Arts, The Bobbs-Merrill Co. Inc., New York, 1961.

Winkler, K. P., 'The New Hume', *The Philosophical Review,* vol. C, no. 4, 1991, pp. 541 - 579.

Wittgenstein, L., *Tractatus Logico-Philosophicus,* trans. D. F. Pears and B. F. McGuiness, Routledge and Kegan Paul, London, 1958.

Woolhouse, R. S., *Locke's Philosophy of Science and Knowledge,* Basil Blackwell, Oxford, 1971.

Wright, G. H. von, *The Logical Problem of Induction* (2nd revised edition), Basil Blackwell, Oxford, 1957.

Yolton, J. W., *John Locke: An Essay Concerning Human Understanding,* abridged and edited with an introduction, J. M. Dent Ltd, London, Everyman's Library, 1976, reprinted 1992.

INDEX

A

B

C

D

E

F

G

H